Fantasies

BOLLYWOOD Love Thief

ALSO BY STEPHEN ALTER

Elephas Maximus:
A Portrait of the Indian Elephant

Sacred Waters:
A Pilgrimage up the Ganges River to the Source of Hindu Culture

Amritsar to Lahore:
A Journey Across the India-Pakistan Border

All the Way to Heaven:
An American Boyhood in the Himalayas

The Phantom Isles

Aranyani

Aripan and Other Stories

Renuka

The Godchild

Silk and Steel

Neglected Lives

Fantasies *of a* BOLLYWOOD Love Thief

Inside the World of Indian Moviemaking

STEPHEN ALTER

A HARVEST ORIGINAL • HARCOURT, INC.
Orlando Austin New York San Diego Toronto London

www.HarcourtBooks.com

Photographs by Abhik Sarkar, courtesy of Big Screen Entertainment.

Library of Congress Cataloging-in-Publication Data
Alter, Stephen.
Fantasies of a Bollywood love thief: inside the world of Indian moviemaking/Stephen Alter.—1st ed.
p. cm.
"A Harvest Original."
Includes index.
1. Motion pictures—India. 2. Motion picture industry—India. I. Title.
PN1993.5.I8A73 2007
791.430954—dc22 2006039096
ISBN 978-0-15-603084-7

Text set in Adobe Garamond
Designed by Liz Demeter

Printed in the United States of America

First edition
A C E G I K J H F D B

For Jeffrey Campbell and Woodman Taylor
with fine memories of
listening to Mohammed Rafi
circa 1975

CONTENTS

AUTHOR'S NOTE

THIS BOOK would not have happened if it weren't for my cousin, Tom Alter, who has acted in more than two hundred Hindi films. His contacts and introductions opened many doors and gave me access to individuals, studios, and sets. Nevertheless, Tom bears no responsibility for my observations and opinions. I am equally grateful to Vishal Bhardwaj and the entire *Omkara* unit for generously letting me follow the process of making this film. Special thanks to Abhishek Chaubey for commenting on the manuscript and to Abhik Sarkar for the use of his photographs. Kumar Mangat, the producer, has been very gracious and accommodating. I am also indebted to Robin Bhatt for his many insights and sage advice. The conversations recorded in this book have been transcribed as accurately as possible, though shifts in language, between Hindi and English, often necessitated paraphrasing within quotes. Translation and transliteration of names, titles, and dialogue in Hindi films can become a challenge. Every effort has been made to conform to conventional spellings, though the recent craze of numerology has film personalities adding and dropping vowels with impunity. Whenever a Hindi film has been released with a parallel title in English, this has been included in parentheses. Otherwise, direct translations of titles have been provided wherever it seemed appropriate. At points I have included a few words and sentences in Hindi to convey the cadence and texture of the language. Most of these are translated in parentheses but common exclamations like *arrey* (hey), *abhey* (yo), and *yaar* (my friend) don't have appropriate equivalents in English. Similarly, expressions like "time pass" and "item number" can only be understood within the lexicon of Bollywood. Two other words require definition. These are the common units for counting money in India: One lakh of rupees is 100,000 ($2,250) and one crore is 10,000,000 ($225,000).

Fantasies *of a* BOLLYWOOD *Love Thief*

SHAKESPEARE REMIXED

IF THIS WERE Venice there might have been an arched bridge of sculpted marble over a romantic canal, ornate balconies, and drifting gondolas.

Instead, we are somewhere in rural India, three hours' drive southeast of Mumbai, near a small village called Takave. According to the script it's supposed to be another place altogether, the badlands of Uttar Pradesh (U.P.), in a different part of the country, more than a thousand kilometers to the north of here. Despite a dislocation of geography, the arid countryside is close enough to match—hard, dry soil cracked by winter drought, yellow thistles and congress weed, sparse fields of maize withering under a fierce sun. Cattle egrets wade in the shallows of a stagnant river spanned by a narrow footbridge built on pillars of crumbling cement.

First day of shooting—Friday, January 13, 2006.

The film is *Omkara,* Vishal Bhardwaj's adaptation of Shakespeare's *Othello, the Moor of Venice.* The Bard goes Bollywood.

Seated on the concrete bridge, Iago and Roderigo get drunk in the afternoon.

ACT I, SCENE III

RODERIGO: I will incontinently drown myself.

IAGO: If thou dost, I shall never love thee after. Why, thou silly gentleman!

RODERIGO: It is silliness to live, when to live is torment: and then have we a prescription to die, when death is our physician.

Instead of speaking Elizabethan English the two actors deliver their lines in colloquial Hindi. Roderigo is Rajju and Iago is Langda Tyagi, two small-town gangsters mixing bile with whiskey.

SCENE 37, SHOT I, TAKE I

RAJJU
Dolly key liye hum apni jaan bhi dey sakhtey hain . . . such hai . . . nadi mein kudh jayenge . . .
(I'll give my life for Dolly . . . It's true . . . I'll jump in the river . . .)

LANGDA
To mainey gotiyan pakad rakhi hai kya teri . . .kudh ja.
(Have I got hold of your balls? . . . Go ahead, jump.)

RAJJU braces himself and jumps into the river, shouting out.

RAJJU
Dolly . . . !!
Desdemona . . . !!

The names have been changed but most of the initials remain the same. Othello is Omkara. Omi. O. The gang leader, a killer, he is ruthless in crime and ruthless in love—a man whose motives are as dark as his complexion. This is his tragedy, fueled by sex and violence, two of the most combustible ingredients in any culture of cinema.

Langda and Rajju are supposed to be alone on the bridge, though more than three hundred people are watching them perform. Aside from the director and his crew, camera and sound technicians, grips and tea boys, the producer and financiers have come to witness the first shot of the film. Months have been spent in preparation—writing, casting, composing songs, raising money, scouting locations—but this is the moment that everyone has been waiting for, when the clapper comes down and the production is under way.

Though the film is being made in Hindi, at least five languages are operating on the set. English is used for most of the direction, along with Hindi. The dialogue is all in Hindi dialect. The financiers converse in Gujarati, while most of the crew speaks Marathi and jokes are told in Punjabi.

Technically, the first shot is relatively simple, a minor scene that occurs thirty pages into the script. The sequence will eventually be edited down to a couple of minutes in the final print but it takes an entire day to film.

Vishal Bhardwaj stands on the bridge as he discusses the shot with associate director Abhishek Chaubey and cinematographer Tassaduq Hussain. Vishal positions the actors, Saif Ali Khan and Deepak Dobriyal. Saif is a star, with two Bollywood hits in 2005—*Parineeta* (A Married Woman) and *Salaam Namaste* (Greetings Hello). In this film, though, he takes on the negative role of Langda Tyagi—Iago. Shakespeare's greatest villain is transformed into an embittered thug with a clubfoot. Playing opposite Saif, Deepak is an unknown actor, a new face. His character, Rajju, is a pathetic fool hopelessly in love with Dolly. Langda uses him to get his revenge for having been passed over as Omkara's lieutenant—his *bahubali.*

"Lock sound!"

. . .

"Silence, please, going for take."

. . .

"Rolling."

On a low hill overlooking the river, a crowd of villagers have gathered to watch the shooting. The women squat in a line, their colorful clothes forming a bright hem along the top of the ridge. The men are dressed mostly in white, many of them wearing turbans. From a distance they can barely see the action or hear the lines. But it is the spectacle of filmmaking that attracts them, as much as the presence of a star like Saif. There are no songs or music today, not even a fight scene. The villagers are audience to the slow, deliberate process of creating cinema. They sit patiently for hours in the burning sun as the scene plays out, the camera moving from one angle to another. Later, some of them may watch *Omkara* in an air-conditioned picture hall, but today they witness a film that is just beginning, the first shot taking place in their own backyard.

The making of a Bollywood movie follows the conventions of cinema around the world. As anywhere, it is a process that combines creativity with technology, an essentially modern idiom and industry. At the same time, filmmakers in India possess their own aesthetics, their own expectations, their own language and artistic mannerisms. They also depend on an audience as diverse as it is demanding. The villagers of Takave, in their colorful saris and turbans, may fit a stereotype of rural rusticity but when it comes to motion pictures they have sophisticated tastes.

Just like audiences in seventeenth-century England, who flocked to Shakespeare's plays, Indian filmgoers pay to enter a theater to watch their own desires, fears, and guilts projected in front of them. They want stories that move and amuse them. For the most part, they know what is false and what is true, even if a writer or director attempts to deceive them. The villagers of Takave, as well as metro audiences in big cities like Mumbai or Delhi, are not naive viewers. They understand that a film is constructed, somewhat like a bridge or a road. It is an artifice of imagination, conceived, planned, surveyed, and built over time, out of many different materials, by hundreds of different hands. That is part of the fascination of watching a film shooting, to observe a production in process. Instead of suspending their disbelief, as the cliché suggests, the audience willingly embraces a conceit.

FILMI MASALA

2 finely diced onions
1 tablespoon crushed garlic
1 tablespoon crushed ginger
3 green chili peppers
1 teaspoon turmeric powder
1 teaspoon ground coriander
1 teaspoon ground roasted cumin
1 teaspoon red chili powder
4 tablespoons ghee for frying

The precise ingredients for a good blend of masala may vary according to the cook, but no matter what the recipe, this pungent concoction of spices excites all five senses.

Masala is the word most often used to describe a combination of elements that go into making a successful Bollywood film. Once again, the ingredients and quantities may be adjusted, with extra measures of romance, sex, violence, or suspense, depending on the script. All of these are simmered together to form a saucy cinematic curry that keeps audiences coming back for more.

It's not unusual that the most prevalent metaphors concerning Bollywood films have a culinary flavor; audiences in India relish a good movie as if it were a feast. Renowned filmmakers like

Prithviraj Kapoor and his son, Raj Kapoor, were insatiable gourmands, as well as being voracious cine-aesthetes. A film that contains racy sequences is referred to as non-veg, as against a blander vegetarian diet that the censors certify for family consumption.

The expression "Bollywood" is a relatively recent invention (claimed by at least one journalist to have been coined in 1991). Though it refers primarily to Hindi-language films produced in Mumbai (formerly Bombay), Bollywood encompasses a style of filmmaking that extends to cinema in many of India's other regional languages. Superficially, it describes movies that splice together elaborate plots involving plenty of dramatic action and leaps of improbable imagination, intercut with song and dance. Nevertheless, Bollywood is more than just the sum of its many stereotypes. It is a culture all its own, with a pantheon of celebrity icons and a fan base larger than the population of Europe and America combined.

The Indian film industry produces more than nine hundred movies a year, including everything from soft porn to highbrow flicks with a social or political message. "Art films" have had a niche audience since the 1970s, but it is commercial cinema, with big budgets and superstars, that drives the industry. For the most part, Mumbai's Bollywood and its regional cousins in cities like Chennai, Hyderabad, Bangalore, Trivandrum, and Kolkata recycle the same formulas that have worked from one decade to the next.

Despite time-tested clichés and rehashed plots of separated twins, family sagas, good sons and evil brothers, fallen women who redeem their virtue, and the inevitable struggle between rural and urban society, making a Bollywood film involves enormous risks. The majority of movies produced in India lose money, and only about 10 percent of the films can claim to be hits. Many end up, as one aspiring director described them, "superduper flops." Raising money for a producer has often involved illegal financing.

During the 1980s and 1990s, Mumbai's criminal underworld became a source of funding. A number of Bollywood celebrities became indebted to mafia dons, who resorted to extortion and murder when their investments failed. Only in 1998 did the government of India recognize filmmaking as a legitimate industry, allowing producers to get bank loans and more transparent financing. This has helped clean up Bollywood's public image but not necessarily its bottom line. Each year, dozens of films remain unfinished—unrequited dreams and a waste of millions of rupees. Even those that are completed often fail to find distributors, who control territories on the subcontinent like feudal filmlords paying tribute to Mumbai's reigning moguls.

Romance is the key ingredient of almost every successful film and story lines can often be traced back to the ancient narratives of India—*The Mahabharata* and *Ramayana.* Big Bollywood films have the operatic scope of epics, with lavish sets and soundtracks. Most productions are over two and a half hours in length. Any shorter and an audience won't feel they've got their money's worth—*paisa vasool.* Another expectation, which is usually fulfilled, requires at least three songs. Often twice that number are incorporated into a film, accompanied by dizzying choreography and costumes. It isn't unusual for actors to change outfits a dozen times in a single song—starting with a chiffon sari and ending up wearing a bikini.

In contemporary India, the cultural impact of Bollywood song and dance is virtually universal. It can be seen in television competitions like the recent *Nach Baliye,* where couples choreograph their own dance routines and are voted on or off the show by audiences from every corner of the country. The format follows *American Idol,* but with pairs of dancers who lip-synch to popular film songs. Dancing at weddings has always been a tradition, especially in north India, but now there are choreographers who teach a bridal party how to shake their hips in unison to songs from family dramas like *Hum Aapke Hain Koun . . . !* (What Am I to You . . . !). In some instances, even the bride, who traditionally keeps her head demurely covered and bowed during a Hindu wedding, drops her veil and does a nuptial cabaret for the groom and guests. At dance bars in Mumbai, young women entertain patrons by putting on gauzy outfits straight out of the wardrobes of Hindi films. These bar girls dance and lip-synch lyrics to film songs like "Tu Hai Khushboo, Tu Hai Jadoo" (You Are Perfume, You Are Magic). Mumbai's dance bars have recently been outlawed on moral grounds, even though the women don't shed their clothes. Instead, they perform a pantomime of musical passion, allowing their male audience the vicarious fantasy of being film heroes for an evening.

While sexual innuendo and scenes of lovemaking regularly appear in Hindi films, the industry is still prudish about displaying flesh. Until recently, kissing was taboo, even in pictures rated "A" for adults. On the other hand, dances invariably include enough pelvic thrusting to give an Elvis impersonator a slipped disk. Similarly, a heroine's breasts, covered by a sequined choli or skimpy bustier, remain a cinematographer's benchmark. Raj Kapoor, probably the greatest showman of the Hindi screen, put his trademark on wet sari scenes. For his fans, nothing compares to the eroticism of six yards of drenched cotton clinging to the ample contours of a starlet's body.

The Kapoors are the first family of Bollywood, having produced four generations of stars. They are not the only dynasty, however, for films in India are a family business. At times it feels as if everyone in the industry is related, with sons and daughters, cousins and nephews cashing in on their family names. Nepotism has often spawned mediocrity, though it also provides an ongoing sense of tradition and strong links with the past.

It is almost impossible to compare Bollywood to Hollywood. Instead of being two opposite sides of the same coin, they are separate currencies altogether, with a wildly fluctuating exchange rate. At times, the similarities are obvious—studios and stars, the glamorous premieres and events like the Oscars or the Filmfare Awards. (In the United States the statuette is male and in India it is female, but there are the same bad jokes and teary speeches.) Yet Hollywood and Bollywood speak different languages—not just the actors' dialogues but the visual vocabulary as well—conflicting illusions of reality. More than anything, the role of music sets Indian cinema apart. While Hollywood has produced plenty of musicals, Bollywood depends on its songs, not only to punctuate plots but also to sell its products. The release of a music album precedes the release of a film and the success or failure of a production often depends on the public response to its songs. Unlike anywhere else in the world, playback singers, whose voices carry the melodies and lyrics, enjoy a level of celebrity that matches the stars. Male vocalists like K. L. Saigal, Mohammed Rafi, Mukesh, and Kishore Kumar are often remembered with greater fondness than the actors who lip-synched their songs. And playback divas like sisters Lata Mangeshkar and Asha Bhosle have given voice to female actors for several generations and are still singing into their seventies.

Though grounded in Indian folk and classical traditions, Bollywood composers borrow from every continent. An eclectic exuberance marks the songs in most Hindi films, which blend ragas with rap and disco or bhangra with Beethoven. Each era of film music has its own distinct sounds. Tunes from the fifties mixed jazz and samba with waltzes and *ghazals.* Within a single song, the beat can change from a traditional *teen taal* played on tabla to the driving rhythms of rock and roll or African drumming. Hindi film composers discovered world music long before anyone else.

Bollywood has now become a global phenomenon. Indian expatriates, referred to as Non-Resident Indians (NRIs), have emigrated to every country in the world, carrying with them an appreciation for Indian cinema. Most airlines that fly to India screen Hindi films en route, helping travelers make the transition between West and East. Filmmakers like Yash Chopra often cater to an NRI audience—exploring displaced identities and longings for a distant homeland. Indian grocery stores in the United States and other countries provide their customers with a selection of Hindi films on DVD and video alongside hard-to-find spices and staples. Even as Bollywood conquers new territory and wins over younger audiences, it evokes nostalgia for films from the past. Karan Johar's recent *Kabhi Alvida Naa Kehna* (Never Say Goodbye) may be set in New York City in 2006 but it takes its title from lyrics by Amit Khanna for a Kishore Kumar song from *Chalte Chalte* (Moving Along), made in 1976.

Anyone who writes about Bollywood risks venturing into a subject on which literally millions of people claim to be experts. Simply mentioning the title of a particular film, or the name of an actor, director, or playback singer, will spark a discussion—even among strangers—that reveals a widespread knowledge of cinema trivia and lore.

When was the golden era of Hindi films?

While most people will concede that the 1950s were the gilded age of motion pictures in India, everyone has their own answer to this question. It usually corresponds to the years when a person was between sixteen and twenty-five. I watched my first Hindi films in the late 1960s and early 1970s. For me, the most memorable movies are romantic classics like Kamal Amrohi's *Pakeezah* (Pure One), starring Raaj Kumar and Meena Kumari; Vijay Anand's thrillers *Jewel Thief* and *Johnny Mera Naam,* both starring Dev Anand; and Hrishikesh Mukherjee's unforgettable *Anand,* with Rajesh Khanna in the title role and introducing a young and dashing Amitabh Bachchan. While these names may mean little to most people in the West, they are as familiar in India as Sean Connery, Elizabeth Taylor, or Marlon Brando.

What are the top-ten Bollywood films of all time?

No ranking will ever satisfy everyone, even two members of the same family. *Mother India* (Mehboob Khan, 1957) would probably figure on most lists, along with *Pyaasa* (Thirst, Guru Dutt, 1957) and *Mughal-e-Aazam* (The Great Mughal, K. Asif, 1960). *Sholay* (Embers, Ramesh Sippy, 1975) finds a place in almost every filmography. After this the choices become so subjective as to be meaningless. I would add *Barsaat* (Rain, Raj Kapoor, 1949) and *Guide* (Vijay Anand, 1965), as well as *Bhumika: The Role* (Shyam Benegal, 1977), the comedy *Jaane Bhi Do Yaaron* (Who Pays the Piper, Kundan Shah, 1983), and *Rangeela* (Full of Color, Ram Gopal Varma, 1995). To make it ten, I'd flip a coin to choose between *Mr India* (Shekhar Kapur, 1987) and *Lagaan* (Land Tax, Ashutosh Gowariker, 2001).

Who is the greatest tragic hero of Hindi cinema?

Devdas—in the many films made in his name. Based on a Bengali novel by Saratchandra Chattopadhyay, *Devdas* is the story of a lovelorn man who drinks himself to death because of his childhood sweetheart, Paro. Whether it is K. L. Saigal, Dilip Kumar, or Shah Rukh Khan playing the lead, this self-destructive tragedy always floods the gallery with tears.

Of all the archetypes in Hindi films, however, perhaps the most appealing is the love thief, a character who steals another's heart. He is a criminal whose only crime is passion. For him, seduction is a form of burglary, a surreptitious game in which he uses charm and guile to gain entry into a woman's guarded affections.

Like so much else in Bollywood, the love thief is an adaptation of mythology. While he appears on-screen in modern guise, his manner and his motives reach back to ancient Sanskrit poetry. The *Chaurapanchasika,* or *Phantasies of a Love-Thief,* is attributed to Bilhana, an eleventh-century poet from Kashmir who was imprisoned because of an affair with the king's daughter. In highly erotic stanzas, he recalls the passionate crimes that put him behind bars.

Of course, the ultimate love thief is Krishna, who not only steals the cowgirls' clothes when they are bathing but also absconds with their desires. Krishna is the blue-skinned god who woos the fair and lovely Radha, enjoying illicit trysts and stolen glances. Dadasaheb Phalke, India's founding filmmaker, made the early mythological *Shri Krishna Janma* (Birth of Shri Krishna, 1918), in which the youthful Krishna steals butter from his mother's kitchen, foreshadowing erotic thefts to come.

In the *Ramayana* epic, the love thief is the demon Ravana, the dark lord of Lanka, who steals the chaste and pale-skinned Sita. The criminality of romance appears in so many Bollywood films, from Raj Kapoor's *Shree 420* (the number in the Indian penal code assigned to crimes of deception) to Manmohan Desai's *Bluff Master* and Basu Chatterjee's *Chitchor* (Heart Stealer). A trickster, a pickpocket, sometimes even a smuggler or extortionist, the love thief is generally male, though the role has also been played by women like Nadira or Helen. More than any other actor, Dev Anand has played the love thief—from *Baazi* (A Game of Chance) to *Jewel Thief*. In the second of these he plays a double role. The hero pretends to be the villain, while seducing Vyjantimala and solving the crime. (He also performs a podoerotic striptease that takes Bollywood's foot fetish to the extreme.)

Omkara may not fit the mold of a conventional love thief, but he is a gangster who steals the bride on her marriage day. As in the epics, he is dark and she is fair. Their love story is a forbidden tale that breaks the rules of family and caste, a stolen romance that ends in tragedy. Omkara's jealousy arises, at least in part, because he knows that he has taken Dolly against the wishes of her father. As an antihero, he remains a ruthless criminal, though it is love that makes him human.

At the beginning of Shakespeare's play, Iago and Roderigo rouse Desdemona's father in the night, shouting: "Awake! what, ho, Brabantio! thieves! thieves! thieves! Look to your house, your daughter and your bags! Thieves! thieves! . . . Sir, you're robb'd . . ."

In a parallel scene from the movie, the jilted bridegroom, Rajju, comes rushing to Dolly's father and blurts out: "*Omi Shukla ney Dolly ko 'tha liya.*" (Omi Shukla has lifted Dolly and taken her away.) A short while later, the title song begins, a folk ballad that celebrates Omkara as a half-caste hero, a contemporary Robin Hood who wins the hearts of his people even as he steals the affections of a Brahmin's daughter.

Ajay Devgan and Kareena Kapoor, surrounded by fans, during the *Omkara* shooting in Lucknow.

MAQBOOL

HINDI FILMS have turned to Shakespeare for inspiration more than once. Baburao Painter's *Savkari Pash,* released in 1925, was based in part on *The Merchant of Venice.* Mehboob Khan made *Taming of the Shrew* as *Aan* in 1952. *Romeo and Juliet* has inspired dozens of films, like Raj Kapoor's 1973 hit, *Bobby. The Comedy of Errors* was remade by Gulzar in 1982 as *Angoor* (Grapes). Almost all of Shakespeare's work has been translated into Hindi, as well as India's sixteen other regional languages. Plays like *Othello* and *Julius Caesar* are part of the curriculum at high schools and universities. The characters and stories are as familiar to educated audiences in India as the works of classical Sanskrit dramatists like Kalidasa. *Shakespeare-Wallah,* James Ivory and Ishmail Merchant's early film, follows the story of a repertory company performing the Bard's oeuvre in small towns and cities across the subcontinent. Rather than being a literary hangover from British colonialism, these plays have been absorbed and integrated into the collective imagination. India has adopted Shakespeare as its own.

Vishal Bhardwaj has already made one film based on a Shakespeare play. *Maqbool,* a reworking of *Macbeth,* was one of the most powerful and disturbing films of 2003. Its critical and commercial success established Vishal's reputation as an innovative and ambitious filmmaker. He transposes Shakespeare's tragedy rather than translating it, though he preserves many of the essential elements, including predictions of doom and indelible bloodstains. Foggy moors and dank castles give way to mildewed *havelis* and the stark cityscapes of Mumbai. Horses are replaced by Mercedes-Benzes and swords with pistols. But the real magic of the film lies in the way Vishal is able to reconstruct a Scottish melodrama within the dangerous and twisted domain of Mumbai's criminal underworld. Not only does he relocate the story in a different time and place but, like a familiar theme in music that gets remixed, Vishal sets it in another key.

Maqbool owes as much to *The Godfather* as it does to *Macbeth,* but this is not the usual imitative fare of Bollywood's generic copies, which sometimes seem to have been produced with a Xerox machine rather than a cine camera. Vishal knows how to punctuate the moment before a gun goes off, just as he knows how to spatter blood or exploit the erotic possibilities of a mosquito net. *Maqbool* is a serious movie that fastens you to your seat.

"Any film that deals with criminal mafia, wherever it is, has to refer to *The Godfather* in some way." Vishal admits that he has always been fascinated by the underworld. He composed the songs for Ram Gopal Varma's *Satya* (1998), one of Hindi cinema's most memorable gangster films.

"Violence catches your attention. If you take out a gun people will listen to you. It happens in a film as well. With *Maqbool* I didn't want to make the usual kind of film about the underworld, which always becomes a story about gang wars. People are killed but most of the time we don't show it directly. And the underworld I have depicted isn't what really exists. Bombay's mafia have become terrorists. Instead, *Maqbool* is a fantasy shot realistically."

One of the strengths of *Maqbool* lies in the performances. Pankaj Kapoor plays mafia don Abbaji with such intensity that he almost steals the show from Irfan Khan in the title role. Abbaji's hooded eyes, lined with kohl, make him as menacing as any criminal on-screen. Love is little more than a cover for jealousy, like the heart-shaped paan leaves that contain betel nuts, tobacco, and lime. When Abbaji prepares paan for his guests, he does it with a maliciousness that makes one feel the betel must be poisoned by his touch. This is not your usual potboiler villain, and when Maqbool finally puts a bullet through his heart we feel almost relieved. Better known for his theater performances than as a screen actor, Irfan Khan takes on Maqbool with suppressed vulnerability, a gangster and lover who is tormented by guilt. He also conveys an insolent sensuality full of passion and betrayal. As the female lead, Tabu is superb playing Nimmi, Abbaji's mistress and Maqbool's lover—Lady Macbeth—a woman maneuvering to get her way in a man's world. In supporting roles, Om Puri and Naseeruddin Shah provide a comic counterpoint as corrupt policemen, turning Shakespeare's witches into fools.

When I first meet Vishal Bhardwaj he is playing cricket in Mussoorie, the hill station where I live. My cousin, Tom Alter, and Vishal are members of the Mumbai Cricket Club, which consists mostly of players who have film industry connections. Both Tom and Vishal are as fanatical about sports as they are about cinema.

Dressed in cricket whites and padded up to bat, Vishal doesn't look like a filmmaker. A quiet, compact man of forty, with a trim mustache that frames an easy smile, he defies the popular image of a Bollywood film director. There is neither the impulsive flamboyance nor the tormented angst of an egotistical auteur. But the more one gets to know him the more his creative side is revealed. He has a restless personality, a preoccupied impatience that shows in his eyes. As his wife, Rekha, explains, "He is always working on something, a song or an idea for a film. It's constantly on his mind."

Often, during the middle of a conversation one can see that his thoughts have wandered—not in a rude or condescending manner, simply diverted by his imagination.

Vishal entered filmmaking through music. After struggling for more than a decade he made his name as a composer, then worked his way up to directing films of his own. Watching his movies, one has a feeling he composes his films, almost as if they were based on a musical score rather than a script.

"There is a rhythm to every film, just like a song. You give it a certain tempo. I tried to do that with *Maqbool.* Being a musician has helped me a lot in directing. I understand the pace of a scene. If an actor takes a second more than he should, or a second less, it can ruin a shot. The other thing is the pitch of an actor's voice. Take Pankaj Kapoor in *Maqbool.* He plays a character who has been chewing paan for fifty years. You can hear it in his voice."

One of the distinctive aspects of *Maqbool* is that it was shot in synch-sound, whereas the dialogue and audio effects in most Hindi films are dubbed in a recording studio—a tedious process in which the actors must match their voices to the movement of their lips.

"With synch-sound you get much more intensity," Vishal explains. "With dubbing, actors become lazy. They know that they can correct themselves later in the studio, but when it's shot in synch they have to concentrate."

India's early talkies used synch-sound and it was only in the 1950s that dubbing became prevalent, as filmmakers moved out of the studios and began shooting on location. The technology for music recordings has moved in the opposite direction. Until the 1970s film music was performed by an orchestra, accompanying the playback singer, as if it were a live performance. Now musicians play separately and the singers record their tracks over the orchestration.

"Technically, the quality of the music is much better and it's easier to correct mistakes," Vishal explains. "But I would say, the earlier recordings had more emotion, when a playback singer performed the songs with the orchestra."

Unlike many Hindi films, where the shift from action to song is abrupt and often awkward, in Vishal's films there is a seamless quality to the music and images he presents. The songs in *Maqbool* are woven into the narrative. This includes one musical sequence in which a female dancer performs in front of an audience of inebriated men. Though the situation and setting is stereotypical of Bollywood dance numbers, Vishal tweaks the cliché by intercutting it with scenes from a bridal party of women dancing among themselves. Though none of the actors suddenly breaks into song, the background score of the film accompanies and amplifies their roles.

Maqbool contains three songs, all of which occur in the first half. "We had a fourth song but I had to take it out." Vishal expresses some regret. "It was in the second half and people were impatient. They wanted to know the end. It was my favorite song in terms of picturization. Tabu is trying to wash blood off her face. The song was beautiful but had to be sacrificed for the sake of the story.

"The most difficult part of making a film is getting the right story. In India we don't have many good screenplay writers. That's why we borrow so many stories from Hollywood. The problem with a story is always resolution. For an hour and a half I can hold your attention with almost anything. But the final half hour is the problem."

Vishal gestures to a line of flowerpots beside us. "For instance, I could put a lemon under this pot and keep you guessing what is there for most of the story, but when I finally pick up the flowerpot, you'll say, '*Arrey yaar,* it's just a lemon.'"

Even after living in Mumbai for fifteen years, Vishal remains something of an outsider. Coming from Meerut, a small town in

Uttar Pradesh, he entered the film industry with few connections. Unlike many filmmakers, who have inherited their positions through family legacies, Vishal has had to make his own way. At the same time, films have always been in his blood.

"My father was a poet and a lyricist. He worked as a government servant in Meerut, where I grew up. During holidays we would go to Bombay, where my father wrote songs for Hindi films. As a boy, I listened to film music all the time, mostly on the radio. At an early age I decided to become a music director. My influences were all of the great composers like Laxmikant-Pyarelal, Madan Mohan, S. D. Burman and R. D. Burman, Salil Choudhury."

A self-taught musician, Vishal lets his ear and instincts guide him rather than formal training. As a student at Delhi University, he met his wife, Rekha, a classical singer. She introduced him to the more traditional aspects of Hindustani music and they have collaborated on many of his songs. Vishal has his own recording studio in Mumbai where in 2003 they produced an album, *Ishqa Ishqa,* of Rekha singing the Sufi-inspired poetry of Gulzar, their mentor.

One of the most respected filmmakers in India, Gulzar has directed more than a dozen feature films, including the controversial *Aandhi* (Storm) and *Maachis* (Matches). At the same time Gulzar has made children's films for television and a serial based on the life of the Urdu poet Ghalib. Gulzar himself is a poet, who has written some of the most popular lyrics in Hindi cinema, including the 2005 hit song "Kajra Re" from *Bunty aur Babli.*

"My ambition was always to work with Gulzar Saab," Vishal recounts. "He is a writer I admired very much. I memorized all of his poems. You can mention any line of his, and I'll complete the couplet.

"One day, when I was in college, I heard that Gulzar Saab was coming to a recording session at a studio in Delhi, so I went to try and meet him. It was eleven o'clock at night and I was sitting there waiting. Suddenly the phone rang and no one else was in the room to answer it. When I picked up, Gulzar Saab was on the line. He said he was lost and couldn't find the studio. I told him I would come and get him. He was near the sweetshops at Bengali Market. So I went across and brought him to the studio. On the way I told him I was a fan of his and introduced myself. Later, when we met again in Bombay, he remembered me and we began to work together on a few television shows."

Some of the earliest songs they wrote together were for the Hindi version of *The Jungle Book.* Since then they have collaborated in several films. Vishal composed the music for Gulzar's *Maachis* and Gulzar wrote the lyrics for *Maqbool.*

"As Gulzar Saab says, 'There are two things in India that everyone thinks they can do better than anyone else: one is play cricket, the other is make films.' If you ask any man on the street, he will immediately give you an opinion. '*Arrey yaar,* if Sachin hadn't played that shot he wouldn't have got out.' It's the same with movies. '*Arrey yaar,* if the director had only cut that shot it would have been a better scene.'"

In addition to *Maqbool,* Vishal has made *Makdee* (The Web of the Witch), a whimsical but frightening horror film about a pair of twins who get lured into a haunted house inhabited by a witch who has the temperament of a venomous arachnid. Though it was made on an extremely low budget, the film starred Shabana Azmi as the witch and attracted an enthusiastic audience of adults as well as children. This was followed by *Maqbool,* after which Vishal made *Chatri Chor* (The Blue Umbrella), based on a children's story by Ruskin Bond.

Adapting *Othello,* Vishal has the opportunity to build on his earlier successes. *Omkara* is a big-budget production with seven well-known Bollywood stars. In scale and vision it is a much bigger film than *Maqbool,* and for that reason it takes far greater risks. Financially there is more at stake, but with a return to

Shakespeare, Vishal also risks falling back into a predictable genre, repeating himself.

Filmmaking is an industry that continually imitates success while trying to create something that's never been seen before. Bollywood is often accused of being derivative, of borrowing story lines from the West. Though some Hindi films may infringe on intellectual property rights, there are many others that break new ground. Movies have always been indebted to literature and the language of film is often lifted from the page onto the screen. *Othello* has been turned into a film at least a dozen times, most notably Orson Welles's black-and-white classic of 1952. Shakespeare himself adapted his stories from other sources, usually without citation. The tragedy of Desdemona and the Moor of Venice was taken directly from Giraldi Cinthio's *Hecatommithi,* a collection of tales originally written in Italian. At the same time, Cinthio's cycle of stories, along with other Italian anthologies like the *Decameron,* was probably inspired by the *Arabian Nights.* Salaciously translated by Sir Richard Burton, *The Thousand and One Nights* contains several episodes about fair damsels falling into the arms of lusty "blackamoors." Whatever the provenance of the tale, four centuries after Shakespeare wrote *Othello,* the story now finds itself in a totally new guise, scripted in Hindi and set among gangsters in northern India.

ONE WAY TO BOMBAY

YOU CAN'T buy a ticket to Bollywood. There's no such place. You won't find it on any maps. The name isn't spelled out in giant letters on a hillside. There's no railway station or bus stop that bears that name, no telephone directory, municipal authority, or post office to give it a stamp of legitimacy. Bollywood is little more than a label, a brand that hasn't even been copyrighted, an idea that blinks and flashes like a neon sign.

The closest you can come to locating Bollywood is somewhere in the northern suburbs of Mumbai, between Mahim Creek or the sea rocks at Bandra and the upper reaches of Juhu Beach, possibly in the vicinity of Pali Hills. While most of Mumbai's landmark cinemas lie downtown in the pendant heart of the city—Eros, Regal, Minerva, Maratha Mandir—Bollywood could just as easily be located at Chembur, within the lengthening shadows of R. K. Studios, or on the other side of Santa Cruz and Vile Parle, in Andheri, either east or west, an ambiguous, amorphous place within the expanding margins of the city. Mumbai never seems to end, growing outward like an alluvial delta veined with streams of traffic and railway lines, formed by tidal surges of commuters.

Nobody seems to like the name "Mumbai" except for the

Maratha chauvinists who insisted on changing it from Bombay ten years ago, an awkward juggling of consonants and vowels that asserts a political identity. Most residents still call their city Bombay, though the name has been respelled on all the signboards. At the same time, not everybody likes Bollywood, either. Because it's derivative. Because it seems like a cheap joke, a second-rate Hollywood, borrowing its shine, its drama, its glamour.

The Hindi film industry has been around for more than a hundred years. It produces more movies than Hollywood, with bigger stars and larger audiences around the world. Why should it have to assume a screen name, take on an alias, adopt a tacky pseudonym?

Perhaps because cinema itself is a derivative medium. There is nothing particularly original about Hollywood, either, which adopted its name from a village in Ireland that sent its sons and daughters to America. The ancestral town in County Cork is famous for the Hollywood stone, a rock on which is etched a medieval labyrinth that looks like a tangled spool of film.

Names are changed at the drop of a comedian's hat. Norma Jean becomes Marilyn Monroe. Yusuf Khan becomes Dilip Kumar. Dastagir becomes Sabu. Columbia Pictures becomes TriStar. Othello becomes Omkara.

One of India's most romantic trains, the Frontier Mail, is now called the Golden Temple Mail. It used to run from Peshawar, in the North-West Frontier Province near the Khyber Pass, all the way to Bombay. But after India's partition in 1947, the journey was cut short and now begins in Amritsar, on this side of the border with Pakistan. Though the name has changed, almost everyone, from travel agents to railway porters, still refers to it as the Frontier Mail.

For Hindi cinema, this train has special significance. It brought many of the great filmmakers to this city. The Frontier Mail is the umbilical cord that connects Punjab with Mumbai. As unknown artistes, full of expectations and hopes, actors like Prithviraj Kapoor, Dilip Kumar, Dev Anand, and so many others rode these rails into the city of dreams. Today, film stars jet about in airliners that take a tenth of the time to travel the same distance, but many still make the journey with nothing more than a second-class ticket and unreserved hopes in their pockets.

There's an old Hindi film called *Miss Frontier Mail,* starring Fearless Nadia—the dashing stunt queen of the 1930s and 1940s, who always wore a mask, as well as shorts that exposed her ample thighs. According to biographer Dorothee Wenner, Nadia was born Mary Evans, the daughter of a Scottish soldier and a Greek belly dancer. Fearless Nadia took on the roles of Indian women before independence, when there was a stigma attached to female actors. Playbills of *Miss Frontier Mail* depict a luxurious train, with passengers seated on overstuffed sofas, evoking an era of gracious rail travel. There is also an image of Fearless Nadia leaping from carriage to carriage atop the moving train.

Departing Amritsar each evening, the Frontier Mail travels through the night to Delhi and continues on from there at eight in the morning. The entire journey takes a little over thirty hours. There are faster trains, but the Frontier Mail is freighted with nostalgia. Retracing this journey, it's not difficult to imagine the impatience and expectations an aspiring actor would feel. The enforced idleness of riding this train encourages daydreams. Like a moving picture, the carriage window frames the passing scenery outside—buffalo wallowing in a village tank, trucks lined up at a level crossing, farmers burning chaff in their fields, the rugged ridges of the Aravalli Range outlined with sandstone fortresses. But your mind is somewhere else, traveling a parallel vision. Film magazines purchased from a platform vendor—*Star and Style, Filmfare, CineBlitz*—offer glossy fantasies of the future. You dream of fame and fortune, but more than that, of a sense of engagement, of being part of the film world, a personality, a presence, a hero. The Frontier Mail carries you forward but your mind is already there. You have left behind the small town where you were born and now you will make a new name for yourself in the big city. You picture yourself surrounded by celebrities, the masquerade of movies, beautiful men and women in the bright glare of camera lights, attending parties, signing autographs.

Mumbai Central Station has none of the architectural grandeur of Victoria Terminus—now known as Chatrapati Shivaji Station—but as its name suggests, this is the hub of the city. Most of the trains from all across India, including the Frontier Mail, arrive at Mumbai Central. Once you leave the gates of the railway station, it isn't a promising sight. You stand there dazed from your journey, alone in the swirl of traffic. You have arrived in Mumbai but there is no welcome—only the jostling of others who have disembarked. A garbage truck is being filled with refuse, men shoveling rubbish into its rusty maw. The stench of garbage stays with you as you cross the street along with a herd of other pedestrians. There are food stalls and sweetshops, as well as dance bars—Samudra Mahal, Captain Cook, Sea Prince—offering happy hours all afternoon.

But as you turn back and retrace your steps, already lost in the tumult of this city, you spot Maratha Mandir. In the unfiltered glare of daylight, the cinema looks seedy—a sooty yellow-and-red exterior. Only a few touts and parking attendants loiter outside.

On Friday, April 15, 2005, the longest-running film in Indian cinema history celebrated its five-hundredth week at Maratha Mandir. *Diwale Dulhania le Jayenge* (The Brave Heart Will Take the Bride) has had a long run of good fortune. Produced in 1995 by the veteran filmmaker Yash Chopra and directed by his heir, Aditya Chopra, *DDLJ* (as it's commonly called) is a family drama fully laden with romance and heartbreak, quintessential Bollywood. It was also one of the first films to explore the Indian diaspora—the experience of Non-Resident Indians.

DDLJ has been deconstructed and analyzed by film scholars over the ten years it has been showing. But for the crowd that lines up in front of Maratha Mandir every day, the matinee show offers two and a half hours of pure entertainment. Reduced prices—20 rupees for balcony, 18 for dress circle, and 16 for the stalls—help draw loafers and loiterers off the street. Maratha Mandir has more than 1,000 seats and when I bought my ticket, in the 499th week, the balcony was full.

The crowd of young men, along with a few couples and families, wait impatiently outside the doors until the ushers finally let them in. The cool suction of air-conditioning draws you into a lobby decorated like a wedding cake with pink-and-white molding. A life-size image of Sathya Sai Baba (an ascetic saint revered for his posthumous blessings) is enshrined on the ground floor. As the cinema fills, a lively jazz medley plays over the loudspeakers, a fusion of Herb Alpert and Ravi Shankar. The atmosphere and decor at Maratha Mandir is sixties kitsch with no apologies.

Only after the movie begins, preceded by the national anthem, does the audience erupt in cheers. All around me I can hear the murmuring of voices reciting the opening monologue, as Amrish Puri's character feeds pigeons in Trafalgar Square. Hoots and whistles greet the appearance of Kajol, who plays his daughter—Simran. Even louder whistles and applause erupt as Shah Rukh Khan—Raj—arrives on-screen, rushing toward the touchline in a rugby match. The first half of the film is set in England and Switzerland where the characters travel on Eurail passes. For the audience, most of whom come from the poorer neighborhoods surrounding Maratha Mandir, it could be another planet but they are willingly transported there. During the songs, two men in the row behind me sing every word. I can feel anticipation building for a favorite scene as people begin to laugh even before a joke is told.

Because of *DDLJ*'s 500th week, two television crews are set up in the lobby during the interval. One is from Japan, the other a

Mumbai channel. As the crowd disperses into the lobby, buying popcorn or heading for the toilets, TV journalists thrust microphones in their faces, asking how many times they've seen the film and why they think it's so popular. Bollywood always makes news.

After the interval, *DDLJ*'s setting shifts to India, as the characters return to their homeland, the beloved soil of the Punjab with its brilliant yellow mustard fields. Though we are sitting in Maharashtra, the film evokes a universal fantasy of the Indian heartland, the rural home for which an urban audience yearns.

Later, during the penultimate scene, when Raj decides to leave Simran because he can't persuade her father to let them marry, one of the television crews bursts into the balcony. A parallel shaft of light intrudes like a second projector beam and a director waves at the audience, gesturing for us to turn around and look at the screen. Thankfully, the TV crew retreats a few minutes later, to let us watch the rest of the film, the dramatic fight scene on the railway platform and the poignant moment when Simran's father releases her hand so that she can run to join Raj on the departing train.

Watching this scene, it feels as if all of us are passengers on the same train, riding through the mustard fields of the Punjab, traveling second class on the Frontier Mail . . .

MONSOON BRAINSTORM

FLYING INTO Mumbai during the monsoon is always turbulent. As our pilot banks the jet to avoid thunderheads, the plane begins to shudder and dip. Because of its location along the coast, Mumbai attracts storms from June through August, moist air currents off the Arabian Sea colliding with the hot anvil of the subcontinent.

As we descend through gaps in the clouds, pleated ridgelines appear below us, unfolding into wetlands and estuaries along the coast. The monsoon has a distinctive shade of green, both brilliant and dull at the same time, a murky, mossy verdure. Circling over the sea, the plane veers suddenly and rolls before dropping into a trough of air. The clouds are above us now and Mumbai is beneath us. Blue plastic tarpaulins are spread everywhere, covering leaks on red tile roofs and rusty jigsaw puzzles of corrugated tin. The bright synthetic blue is a sharp contrast to the muddy slums slipping beneath our wings. We drop again and the saturated ground comes up to meet us, plumes of water spraying out as we land.

"I need five romantic stories. Classics," Vishal demands, adding with practicality, "all out of copyright."

We are at his recording studio in Andheri, along with Abhishek Chaubey, associate director of *Maqbool* and a cowriter on *The Blue Umbrella.* Outside the window, rain is still coming down, beaded curtains of moisture.

Vishal hands me a script that he and Abhishek have just finished writing: *Romanchak.*

The title is a composite of English and Hindi. Its root is "romance" but the suffix "*chak*" means to taste with the tip of your tongue.

"It means thriller or thrilling," says Vishal.

"Like pulp fiction," Abhishek explains. "Cheap Hindi novels are described as *romanchak* stories."

Now that they have finished the script, there is a problem. "I don't have time to shoot this film," Vishal says in frustration.

His next project is supposed to be a movie with Aamir Khan and Kareena Kapoor entitled *Mr. Mehta and Mrs. Singh,* but Aamir Khan's dates have been postponed to next July, a year from now. Shahid Kapoor, whom Vishal wants to cast as the lead in *Romanchak,* can't give him dates until January, which doesn't leave enough time to complete the film.

Caught between projects, Vishal is not someone who likes to sit idle for long. After a month of scriptwriting, he's ready to do something else, anything to engage his imagination. He has directed a couple of ad films, but doesn't find the work satisfying.

"The money is good," he admits. "But only ten percent of it is creative. The rest is just hard work."

After the success of *Maqbool,* very few people have approached him to compose music. Now that he is known as a director they seem hesitant to ask him for songs. The most recent *Filmfare* has a long article about Vishal, with a glamorous photograph of him looking pensive and thoughtful. The writer quotes him as saying, "Please emphasize in bold letters that I'm open to assignments. When I began directing films, the impression was that I wouldn't be interested in scoring music. But that's not the case."

He has been traveling to Uganda for a film festival and workshop with Mira Nair, director of *Monsoon Wedding. The Blue Umbrella* is going to be shown at festivals in Seoul and Goa, but the commercial release has been delayed. His desk is piled with DVDs and books, including Quentin Tarantino's published script of *True Romance.* Vishal is a director in search of a story, bouncing ideas off the walls.

Earlier, his wife, Rekha, had come to the studio to listen to a remix of the title track from *Ishqa Ishqa,* the Sufi-inspired album she recorded in 2003. Hitesh Sonik, a musician and composer who works with Vishal at the studio, adjusts the levels on the sound system.

"I wanted to make it a little different," Rekha explains. "After two years of singing these songs, it gets boring to repeat it again and again without variations, as if I were lip-synching." She wears a blue kurta, dopatta, and jeans. Her voice is muted outside the speakers and the vacillating lights on the sound console.

They discuss the song—she sings a few lines, Vishal sings a few lines. "*Tere ishq mein, tere ishq mein . . .*" (In your love . . .) The devotional passion of Sufi mystics blurs with the romantic lyrics. They replay a phrase.

"We can leave out the flute," Vishal says to Hitesh, then tells me, "We've agreed to a deal with Sony. They're doing a new album of Rekha's songs. Along with this we're making five short films. Each will be a love story to be shown on television. The songs will be included, like a music video but longer. I want to have Rekha and her band as part of the story, in the background . . ." Vishal is thinking aloud. "Or each film can begin with the band traveling to a different destination. But first we need five good romantic plots," he insists.

Thinking back to texts I've assigned in creative writing classes, I narrate Kate Chopin's "The Story of an Hour." It's about a woman with a weak heart, whose husband is killed in a train accident. When her family breaks the news to her as gently as possible, she locks herself in her room and experiences a strange catharsis. Though she loved her husband, she is "free at last." Her grief is mixed with relief. The story is only three pages long and takes place within an hour, but Chopin ends with a plot twist that undercuts everything that went before.

Vishal likes the story.

"This is a good one," he says. "We can add to it. In flashbacks we can show how the main character remembers her marriage, how she loved her husband but now that he is dead she feels completely free. It's very subtle. And almost any song will go with this."

Both Vishal and Abhishek light up India Kings—and as they smoke, their imaginations seem to fill their eyes. Abhishek is tall and lanky, with long hair and glasses, in his early thirties. Vishal is older but with a youthful face covered in three weeks' growth of beard.

Our conversation moves back and forth between Hindi and English. The idea of these five films fitting together as a sequence intrigues Vishal. He rings for his personal assistant, Shailender, and asks him for an anthology—*A Hundred Great Love Stories.* The book has been put away in a cupboard somewhere. While Shailu searches, Vishal stares out the window.

"There's a woman over there, in the apartment across the street. Every day she comes out on the balcony to sit and drink tea, have a cigarette, read . . . Sometimes when I am composing, I find it distracting and I have to close the curtains."

Abhishek and I look across at the woman, a distant figure amid the anonymous apartment blocks in Andheri. The rain is still falling lightly and the clouds are close above us. On the street below an autorickshaw drives through a puddle sending up a spray of water. The woman doesn't know that we are watching her. Creative voyeurs. Brainstorming about love. All we need are five good stories . . . out of copyright.

Whether it is Sanskrit poetry from the fifth century or Bollywood films of today, monsoon clouds have always represented passion and desire. Their dark, tumultuous shapes form the backdrop for love stories from *Shakuntala* to *Kashmir ki Kali* (The Blossom of Kashmir). For Hindi filmmakers the monsoon has always provided a dramatic visual device to suggest the onslaught of love, be it the black-and-white storm clouds in *Do Bigha Zameen* (Two Acres of Land), the Technicolor palette of *Mausam* (Season), or the digitized hues of *Dil Chahta Hai* (Do Your Thing).

As much as anyplace on the Indian subcontinent, Mumbai absorbs the monsoon in all its ferocious fertility. Cloud banks approach across the ocean, rearing up above Nariman Point and Malabar Hill, like a slow stampede of elephants. Those sultry, humid moments before a storm are like the aching fullness of desire.

I'm staying in Colaba, at the southern tip of Mumbai. When I set off for Vishal's office the next day, the sky is overcast. The first few drops of rain start to fall, spattering the pavement, as I hail a taxi. Within seconds a cannonade erupts. The driver warns me it will take at least two hours to reach Andheri. Beggars wade out to the cars, draped in clear plastic, their pathetic gestures all the more disturbing because of the rain. Inside the taxi I can hardly breathe but the minute I open the window rain pours in to soak the seat.

Three hours later, when I come dripping into his office, Vishal hardly seems aware of the rain outside. Before I have a chance to discuss *Romanchak* he tells me that he narrated "The Story of an Hour" to an actor he's considering for the role.

"She was totally zapped! She wants to do this part."

As in most of our conversations, we carom from one idea to the next. Vishal is still searching for more love stories. He digs out a collection of Hindi stories by Sharad Joshi in which there is a spoof of *Shakuntala,* with a detective who helps find her lost lover.

"I've been thinking of making this as a full-length feature for some time. I want to make it like a James Bond film with chopper shots and everything—or like *Crouching Tiger, Hidden Dragon,* a martial arts movie. Set in the period but with a detective."

Finally, we return to the *Romanchak* script and I tell him which characters I like, particularly Colonel Ranjit Singh, the hero of a cheap mystery novel that you might buy on a railway platform. Vishal and Abhishek's script is a rough draft, still unpolished. It moves between English and Hindi, with references to early Bollywood films, particularly famous screen villains like K. N. Singh, Jeevan, and Premnath, as well as the most famous screen danseuse of all time, Helen—crowned "Queen of the Nautch Girls."

"I'm still not happy with the climax," Vishal says. A briefcase that contains the vital secret of the story doesn't really work. There is a metaphorical reference to a parakeet—a *tota.* We discuss having a live parakeet instead of a briefcase.

"Yes, I like this," he says. "We'll make it a talking parrot and it has the secret memorized, some Web site . . . www.something.com. This is much better."

One of the worst monsoon storms in Mumbai's history strikes the city the day I am supposed to leave. Twenty-nine inches of rain falls in twenty-four hours. A hundred people are killed within Mumbai itself, close to a thousand casualties in the state of Maharashtra. Not only is my flight canceled but the airport terminal is flooded and all of the computers and security equipment stop working. Unlike most passengers who spend the night ankle deep in water, I am lucky to find a room at an airport hotel. At least I am dry, even if there is no electricity, drinking water, or telephones. The entire city has shut down. Roads and railway lines are flooded. Houses collapse. Drivers are asphyxiated in their cars.

Two days later, when the television finally comes on in my room, I can see pictures of devastation: mud slides that killed dozens of people, the carcasses of dead buffalo, stalled lines of traffic. Some film stars have helped rescue victims, other celebrities have sought shelter in five-star hotels.

One TV channel broadcasts a special program of film songs related to the monsoon, an antidote to the misery and suffering caused by the storm. Musical clips have been chosen from different films, all of them celebrating the romantic side of the monsoon. This may not offer much solace for those who are waist deep in water that is swirling with sewage, dead rats, and other debris, but for most people stranded at home it provides a diversion. Each medley of songs is introduced with the logo "Rain Is Falling" and the symbol of an umbrella from Raj Kapoor's *Barsaat* (Rain). I tune in to a song from *Lamhe* (Moments), with village women pushing each other on swings during a monsoon shower. This is followed by a song from *Sir,* in which Naseeruddin Shah plays a guitar as his students flirt in the rain. The twirling umbrella is a repeated motif. *Yeh Dillagi* has a song with Kajol frolicking in the rain, wearing drenched denim shorts and a T-shirt instead of a wet sari, which appears in the next song from *Dil Hai Betaab.* Ajay Devgan and his heroine dance around a flooded petrol pump. Though Devgan isn't known for his dancing, today he seems to dominate the monsoon melodies with songs from *Sangram* and *Platform.* His leading ladies throw themselves into mud puddles and writhe with desire. My favorite song, however, is a Sridevi number from *ChaalBaaz,* in which she twirls her umbrella along with a garage full of motor mechanics, all of whom are dancing in the rain. Nobody seems to have as much fun in the monsoon as Sridevi.

Compared to the catastrophe that destroys the lives and homes of so many people, it's a small disaster, but Sony's offices in Mumbai are flooded during the storm and their computer files and papers are destroyed. Vishal's agreement to produce five love stories, accompanying Rekha's songs, is literally washed out. The project is canceled.

A month later, toward the end of the monsoon, I return to Mumbai. Vishal invites me over to his flat for a drink. We sit on the terrace, facing a forest of mangrove trees.

"You can't get this kind of view anywhere else in Bombay," he says, as we look out over acres of green with only a few high-rise buildings to the west. A breeze blows in, carrying with it a sprinkling of rain.

We pour ourselves pegs of Vat 69—the screen villain's drink of choice—the same scotch that Premnath and Jeevan would be drinking in *Romanchak.* Abhishek arrives, though he has been running a fever. As soon as he joins us, Vishal begins to talk about making *Othello* in Hindi. The main character will be Omkara. Instead of Shakespeare's Moor, he'll be a lower-caste man in love with a Brahmin's daughter. Like *Maqbool* it will be a gangster film but not the underworld of Mumbai.

"I want to set it in U.P.," says Vishal. "In a kind of lawless, Wild West sort of setting."

This is the part of India he knows best, having grown up in Meerut. We talk about the language of this region, the colloquial Hindi dialect. We also discuss forms of abuse, especially the word *chootiya.* Vishal has the first line of dialogue already composed in his mind; it describes the difference between a *bewakoof* and *chootiya.* One means "fool" and the other "fucking idiot." "*Bewakoof aur chootiya mein dhaga bhar ka pharak hota haiga bhaiya . . .*" (Between a *bewakoof* and a *chootiya* there is only a thread of difference . . . pull out the thread and who is the *bewakoof* and who is the *chootiya* . . . that's a question worth a crore of rupees.)

In U.P., *chootiya* is such a common expression that it has almost lost its obscenity. We discuss the pronunciation of *chootiya,* the way the vowels can be extended to increase the insult and also the way it is often phrased, "Do you think I'm a *chootiya*?"—which means the insult is not directly implied but reflects back on the speaker. The nuances of profanity (*gaali*) are as subtle as the idiom of romance. Pouring a second drink, I try to imagine Othello as a small-town hoodlum from U.P., with Iago lurking in his shadow. Instead of lines like "Zounds, you rogue, you rascal!" one turns to the other and mutters, "*Abhey chootiya!*"

Omkara and Langda.

SEX, FILMS, AND SMS

INTELLIGENT AND SUBVERSIVE, Mahesh Bhatt is one of Bollywood's most successful yet controversial figures, admired by many, reviled by some. Over the past five years, Bhatt has created his own genre of slick, low-budget, erotic thrillers like *Zeher* (Poison) and *Murder.* He is putting the final touches on *Kalyug* (*Dark Age*), his latest film with director Mohit Suri. The editing studio where we meet is the antithesis of the Marriott hotel across the road, a five-star pleasure palace facing the sea. The filmmakers are seated in the cramped living room of a ground-floor flat. It's after dark and the housing colony in Juhu could be the shadowy set from one of their films.

Mohit Suri has a boyish face and lank black hair. He and the editor look like a pair of graduate students who've just pulled an all-nighter. Bhatt is professorial, bespectacled, with a comfortable look of dissolution. He wears jeans and an open-collared shirt, swatting at mosquitoes as he talks.

With few preliminaries, Bhatt launches into a lecture on Hindi films, a postmodern rant, delivered in a cosmopolitan drawl. "The expression 'Bollywood' is here to stay . . . there's nothing wrong with it. After all, we owe so much to Hollywood." He shifts his weight on the sofa, warming up. "But this obsession with trying to win Oscars is absurd . . . Mehboob Khan's *Mother India* was nominated but it was not a big thing . . . Now the Oscars are a badge of slavery. We don't want your prizes, we want your dollars and pounds sterling . . . *Mother India* was such a great film . . . part of our collective memory . . . but today Bollywood has erased the rural poor, they've disappeared from our films . . . Entertainment has become a narcotic, an audio-visual drug . . . everything is getting demystified . . . credibility has collapsed . . . People are making more money selling Bollywood than Bollywood makes itself. In England they are using Bollywood as a catchphrase for multiculturalism to fight the fundamentalists."

Bhatt was recently in England, lecturing on Hindi cinema. His words and phrases come spilling out in a seemingly random medley, a one-man jam session of ideas.

On the wall is a poster from *Kalyug*. The two young actors, Kunal Khemu and Smiley Suri—the director's sister—are running away from a street full of pornography. Both are wearing tight black leather.

"We just finished editing today," Bhatt announces. "*Kalyug* is about the total collapse of society. It exposes the flesh trade . . . When people can come into your bedroom and show you fucking it fucks you up. It's fiction based on fact."

Kalyug takes on the topical issue of intrusive pornography, which has been making headlines. Over the past year there have been several exposés of hotels in India that install hidden cameras to capture their guests having sex. This is the premise of *Kalyug*—an innocent young couple, Renuka and Kunal, get sucked into the world of cyberporn.

"It's everyone's fear, that someone will be watching their most intimate moments," says Suri.

"They take these videos and put them on porn sites," Bhatt explains. "There's a huge audience for *desi* porn. Indians, here and abroad, have seen Europeans having sex, now they want to see Indian men and women doing it."

Always ready to challenge false morality, Bhatt has little time for the prudish side of Bollywood. "You must understand that kissing was permitted in early Hindi films. It was done away with as part of the freedom struggle. Kissing was seen as something European." Bhatt has written an article on the subject and he summarizes his thesis, arguing that kissing and sex are age-old subjects in Indian literature and art. Rather than a moral choice, not showing kissing in a Hindi films was a political decision, a form of patriotic self-censorship by filmmakers during the independence movement.

One of Bollywood's most accessible filmmakers, Bhatt has always been good for a quote, speaking out against the closure of dance bars or voicing his opinion on legalizing prostitution. He has also been associated with a number of social causes—a renegade liberal who treads a thin line between hyperbole and hypocrisy. Bhatt has gone through many different incarnations as a filmmaker, from the socially concerned director of successful art films like *Arth* (The Meaning) and *Zakhm* (Wound) to the fisticuffs and gratuitous gore of Sanjay Dutt thrillers in the 1980s, as well as family comedies like *Hum Hain Rahi Pyar Ke* (We Are Travellers on the Path of Love). In his latest avatar, he's making films straight out of the tabloids.

"That's where we look for our stories," he says. "Box-office success means you have to make concessions . . . a popular product is shackled to traditional value systems . . . We find our stories in the headlines . . . People want narratives from the news."

Ideas ricochet off his tongue but he stops himself and waves at Suri. "Why don't you show him the film?"

Kalyug begins with a deceptively naive love story, as well as background narratives about displaced Hindus from Kashmir. (Earlier in the day, Bhatt was speaking to one of the Mumbai

Rotary Clubs on the subject of Kashmir.) The actors have an endearing innocence and their honeymoon takes them to an idyllic, unnamed location, which has undertones of a creepy fairy tale. All of this is shattered when the police arrest them for appearing in a porn film and the story takes a sharp left turn into an odyssey of revenge. Determined to destroy his destroyers, Kunal travels to Switzerland, from where the porn site is controlled. Though the film has railway-station moments that evoke *DDLJ,* this is definitely not Yash Chopra's Switzerland. Instead of the picture-postcard world of the Alps, we enter a Zurich sex shop where Emraan Hashmi is singing "Bheegi Honth Tere" (Your Wet Lips) and tries to sell the hero an inflatable doll.

INTERMISSION appears on the screen and one of the assistants comes in and shuts off the system. In the room outside, Bhatt is reading a novel. He summarizes the second half of the film, as Suri joins us.

Amrita Singh plays the villain in the story, an expatriate Indian who controls an empire of cyberporn. In the film she looks like a jet-set socialite in tailored suits—a dominatrix dressed up by Yves Saint Laurent.

Bhatt refers to her simply as "the vamp. She wants to be bigger than *Playboy, Penthouse,* and *Hustler,*" he says. A female Larry Flynt, preying on South Asian desires. Bhatt sketches out the climax in which the hero uses the vamp's daughter "who has lesbian tendencies" to get his revenge on the mother. "Even though she runs this empire of sin, she still holds on to her traditional Indian value systems." She cannot bear to see her own daughter having sex with another woman and finally shuts down the porn site.

Whatever value systems may be operating in Bollywood, Bhatt argues that erotica is here to stay. "According to research done in Mumbai beauty parlors, a lot of women are watching pornography. They go home and switch it on in the afternoons while their husbands are at work."

Still, there are limits to what can be shown in a Hindi film. Though we catch glimpses of an X-rated video playing in the sex shop, the scenes are relatively tame, veiled nudity and throbbing music. When Renuka and Kunal make love it is soft-focus, mildly erotic.

"In the sex-shop scene," Suri says, "I had to move a lot of things out of the shot because they wouldn't have passed the censors."

Bhatt laughs. "There were so many sex gadgets. While doing our research, we had a lot of distractions."

One of the most successful aspects of Bhatt's films is the music, a synthetic blend of global pop and qawwali rhythms, the lyrics laced with innuendo.

"The best music comes from Pakistan," he says. "'Bheegi Honth Tere' was a Punjabi folk song remixed for *Murder.* In *Kalyug* we've used Rahat Fateh Ali Khan, Nusrat Fateh Ali Khan's nephew."

Once again Bhatt slips into an intellectual mode. "Bollywood began as a preliterate medium. Many of the early filmmakers were illiterate—Mehboob Khan, for example . . . None of them could read a script. They hired poets to write the dialogue but it was a verbal and visual medium from the start . . . As Spielberg says, 'If you want to find out who you are, you need to find out who you were.'"

While we're talking Mohit Suri checks his phone and interrupts with a laugh.

"I just got an SMS," he says. "Of the five top ringtones, four of them are ours."

A preliterate medium in a postliterate world.

SCRIPTING *OMKARA*

AT THE BEGINNING of October, Vishal Bhardwaj phones to say they are moving ahead with *Othello.* He sounds elated. A producer has agreed to finance development of the project and Vishal wants to come up to Mussoorie to write the screenplay, away from the distractions of Mumbai.

The town of Mussoorie is about as far removed from Bollywood as anyplace in India. At 7,000 feet above sea level, in the foothills of the Himalayas, this hill station is a quiet settlement of schools and resort hotels that cater to seasonal tourist crowds. Most people in Mussoorie go to sleep by 10:00 PM, which is when nightlife in Mumbai starts waking up. There used to be seven cinemas in Mussoorie but all of these have closed, victims of the ingress of television, video, and DVDs. I watched my first Hindi films at the Picture Palace and Rialto cinemas along Mussoorie's Mall Road, but these have been boarded up for the past two decades. The 1980s and early 1990s were a time of crisis for India's film industry, which has recently rebounded with new directors, more professional approaches to production and marketing, and multiplex cinemas in urban centers. But many of the old movie halls in towns like Mussoorie are unlikely to reopen, relics of an earlier era when cinemas faced little competition.

A week after he calls, Vishal arrives with Abhishek Chaubey and Robin Bhatt. By the first afternoon, they're already at work. Vishal's hotel suite has a balcony overlooking the town, but they are camped out inside. Robin has his feet drawn up beneath him and leans back against the cushions. He is the brother of Mahesh Bhatt and a veteran of the film industry who has produced and directed films of his own. Across the room, Abhishek has folded himself into an overstuffed chair, a laptop perched on one arm. Vishal paces about restlessly, shifting from one seat to another. The three writers form the corners of a triangle and their conversation traverses this geometry, with Vishal at the apex and the other two directing ideas at him.

Giving me a printout of the script so far, Abhishek warns, "It's only sketches, not very reader friendly."

He narrates a section where Cassio gets drunk and Othello demotes him. Vishal and Robin suggest a few changes, after which they work on a scene where Iago is shopping for Desdemona, dragging a Delsey suitcase through a bazaar.

"We need some humor in this scene," Vishal insists. "He is a gangster but he has to purchase things for the home . . ."

Robin suggests that Iago has to buy a bra, but he doesn't know what size.

"D cup? C cup? He isn't sure, so he buys them all."

This seems too crass for the others.

"What about lipstick or cold cream?"

"Yes," says Vishal, bringing his hands together in satisfaction.

The team moves on to a sequence in which Iago first hints at a relationship between Cassio and Desdemona. Already there is a blurring of texts. The characters are alternately referred to by their Shakespearean names and by the names in the script. Othello is Omkara. Desdemona—Dolly. Cassio—Kesu. Emilia—Indu. Iago—Langda (which means "lame" since he's been given a clubfoot). They discuss one of the strengths of Shakespeare's play—very little is stated directly. Vishal recites a line of Langda's dialogue that he has written earlier: "Don't listen to me. My mind is full of filth. A drain runs through my mind . . . Yet . . . I wonder why Kesu is spending time with Dolly."

While most American stage productions and films of *Othello* inevitably focus on the issue of race, *Omkara*'s scriptwriters deal with this theme in more subtle ways. Part of the reason is that race carries different connotations in India, though prejudices against dark complexions are prevalent. Caste, regional background, and ethnicity are all part of the equation, but in the screenplay these elements are touched on lightly and only hinted at in the dialogue.

"We're focusing on the jealousy more than racism," Vishal explains. "It's there, but not in the foreground."

The story remains Shakespeare's, but the writers have reimagined it together. As Abhishek rapidly types into the computer, Vishal announces, "Let's take a walk."

We set off on a trail that circles the hotel. Along the way, Vishal explains that he began thinking of this project about eight months ago. "Originally we had the idea of retelling this story using the background of the Indian cricket team. Othello would be the captain and they would go on tour to the West Indies. After that we thought of setting the film on a university campus."

He gestures to Abhishek, who explains that they had an opening shot in which students were seated in a classroom and the lecturer was reading aloud from Shakespeare's play. "Then the camera travels out of the window and there on the lawns sit Iago and Roderigo. We wanted to set it against the politics of Delhi University, where you have student leaders who stay on into their thirties."

Though the idea was rejected it still teases their imagination and the character Kesu is a student leader as well as a member of Omkara's gang. The team has worked together on two other scripts—*Timbuctoo* and *Mr. Mehta and Mrs. Singh.*

"*Omkara* will be the first of our films that is actually made," Vishal says. "Last February, Robin and I went to see Ajay Devgan and explained that we wanted to do *Othello.* He liked the idea but couldn't give us dates. Two months later, he came back to me and said his shooting had been canceled and he was ready to do it. But by that time, I was committed to *Mr. Mehta and Mrs. Singh.* My dates were locked. Then Aamir Khan postponed, so we went back to Ajay and he was ready to go ahead." As soon as their calendars had been reconciled, the project went on a fast track. The producer is Kumar Mangat, Devgan's secretary and business manager.

Before coming to Mussoorie, Vishal and his team visited potential locations in U.P. In Meerut they interviewed a jailed gangster who was on trial for murder.

"Every criminal culture is different, whether it is the Mumbai underworld, Veerappan, Chambal dacoits, or criminals in U.P. Not all are the same," says Vishal. The murderer in Meerut jail is a man named Mohinder Yadav, whom Vishal heard of through his contacts in Meerut.

"He's sitting there in the jail cell on a mattress covered with a white sheet, leaning against bolster cushions. He's wearing a starched white kurta and expensive rings on his fingers. We are served tea and snacks inside the jail." Vishal shakes his head. "This man had seen *Maqbool* and told me how much he liked my film. He openly admitted that he had killed his mentor, a politician. Yadav said that he regretted what he'd done. 'Taking another human being's life is not a good thing,' he told us. But even behind bars the man held power."

Getting inside the jail to see him was a challenge because of a court order restricting visitors to only those whom the gangster approved. After keeping them waiting for more than an hour, Yadav gave permission for the filmmakers to enter his cell.

"For a long time he didn't look us in the eyes and he spoke softly—a thin voice. We talked with him for two hours about his experiences. At one point a jailer came and said that visiting hours were over. Yadav waved him off, saying, '*Dubara aaney ki zaroorat nahin.*'" (There's no need for you to interrupt us again.)

This is one of several lines that Vishal has used as dialogue. Yadav has become a character in the script, a mobster-turned-politician named Bhaisaab, who plays the equivalent of the Duke of Venice. They have decided to hold the trial scene, when Othello is confronted by Desdemona's father, inside the walls of Meerut jail. All three writers were affected by their meeting with Yadav. As Vishal says, "We decided right there . . . we knew what we wanted and we came straight up to Mussoorie and started writing."

"*Us sey humein ek sur mil gaya,*" says Robin. (It was as if we had found the opening phrase of a song.)

Vishal goes on to summarize the plot. "We've decided that instead of having Othello and Desdemona married at the beginning [as in the play], astrologers have told them that they need to wait a month for an auspicious date." This is the period during which they are in Cyprus, where Shakespeare sets the second half of his play. Instead of the invading Turks, whom Othello is sent to defeat, an election is coming up and Omkara has been offered a party ticket. For this reason he has to shed his criminal activities and appoints Kesu as a lieutenant—his *bahubali.* Langda becomes jealous and turns Omkara against Kesu. All of this takes place in the city of Meerut, which serves as Venice, and a fictitious rural village in western U.P. called Cypra.

In addition to using the framework of Shakespeare's tragedy they also hope to use specific lines, like the quote in which Othello describes himself as "one that loved not wisely but too well," and the reference to "making the beast with two backs," a crude metaphor for sex.

"I'm sure we can find equivalents in Hindi," Vishal insists. "We must keep going back to Shakespeare."

October 22. While the team is in Mussoorie, the *Times of India* breaks the news of Vishal's new film in progress. The article focuses on Kareena Kapoor and is titled BOLLYWOOD'S OWN DESDEMONA, accompanied by a photograph of Kareena posing seductively in jeans and a blue blouse. Until now, Vishal has tried to keep the project confidential and refused to be interviewed, though he's quoted in the *Times of India* as saying, "I have to be careful about what I do next. I have left Mumbai to focus on the writing of the script for *Othello.*" Kareena is more candid: "Vishal has offered me the role and I'll be sitting in on a script-reading session . . . I'd love to do it, if all goes well."

Over dinner that evening, Vishal and his team are in an upbeat mood. "We accomplished a lot today. Now we're into the second half. We've been working very hard. In the morning we work on the script, then in the middle of the day I write the dialogues. In the evening we go back to the script again."

Reminiscing about the early days of Hindi cinema, Robin says his uncle worked on *Alam Ara* (The Light of the World), the first full-length talkie made in India in 1931. When I show him some old playbills I bought recently, including one from a 1939 stunt film, *Bijli* (Lightning), Robin points to the director's name: Balwant Bhatt.

"That's my uncle," he says. "My father also worked on this film."

Robin's family has been involved in cinema for several generations. In the 1930s and 1940s, Robin's father, Nanabhai Bhatt, worked on stunt films starring Fearless Nadia.

"Many people ask me why I'm called Robin," he says. "It was Nadia who gave me my name. In 1946 my father was directing one of her films, *Lady Robinhood.* When news reached the set that I was born, Nadia came straight to the hospital from the shooting. She picked me up and said that my name should be Robin."

Though most of the original prints of Nadia's films no longer exist, Robin says he has been able to get a DVD copy of one of his father's first productions, based on the story of Sinbad the sailor. As Bollywood rediscovers its heritage, there's a growing market for film memorabilia. The playbills I found three months ago in Mumbai's *chor* bazaar (thieves' market) are already worth twice what I paid for them.

Pointing to a poster of *Dil Diya Dard Liya* (A Heart Given, Pain Received), Abhishek mentions it was a 1966 remake of *Wuthering Heights.* Robin confirms: "*Wuthering Heights* has been adapted three times but the directors never had the courage to go all the way. In the novel, toward the end, Heathcliff becomes a tortured character. None of the heroes, including Dilip Kumar, wanted to take the role in that direction."

English literature has had a longstanding influence on Hindi cinema. The syllabi for university courses that assign texts like *Othello* or *Wuthering Heights* have made a lasting impression on filmmakers and their audiences. Abhishek studied English literature at university. "I first read *Macbeth* in school and in college," he says. "When we were working on *Maqbool* I knew the story by heart."

"Harivansh Rai Bachchan, the poet and father of Amitabh Bachchan, translated *Macbeth* into Hindi. I read his translation," Vishal adds.

Asked how he transcribes the script, Abhishek says he writes the narrative portions on his computer in English while Vishal writes the dialogue in Hindi. These will later be retyped together, so that the script moves back and forth between the two languages. Unlike many writers who transliterate Hindi words using English letters, commonly referred to as Roman script, Vishal prefers to use the Devanagri alphabet for the dialogue.

"Both Vishal and I like to have our English in English and our Hindi in Hindi," Abhishek explains. At the same time, he admits that the languages constantly converge. "For people of my generation," he says, "we grew up speaking 'Hinglish.' We mix the two languages all the time."

Like Vishal, Abhishek has his roots in U.P. He was born in the eastern part of the state, in a town called Faizabad. "I come from an ordinary, middle-class family but my parents were huge film buffs," he tells me. "We'd go to the cinema together as a family and if we liked a film we'd see it five, six times. Growing up in towns like Faizabad there was nothing to do but play sports and watch films. It was the chief form of entertainment . . . When I was twelve I told my father that I wanted to work in films. He was a bank officer and we were posted in different cities—Patna, Ranchi. Later I went to boarding school in Hyderabad, then to Delhi University."

After finishing his degree, Abhishek moved to Mumbai to do a communications course at St. Xavier's College. While studying there he met Vishal and began working with him on *Makdee* and *Maqbool.* Before starting on *Othello,* Abhishek watched all of the Hollywood versions of the play.

"I haven't enjoyed any of them," he says. "*Macbeth* has been adapted successfully but *Othello* always becomes too dark and depressing."

October 23. Vishal's phone has been switched off all day but around 4:30 he calls and asks me to join them for a walk around the *chukkar,* a road that circles the highest point in Mussoorie, overlooking a panorama of snow peaks.

"*Aaj to hum atak gaye, burri tara,*" Vishal complains. (Today we got stuck. Very badly. We couldn't move forward.)

Different threads of the story are now converging and the writers are having difficulty braiding together strands of the plot leading to the climax. Part of the problem is that many of the minor characters in the play have been given bigger roles. For example, Bianca the courtesan has become Billo Chamanbahar, a dancer and singer, who is Kesu's lover. There are other added complexities. Indu and Langda have a nine-year-old son. In the play, Iago suspects that Othello has slept with his wife. This is part of the jealousy that drives his hatred.

"When he looks at his son, he wonders if it is Omi's child," Robin says.

Our conversation veers off into a discussion of current film stars and how most of them have been caught with their pants down, so to speak. Industry gossip provides comic relief as the team struggles to resolve the infidelities of their characters.

Though Abhishek has left his computer at the hotel, he narrates the sequence of scenes written so far. Recounting the plot, he gestures, points, pretends to fire a gun, all as we walk along. He comes to the scene where Langda tries unsuccessfully to kill Kesu.

"This part will be simple," says Vishal. "We can solve this tomorrow. It's just mathematics. Two plus two." He jumps ahead to the scene where Othello kills Desdemona.

"Should it be outside or inside?" he asks. "I was thinking he could take her back into the forest."

Both Robin and Abhishek disagree.

"It has to be indoors."

"Visually, I have this idea," says Vishal, stopping. "They are on the roof of the house . . . or in a room with a glass roof. A full moon is covered by clouds. As he takes the handkerchief and wraps it around her throat . . ." Vishal acts out the scene. "At that moment, the clouds slip aside and the moon comes out."

"Why not reverse it?" says Robin. "Have the cloud come across the moon when he strangles her."

Everyone pauses, considering the scene.

"It's a bit filmi," says Abhishek.

"Others have done it with the sun," says Vishal, "but not with the moon. I was actually thinking of an eclipse but that wouldn't work because it couldn't be their wedding night." The date of an eclipse is considered inauspicious.

We carry on to a small bazaar called Char Dukan. At the Tip

Top Tea Shop we order tea and sit under a walnut tree that has shed its leaves.

They briefly return to a discussion of the script but agree that no more writing will be done tonight. Tomorrow each of them will sit alone and write from where they stopped, then get together and compare notes.

While we're drinking tea, Robin tells a joke about a man who took his wife to Alaska on his twenty-fifth wedding anniversary. When asked what he is going to do for his fiftieth, he answers, "I'll bring her back."

It isn't very funny but we laugh anyway, not realizing the joke will later find its way into the script.

October 25. Vishal phones to say they are finished.

"We've decided to go back to Bombay tomorrow," he says. "I still have some dialogues to write but I can do that there. Come over this evening and we'll narrate the story."

We get together at 7:00. The team is obviously eager to return home in time for Diwali, the festival of lights, though they were prepared to stay on into November if necessary.

"This morning it took us about an hour. We made some changes at the end and all of us agreed it was done."

While writing dialogue this afternoon, however, Vishal has come up with a couple of scenes he hasn't shared with Robin and Abhishek. In his notebook, he has written the dialogue in longhand. Robin has slid down to the floor, on a level with the coffee table. Abhishek leans back, no longer hunched over a keyboard. Vishal begins.

"There is a pounding on the door. Dolly goes to open it. Omkara is wounded. He comes inside and falls against her, bleeding. Others take him away. His blood is on her clothes. Though Dolly is engaged to marry someone else she has fallen in love with Omkara . . ."

Vishal narrates the story softly, his voice almost a mumble. The dialogue is in the dialect of western U.P.—"*ek launda, ek laundiya,*" a boy, a girl. He explains the shots, part of a montage, flashbacks within flashbacks. He even provides the musical cues.

We move on to a scene in which Dolly holds a razor blade in her hand. It looks as if she is going to cut her wrists. Instead, she slices her finger and writes a love letter using her blood as ink.

" 'To O from D,' she writes on the envelope." Vishal mimes the action. "Then she goes to Kesu and gives him the letter to take to Omi."

Robin and Abhishek murmur approval. Though the language of the criminals is crude, Vishal renders it in a lyrical form. Throughout the evening we are interrupted by phone calls. Kumar Mangat, the producer, wants to know how things are going. Vishal tells him they are done and returning to Mumbai. Another call is from Tassaduq Hussain, the cinematographer, asking how the script is coming along. Now that word is out that the film is under way, a number of actors are trying to get auditions. Most of the calls go unanswered.

Mobile phones play a significant part in the script, adding a contemporary element to Shakespeare's plot and the feudal world of U.P. gangsters. In one case, Dolly takes a photograph of Omkara using her phone—a counterpoint to love letters written in blood. In another scene, Omkara's gang blackmails a political rival with incriminating images recorded on a mobile phone.

Had the technology been developed around the turn of the seventeenth century, Shakespeare probably would have used mobile phones in his plays. Instead of whispered asides, mistaken identities, and accidental encounters, he might have included text messages sent to wrong addresses, secrets divulged over speakerphones, and all of the other mischief of wireless communication to add plot twists and moments of coincidence. Iago might even have created erotic MMS clips of Desdemona and Cassio to feed Othello's jealousy.

FILM CITY

THE LOWER HALF of the Taj Mahal, complete with marble screens and inlaid calligraphy, has been erected on an open lot facing the hills above Goregaon, at the northeastern edge of Mumbai. There is no dome or minarets, only the arched façade, re-created as an outdoor set. More than fifty dancers mill about in the midday sun, drinking bottled water and mopping perspiration from their faces. The choreographer and director are seated beneath beach umbrellas on the plinth of the Taj. Security guards cordon off the area but a large crowd of onlookers have been attracted by the music booming over the loudspeakers.

Marigold, starring Salman Khan, is being shot at Film City. It's a big-budget international production, partly financed with money from abroad and costarring English actors—Bollywood gone global. The crew are holding reflectors that intensify the brightness of the sun and the dancers seem to wilt in the heat as soon as the music stops. The women are dressed in different shades of orange and saffron, with full skirts and gossamer veils; the men bare-chested with gilt turbans, like something out of the *Arabian Nights.*

"Here we go . . . Clear the set, please!" Plastic water bottles are retrieved and turbans pushed into place. The dance director's voice carries a British accent but the music is pure Bollywood, Hindi lyrics with a strong, seductive beat.

As the dancers wag their hips and wave their arms in unison, the director calls out the musical tempo: "One, two, three, four! One, two, three, four!" The sequence requires everyone to sway together, a swirl of color and glitter against the pristine façade of the Taj. Twenty seconds later the music stops and the director calls out: "Okay. That was good!" But he shoots it another three times, just to be sure.

A few hundred meters away the set from Amol Palekar's *Paheli* is being demolished, a Rajasthani palace reduced to rubble. Trucks are carting away debris, as if an earthquake has struck.

Film City is 560 acres of land on the outskirts of Mumbai, where many of the scenes of Bollywood's biggest productions are shot. It is a giant playground for the industry, where fantasies can be erected and torn down like sand castles on the beach.

Brochures advertise the facility with filmi hyperbole:

> **FILM CITY**
>
> **WHERE WE SHAPE YOUR DREAMS**
>
> . . . Where the stars sparkle, even during the day. Where the sun may set, but the lights never go off. A world that lets you put your imagination to the test. And then enables you to shoot out your thoughts . . .

Founded in 1977, Film City is the largest venue for filmmaking in Mumbai. While there are a number of smaller, private studios in the city, none of them can match the scale and range of facilities, both for indoor sets and outdoor locations. Until the 1970s, most studios followed the pattern of Hollywood, with large banners that operated their own facilities and employed an exclusive stable of directors, technicians, and actors. Many of these, like Natraj, Rajkamal, and R. K. Studios, have declined or shut down. Most studios in Mumbai are nothing more than empty spaces, rented out for shootings by independent filmmakers, rather than being production companies that develop scripts, raise finances, and handle the making of a film from start to finish.

Though I've been assured of an appointment to tour Film City, nobody seems to know anything about it. At the reception desk, I am told it is a government holiday: Ambedkar Jayanti, the birth date of Dr. Bhimrao Ramji Ambedkar, India's champion of untouchables and underclasses. A photograph of Dr. Ambedkar has been placed in the entrance hall, garlanded with marigolds. As I wait for the public relations officer to show up, one of the staff lights incense in front of the picture and distributes sweets.

Eventually, the PRO arrives and explains, "We provide locations and studios. Electricity, water, roads, security. The rest is the producer's responsibility. It's a totally artificial environment."

After a few minutes, he assigns his assistant, Suresh Shinde, to show me around. We drive up a winding road, through low foothills. At the first bend in the road, Shinde points out a barren ravine that opens onto an apron of dust.

"This is where desert scenes are shot," he says. "Art directors bring in sand to make it look like Rajasthan." Currently nothing is being filmed on the lot, and a group of young boys have turned it into a cricket pitch.

Further on we pass a bridge that I have seen in half a dozen films. The winding "Khandala Road" leads nowhere but is used for filming car chases. Around the next corner we come to a simple, whitewashed shrine.

"We call this a godless temple," says Shinde, "because there is no idol. The filmmakers have to provide their own deities." On ahead lies a log cabin and a replica of a forest rest house, with a manicured lawn and garden. Red-and-green powder stains the white trunks of eucalyptus trees in the yard. Shinde explains that scenes of Holi—the festival of color—were recently shot here. There is also a replica of a parapet wall from the hill resort of Mahabaleshwar, a favorite site for dance sequences. The entire complex overlooks a reservoir that provides water for Mumbai.

This lake, with forested islands, has been incorporated into many films.

On the other side of the rest house, a group of six men are sitting under a tree, all of them carrying cameras with telephoto lenses. Assuming they are on the lookout for celebrities, Shinde bristles at the sight of these intruders. Putting on an officious tone he asks what they are doing trespassing on government property. Looking puzzled, the men explain that they are bird-watchers. Having hiked up the hill from the reservoir they are simply resting in the shade.

"You must leave immediately. If the security guards find you, they'll take your cameras away," Shinde warns.

The highest point at Film City is a helipad that offers a panoramic view of Mumbai. Shinde first takes me to "Suicide Point," where cars are pushed over the side of the hill to simulate a crash. He explains how the vehicles are wired with explosives, then toppled over the edge.

Film City operates on four shifts a day, starting at five in the morning and continuing throughout the night. It costs from 10,000 rupees per shift for a simple outdoor shoot at a minor location, to more than 35,000 rupees at the major locations.

There are also sixteen studios on the premises. Shinde takes me to the largest of these. The exterior serves as four outdoor locations. One side of the studio replicates the front steps and pillars of the Mumbai High Court. Another façade is a police station, the third a church, and the fourth a chawl—one of Mumbai's inner-city neighborhoods. The studio has been rented out by Star Plus television channel for the show *Kaun Banega Crorepati?,* India's incarnation of *Who Wants to Be a Millionaire.* The set looks like the interior of a spaceship with room for more than three hundred audience members. Amitabh Bachchan, who remains one of the top stars in Bollywood, hosts the show.

As I say good-bye to Shinde near the entrance to Film City,

the dancers are still performing in front of the Taj Mahal. By this time the temperature has risen a couple of degrees but the choreographer's voice still carries an insistent note and the beat of the music throbs with the same intensity.

A few weeks later, when I return to Film City, it is after dark. Walking into Studio 11 is like stepping into a wedding reception. Dozens of men in pink turbans and embroidered sherwanis and women in bright-hued lehngas are milling about with dinner plates in their hands. A buffet is set up on one side of the studio and the crew are helping themselves. As I pick my way through a hedgerow of lights, I can see Prahlad Kakar huddled in front of a video monitor. Music is playing and beyond a reflector screen is the large set of a marriage hall, its arcades decorated with red bouquets. Chandeliers hang from the high ceilings and a remote-control camera is attached to a crane that travels back and forth on thirty feet of track.

Once the shot is finished Kakar offers me dinner and introduces Saroj Khan, the choreographer. Saroj, one of the top dance directors in Mumbai, won seventeen awards for the dances in *Devdas.* "A clean sweep," she says with a satisfied smile. While Kakar looks like a throwback to the sixties, with a Jerry Garcia beard and granny glasses, Saroj looks like your favorite aunt, jovial and sweet-natured. She has become a familiar figure on TV after serving as a judge for the dance competition *Nach Baliye.* Saroj pats the chair next to her for me to sit down and chat between shots, but when the next sequence is ready to be filmed, she turns into a ferocious incarnation of a physical education instructor.

"Okay, boys and girls!" she shouts into a wireless microphone. "Move in closer. Make a circle."

Like Kakar she has a video monitor on which she directs her

dancers, who are fifty feet away behind the barricade of reflectors and lights.

"Sound! Okay, positions! Boys, girls . . ."

The music starts again and the figures on the screen begin whirling, hands in the air.

"Cut!" Saroj is unhappy and scolds her troupe over the microphone. "What is this? You call that dancing?"

The shot is repeated half a dozen times, two concentric rings of dancers moving in opposite directions. Not satisfied, Saroj suggests they skip instead of dancing. This speeds it up. Then she asks the women (Girls!) to remain in one place and twirl, so their skirts billow out, while the men wheel around them. It works.

Kakar signals thumbs-up. The product he is filming for today is BoroPlus, an anti-blemish and fairness cream. It's one of many beauty products in India that promise to lighten a woman's face. The female dancers all wear pancake makeup so their skin looks as fair as possible under the bright lamps. Kareena Kapoor is the star of this ad—the blushing bride on her wedding day. Kareena's pale features, which will seduce the dark Omkara, advertise a skin-care lotion that promises to whiten every woman's complexion.

Kakar began his career as an assistant director on Shyam Benegal's *Bhumika: The Role.* ("We worked as slaves," he says.) Instead of continuing in cinema, he turned to advertising and is one of the most sought-after directors of ad film. Over the past ten years, Kakar has been responsible for projecting the beauty of Bollywood's most glamorous heroines. A number of the models he has worked with have moved on to become actors.

"We made Aishwarya Rai through her Pepsi commercials," he says. Though she was already a beauty queen, Miss World, her face and eyes captured the fantasies of India through the ads she made.

Asked why actors come back to do ads, Kakar shrugs.

"For the money. They can make as much in two days shooting an ad film as they would on a full-length feature."

Clearly this is where the money is for everyone—directors, choreographers, crew. Bollywood stars like Amitabh Bachchan and Shah Rukh Khan are willing to sell Cadbury's chocolates or bathe in tubs full of rose petals to earn an extra crore or two. For all his laid-back style, Kakar has helped create the aggressive marketing culture that drives this industry.

"Do the stars recognize that ads help their careers?"

"I hope they do," says Kakar.

By this time the caterers are collecting the dishes and the next shot is being set up. Saroj's microphone has stopped working and a harassed-looking assistant brings her another. The studio has at least a hundred people inside. All of this for half a minute of screen time, selling a product that makes women's faces smooth and unblemished, so that millions of viewers can believe that their complexions will be as flawless and fair as Bollywood's own Desdemona.

Omkara and Dolly.

1,001 NARRATIONS

THANKS TO a Tata Indicom promotion, Ajay Devgan's face appears on TV every half hour. He and his wife, Kajol—the star of *DDLJ* and other films—extol the virtues of mobile communication in a lighthearted series of advertisements. The star couple are also "brand ambassadors" for Whirlpool appliances, and Devgan endorses Bagpiper whiskey. Earlier in the year he filled the big screen with brooding intensity in films like *Insan* and *Kaal.* A prolific actor, who has played everything from romantic leads to villainous ghosts, it isn't difficult to picture him as Othello, more because of his complexity than his complexion.

Though Devgan has tentatively agreed to take on the role of Omkara, this will be the first time he hears a narration of the entire script. Vishal is tense as we leave his studio. Driving to Devgan's office he says, "This is just the beginning. I have to do four narrations. One for Ajay today. One for Saif tomorrow. He's in London but flying into Bombay for a day. After that I go to Chennai, where Kareena is shooting. Then back here to narrate for Viveik and Konkona."

Though virtually every producer and star in Bollywood now insists on a bound script, very few people actually read a screenplay. Instead, they depend on a narration by the writer or director, who must present the script as an oral performance. Storytelling has a long tradition in Bollywood, going back to a time when all-night script sessions were held by filmmakers like Raj Kapoor, who surrounded themselves with raconteurs. More than words on a page, it is the tale as it is told that germinates into a film. In this way, Hindi cinema owes far more to *The Thousand and One Nights* than it does to the textual formulas of Western scriptwriting. It is an oral tradition that demands a riveting rendition, entertaining enough to keep a Bollywood mogul awake until dawn and spare the producer's sword in favor of a promised denouement. Essentially, the storyteller must recount what Othello calls "a round unvarnish'd tale."

We arrive at Chandan Cinema, one of Juhu's older landmarks. Devgan's office is on the ground floor of a building around the corner. A cluster of young boys lurk near the gate, trying to catch a glimpse of the star.

Hangers-on fill the entry hall, which displays a poster of Devgan's latest film, *Shikhar*. Vishal, Abhishek, and I enter the actor's office. Robin is already there chatting with Ajay, who reclines on a sofa. He wears a pale, striped shirt with a Chinese emblem on the back, unbuttoned to the waist. His rumpled white trousers look like karate pants—the disheveled hero off camera. He seems guarded, chain-smoking throughout the narration.

Kumar Mangat joins us as Vishal moves from one chair to another, getting comfortable. Eventually he ends up in Ajay's executive chair—"I get tired of sitting there," says Devgan. Trophies line a shelf, jubilee souvenirs and other awards, though the rest of the decor is simple, unpretentious.

"Shall we start?"

"Of course. This is the first draft, we'll be revising it . . ." Vishal pauses. "Check the time." Twenty minutes past four. The story begins. With the script in his lap, Vishal leans forward, hands framing the first shot.

"Scene One. Exterior. Arid countryside. Day. Fade in: Shot of a dusty road stretching till the horizon in an arid landscape. There is a breeze in the late-afternoon air and dust floats just above the ground creating a kind of blurry mirage. The camera pans across the landscape as we hear a man's voice on the soundtrack. Voice-over. '*Bewakoof aur chootiya mein dhaga bhar ka pharak hota haiga bhaiya . . .*'"

Though Vishal begins by reading from the script it gradually becomes a telling, as he paraphrases and embellishes the written words. His voice is full of emotion, accompanied by gestures and sound effects. Guns go off—"*Dhar! Dhar!*" Kesu and Langda are playing marbles, the villain limping awkwardly. Every time Vishal says "Cut," he snips the air with his fingers. He reads the dialogue, taking on the role of each character, spitting out obscenities. Though the narration leans toward Omkara's role, even the minor characters are given prominence, including a henchman named Mental.

When Kesu gets drunk, Vishal pretends to tip a bottle back and slurs his speech. Later, during a conversation between Dolly and Indu, his voice grows softer, more intimate. Devgan interrupts the narration only two or three times, for clarification. He listens attentively but does not react when his character first appears. A little later, as Vishal describes the montage of flashbacks in which Omkara first meets Dolly, the hero's eyes flicker—he can see himself playing the role, falling wounded into her arms. A scene in which he pumps water for an old woman obviously appeals to him. Already, he seems to have taken on the mantle of Omkara, riding in a jeep with Bhaisaab, a political procession. He nods his head as Vishal sings Omkara's lullaby: "*Jag ja ri gudiya . . . misri ki pudiya . . .*" (Wake up little doll . . . a packet of sweets . . .) The childlike innocence contrasts with the brutality of the gangster.

Parts of the script have been changed since I heard it narrated in Mussoorie. The scene with the suitcase in the market has been taken out and other sections have been moved around. The narration follows the language of the script—descriptions in English, dialogue in Hindi, though Vishal mixes it up as he goes along. He stops from time to time to explain a scene, offering an occasional aside or visual references—"dissolve to fire." The headlight of a locomotive in the rain. Langda Tyagi licking the blood that trickles down his cheek. And plenty of sounds—motorcycles, guns going off in the night, cries and arguments, drums and whispers.

At several points Vishal acknowledges Abhishek's and Robin's contributions to the script, including the joke about the man who takes his wife to Alaska for their twenty-fifth wedding anniversary. But instead of Alaska, now it's Timbuktu, a sly reference to their earlier script.

After an hour, we come to the interval and take a break. Though Ajay has been smoking, everyone else goes outside to have a cigarette.

"Just telling the story, I feel this script will work," says Vishal, more relaxed, more confident. It's growing dark and the crowd of fans get excited seeing Devgan in the doorway. He paces about, taking calls on his mobile phone. The sign at Chandan Cinema is lit up. Beyond the old picture hall a new multiplex is going up, along with a shopping mall.

When we return inside, tea is served and Vishal plunges back into the story.

Preparations are under way for Omkara and Dolly's wedding but Langda has infected Omkara with jealousy, the tragedy uncoiling. One of the major changes in the script is that instead of a handkerchief (Shakespeare's device) Omkara gives Dolly a silver belt or cummerbund as a gift. "She ties it around her waist. Very sexy." This is used by Langda to feed Omkara's suspicions.

Though the script remains in Vishal's lap, he now refers to it only for the dialogue and narrates the story from memory. During the scenes in which the characters make love, he snips the air at the appropriate moment, like a prudent censor.

Only at one point during the narration are we interrupted by a knock at the door. An important call for Ajay. He waves it off and snaps at his assistant. "I'll call back in fifteen minutes. I'm in the middle of a script."

This is the climax of the film. Wedding celebrations are accompanied by "ominous music." After killing Dolly, Omkara sings the lullaby again. Langda shoots Kesu and Rajju. Indu discovers that her husband is responsible for the tragedy. Kesu, badly wounded, staggers into Omi's room. Confronted with the truth, Omkara points his pistol at himself, recalling others he has killed, then finally shoots himself. The camera withdraws through the skylight and the final image is the bodies of the newlyweds lying lifeless on their wedding bed.

"Fade to black. Titles roll."

After a prolonged silence, Devgan says, "Excellent. This is the kind of movie in which the last ten minutes I wouldn't want to watch." He means this as a compliment.

Ajay also comments that he likes the language—U.P. dialect, interspersed with a few English phrases. He mentions a line where Bhaisaab says, "Go ahead."

"You could do more of this," he says.

There is some discussion about the title. Instead of *Omkara,* Kumarji and Devgan want it to be called *O Saathi Re* (O My Companion), which is a line from one of the songs Vishal is composing.

"It's a love story," Devgan says. "If you call it *Omkara,* then you'll lose half your audience. As an actor I would prefer *Omkara* because I have the title role. But here we have to think of bringing in the audience. That is all that matters in a title."

Vishal doesn't argue with them but makes it clear he disagrees.

"Will Saif be willing to play Langda?" Robin asks.

"He should," says Devgan. "It's a very strong role."

Asked why Omi doesn't strangle Dolly with the scarf, as earlier planned, Vishal shakes his head. "It would be too much. Better not to see her face." She will be smothered with a pillow, as in the play.

The conversation turns to casting. It hasn't been decided who will play Billo, the courtesan. A couple of actors have cornered Vishal, demanding auditions. Though the story is dominated by male characters, the script has fleshed out the women more completely. Indu and Billo have become much more interesting parts, with strong scenes in the second half of the film.

Various actors are suggested for Billo's role.

"Too young."

"Her body is wrong."

Kumarji suggests a name and Devgan shakes his head. "She can't act. Very weak."

The discussion is ruthless. Actors' names are brought up and discarded. Opinions are expressed with a harshness that seems almost as brutal as the script itself.

Locations are the next question. While Vishal had spoken earlier of shooting the film near Meerut, Ajay isn't enthusiastic.

"In U.P., we'll have such a lot of trouble with crowd control. Not only do they mob a car, they actually pick the whole vehicle off the ground." Devgan tells Vishal he should scout locations near a town called Wai, in Maharashtra, where he recently shot another film. The villagers there are used to having film crews and stars around. They've also been taught to act as extras.

Vishal remains noncommittal, saying he's still thinking of shooting in U.P. Glancing at his watch he asks, "Is there anything more to discuss?"

"Nothing. From my side it's fine," says Devgan, his approval of the script decisive.

It's past seven o'clock when we finish. The crowds outside Devgan's office have grown larger, peering in through the gate. As the star emerges, there is a murmur of excitement. He waves to his fans, a broad, generous gesture, then climbs into a car and drives home.

After the narration, Kumarji takes us to his club for a drink—part celebration and part strategy session.

"The best thing," he says, "is that Ajay raised no objections." For him this means the film is on. Being both Devgan's secretary and the film's producer might put anyone else in an awkward position but Kumarji juggles his responsibilities without any apparent conflict of interest. While he makes a few suggestions about story alterations, most of his attention is fixed on financing the film. He is as much of an industry insider as anyone. Not only does he handle Devgan's career but Kajol's as well. Tomorrow he is off to Delhi with her to launch a diamond promotion. His two phones ring constantly and seem permanently attached to his ear.

The Classique Club is a new establishment, unlike Mumbai's older watering holes, such as the Royal Bombay Yacht Club and the Breach Candy Club, where membership is impossible to acquire. The Classique lies behind a shopping mall and does not advertise itself, though inside there is enough marble to cover a cricket oval. We go upstairs to the Shooter's Bar. One wall is taken up by a large-screen TV, on which Shashi Kapoor and Amitabh Bachchan appear in a clip from *Deewaar,* a blockbuster from the seventies. Both heroes are wearing dinner jackets but the dress code at the Classique is casual. Scotch and snacks are ordered as the conversation drifts back to casting. Robin suggests an actor's name for the role of Billo. Kumarji immediately rejects her.

"*Bahut paisa leygi!*" he says, curling his upper lip. (She'll take too much money.)

Of the female roles Billo's is different because she is a somewhat older woman. In Bollywood there's an acknowledged ceiling of thirty years for a heroine. For most female actors the choices after thirty used to be limited to marriage, the odd character role—a vamp if you're willing to show skin—or eventually a return to play the mother roles. Ironically, the only available part in *Omkara* is for a mature woman. Almost jokingly, Vishal puts forward Aishwarya Rai, who is thirty-two. Abhishek approves: "Not a bad idea!" Robin cocks an eyebrow as if to say it would be unlikely she'd accept.

Kumarji's eyes haven't shown any reaction. He fingers his mobile phone as if it were a calculator.

"For Aishwarya Rai, I'd be willing to pay," he says, mentioning her item number in *Bunty aur Babli,* which helped make the song "Kajra Re" a hit.

Later, when I ask Robin about the budget for the film, he estimates twelve to fourteen crore, most of which will go to the actors. A major star like Kareena will take no less than two crore. All of this must be running through the producer's mind as he returns to the issue of locations.

"Forget U.P.," he says. "Security will be too much of a problem. The best thing with Wai is it's close enough to Bombay. If you need anything, it can be ordered by next morning."

Abhishek excuses himself a couple of times. He is already lining up assistant directors. I ask Vishal if he is relieved that the first narration is over.

"Not really. Now the hard part begins," he says, taking a deep breath. Three more stars have to be persuaded and he has all of the logistical issues to contend with, as well as six songs to compose.

With a second round of drinks the mood became looser. Kumarji wants everything tied up by the end of the month. Vishal seems to think it is feasible. Growing expansive, he says he wants to have a small scene that echoes *Maqbool.*

"I was thinking I might ask Naseer and Om to play the pundits who read the horoscope," a reprise of their roles in *Maqbool.* This isn't in the script but Vishal is toying with the idea.

"Eventually I want to make a trilogy," he says. "*Macbeth. Othello.* And *Julius Caesar.*"

THE POET OF PALI HILLS

HOLLYWOOD HAS always exploited the talents of fiction writers to generate scripts, while Bollywood has turned to its poets. As a result, the language of Hindi films is more lyrical, layered with metaphors, rhythms, and rhyme schemes, as well as a vocabulary that isn't often found in prose. The status given to poets in Bollywood is somewhat similar to the patronage they enjoyed under Mughal emperors, with all its attendant privileges, demands, and compromises.

As one of the poet laureates of Indian cinema, Gulzar has composed lyrics for dozens of films, in addition to directing his own movies. At the end of *Angoor* (Grapes), his adaptation of *The Comedy of Errors,* Shakespeare makes a cameo appearance. After the confusion of muddled twins, mistaken identities, and double entendres, the playwright winks at the camera. More than any other writer in Bollywood, Gulzar can appreciate Shakespeare's poetic ironies.

Though a respected and resilient filmmaker, Gulzar remains a poet first. His mother tongue is Urdu, a language with a rich history and an uncertain future. In many ways, Hindi films have helped preserve and promote Urdu by employing its poets to write lyrics and dialogue. A language that evolved out of courtly Persian, or Farsi, and the colloquial dialects of northern India, Urdu was once the most common language of cities like Delhi and Lahore. It was also a language used by the British to communicate with their subjects. The most celebrated Urdu poet was Mirza Ghalib, who died in 1869. Gulzar refers to himself as a "servant" of Ghalib and directed a television serial on the life of his literary mentor.

In his spacious home in Pali Hills, the poet sits behind a well-laden desk, working on an Urdu manuscript. Dressed in immaculate bleached cotton that matches the white brushstrokes at his temples and his trim mustache, he looks every part a man of letters. When Gulzar describes the creative process, he repeatedly uses the verb "indulge."

"When I write a poem it is like painting. I describe the dawn or sunset as if I were re-creating it with a brush, though I am using a pen to write the words. It is the same with music or the call of a bird, which enters into poetry . . . With films you have an opportunity to indulge in all of these different elements—language, color, sound, drama. Of course, there is a problem with film. It is never completely a personal creation. Making a film you rely on so many other people, unlike a poem, which is totally your own.

"In my films I try to do everything I can—writing the script, the lyrics, the dialogue and directing. For those things I cannot do, I turn to others but I tell the cinematographer exactly what I want to see . . . the angle of a shot, the light. In this way, I indulge in every part of the production. For example, I control the actor. I tell him or her that I want a tear to form in the eye but not to let it fall. Hold that tear. Keep holding it there on the rim of your eye. Only when I say, should you let it run down your cheek."

He recounts how the actors in his film *Maachis* (Matches) were completely absorbed in their roles, particularly Om Puri, who plays a Punjabi separatist. At one point he is asked about his family and he replies that all are dead. "*Aadhey saintalees mein, aadhey chaurasi mein.*" (Half of them died in 1947, the other half in 1984.) Om Puri was so caught up in the emotions of that line, every time he delivered it, tears welled up in his eyes. Yet the character was not someone who wept. Eight shots were taken of that scene and each time Om Puri choked up because he felt the tragedy of those words. Finally, he delivered the line with suppressed emotion. Yet those two dates, which are pivotal for most Punjabis—the year of partition and the year of the anti-Sikh riots that followed Indira Gandhi's assassination—provide a tragic parentheses of history.

Gulzar himself is a displaced Punjabi. Though he uses his pen name exclusively—Gulzar means "garden of flowers"—his real name is Sampooran Singh and he came from the town of Deena, now in Pakistan. *Maachis* explores the motives behind separatist violence in the Punjab. After it was released, there were questions in parliament and it was sent back to the censor board for review. They stood by their original decision and let it be shown. Though all of the characters are Punjabis, the dialogue is almost entirely in Hindi and Urdu.

"I added a few words and phrases of Punjabi, just sprinkled them into the dialogue to give a texture of the Punjabi language."

Though Bollywood movies are known as Hindi films, the root language is actually Hindustani, a dialect that has gone out of favor because of Sanskritization. Hindustani, the most common blend of vernaculars spoken throughout north India, is essentially derived from Urdu. All of the great dialogue writers and lyricists—Shailender, Kaifi Azmi, Majrooh Sultanpuri, Khwaja Ahmad Abbas, Anand Bakshi—have been Urdu poets like Gulzar. If a character is expected to make an emphatic statement, whether it be a declaration of love, an oath of revenge, or a philosophical rumination, Urdu is the language in which those lines are written.

"It is Urdu. Of course, it's Urdu," says Gulzar. "But just as there is not one English—whether Oxford or the Queen's English—there is not one Urdu, not one Hindi." As Ghalib points out, in Gulzar's scenario, language changes every fifty miles in India. "Language is always changing. The Urdu that Ghalib spoke in 1850 is not the same language we speak today.

"Most of the early Punjabi filmmakers spoke Urdu and brought it with them to Mumbai. It was the language of Lahore from Mughal times. Urdu has been nourished by writers from the Punjab. In fact the greatest modern Urdu poet was a Punjabi—Faiz Ahmed Faiz. So many other writers, too. Sahir Ludhianvi. Saadat Hasan Manto. Rajinder Singh Bedi."

The last two writers he mentions were responsible for the screenplay and dialogue of the classic movie *Mirza Ghalib,* made in 1954, starring Bharat Bhushan.

When asked if Mirza Ghalib would have written for Hindi films, were he alive today, Gulzar laughs. "Ghalib was always in debt, so he might have agreed to write lyrics for a fee, but he probably would have taken the money and not written a word."

Pausing a moment, with a wry smile, he continues: "Let me answer your question like this: The Almighty decided one day that he wanted to send Ghalib back to earth, so he consulted one of his angels. He said, 'I don't want to send him back as a poet, perhaps something else. What do you suggest?' The angel answered, 'Why don't we ask Mirza Ghalib himself?' So the Almighty summoned the great poet and told him of His intentions. Ghalib folded his hands and answered, 'You can send me back to earth as anything, but please not as Bharat Bhushan.'"

The joke is told in English but the punch line in Urdu.

Gulzar shows me a calendar on his desk, which has a *ghazal* for every day of the week, a compilation of verses from different poets. Today's *ghazal* is by Dard, the nom de plume of a grandson of Bahadur Shah Zafar, the last Mughal emperor. Gulzar has circled one of the couplets and reads it aloud to me. "It's not very good," he says. "It sounds totally filmi." Then he reads the next couplet, which is far better. "You see, if he could write like that, why didn't he delete the verse preceding it?

"Nobody edited his work as much as Ghalib, and he often changed the words. For example *dil* (heart) and *ji* (life). When I was making *Mausam* (Season), you may remember the song, '*Dil dhoondta hai phir vahi fursat ke raat din . . .*' [The heart searches day and night.] It is a verse from Ghalib. The original couplet began with '*ji*' but the music director, Madan Mohan, said it would sound better as '*dil*.' I told him, you cannot change Ghalib's verses but he went and found another edition of his work in which the first word had been revised from '*ji*' to '*dil*,' so that's what we used in the song."

For all of his political films, Gulzar remains a romantic at heart. A simple, unpretentious man, he lives comfortably and surrounds himself with the things he enjoys. As we are talking, a servant brings in two glasses of watermelon juice. Unlike so many filmmakers, he does not clutter his office with trophies and awards. Most of what he has on his desk is literature and manuscripts. At the moment he is working on a screenplay about a nineteenth-century Portuguese wanderer and poet who settled in Bengal and immersed himself in the music and poetry of that region. He became so well known that he defeated several major poets in the "tak-a-tak" give and take of poetic performance. The poet's name is Anthony Firangi and a Bengali film was made about him.

"He was addicted to ganja but they never showed that in the film. For me, that is one of the most interesting things. He also married a widow . . . Not much has been written about the Portuguese in India. The British were here for two hundred years, the Portuguese were here for four hundred years."

Whenever Gulzar recites Urdu poetry, as he does at many points during our conversation, it is never with the flamboyance of amateur recitations—the kind one hears at Rotary Clubs and Founder's Day functions. Instead it has a gentle urgency, rising out of his throat, as if the language comes not from the tongue but from deeper within, enunciating the rhythms of his heart. Each consonant and syllable is pronounced with subtle diction. One hears the language almost before it has been uttered. Even if I can't understand every word, it is possible to feel the meaning in the sound of each phrase.

Vishal Bhardwaj, Gulzar, and Robin Bhatt.

MUSICAL SITTING

SEATED CROSS-LEGGED on a cushioned divan, Vishal picks at the keys of a harmonium with his right hand as his left hand pumps the instrument's pleated diaphragm. The first notes of a melody emerge through the reedy whisper of the harmonium. At the opposite end of the divan sits Gulzar, dressed as always in immaculate white cotton, one leg tucked beneath him. He holds a spiral-bound notebook open on his lap, the pages threaded with Urdu verses and phrases. Accompanying them on guitar is Hitesh Sonik. Nobody speaks until Vishal hums along with the harmonium, then sings a line softly, a plaintive phrase. Gulzar flips a page to find the lyrics.

We are in the poet's drawing room, low furniture with cream-colored upholstery and driftwood sculptures. Paintings cover the walls, including a surrealist oil of a nude figure embracing itself, as well as caricatures of Gulzar by different cartoonists. He has a distinctive face, from which it is easy to draw a likeness—the white mustache, sharp jaw, and eyes that waver between weariness and amusement.

This is one of a series of sessions in which words and music are woven together. At the same time it's a social gathering. Six of us are together in the room, including Rekha, who sits in a chair facing Vishal. Their son, Aasmaan, plays with Gulzar's bulldog Pali, who nuzzles our legs as he prowls the parquet floor.

"We should find that point where we were last time," Gulzar muses. "When it all came together."

But inspiration is elusive. Vishal sings the first few lines again. The music has a lively folk rhythm, a rustic sound that Vishal has chosen for *Omkara,* to accompany his story of rural U.P. Gulzar's lyrics, too, are part of the language of village India.

"*Bheetar bheetar aag jale . . . baat karun to saeink lage . . .*" (Inside me burns a fire . . . if I speak it fans the flames.)

Hearing the first verse and the refrain, as Vishal sings it, Gulzar suggests shortening one phrase. They take out a word and try it two or three times. Hitesh's accompaniment is unerring and unobtrusive, the guitar providing a subtle counterpoint to the harmonium.

After a few more attempts, Gulzar suggests adding a syllable at the end of the line, instead of trimming it. The song has no title yet, though they refer to it as the *namak* (salt) song, because of the refrain.

"*Jabaan pe laaga, laaga re . . . namak isk ka . . . tere isk ka.*" (My tongue has tasted the salt of love . . . of your love.)

This time when Vishal sings it, everyone expresses satisfaction. Gulzar cautions him: "Now this is your beginning. It's perfect. Don't go back and ruin it by adding any more."

"I don't have time to ruin it," Vishal responds. He has to compose six songs in a month and a half, on top of all his other responsibilities as director.

As he sings, the tension eases. His face softens. Instead of his fingers drumming on a desk, they caress the keys of the harmonium. His eyes close. One hand leaves the keys and snakes up, as if to trace the tune.

Music is Vishal's first medium of expression. It is an individual form of creativity outside the ambiguities and uncertainties of film production. Later, when I ask about the process of composition, he shrugs. "The music comes from the air. It gets recorded in my mind and then transferred onto a cassette or CD."

The poet and composer move on to another song, "O Saathi Re," which remains unfinished. Nothing has been written on paper aside from Gulzar's lyrics. But Vishal does not need to refer to these. Every word, every tune, every keystroke on the harmonium is committed to memory and reworked inside the composer's head.

Though orchestration and percussion will be added to the songs when they are mixed in the recording studio, at the moment these are simple folk ballads. Omkara's exploits and passions have been put to music, like tributes to so many rural heroes in India. The music is part *ghazal,* part *thumri*—not standard Bollywood fare but with a filmi energy and playful notes of innocence. While Vishal incorporates other styles of music in the orchestration, the music for *Omkara* is distinctly grounded in the cultural rhythms of U.P.

When we break for lunch, I ask the meaning of a phrase, "*atti batti,*" which is used in "O Saathi Re." Rekha is the first to explain. "It's a children's rhyme. When you quarrel with someone and stop being friends, you click your fingernail against your front teeth and say '*atti.*' "

Both she and Gulzar demonstrate.

"Later, when you become friends again you say '*batti.*' *Atti . . . batti . . .* And if you really want to mean it seriously, that you'll never be friends again forever"—Rekha laughs—"you put your hand under your leg, then click your tooth."

She demonstrates again, one arm cocked under her knee. The phrase is part of the love play between Omkara and Dolly. Thinking aloud, Vishal says he isn't sure if the line works, more because of the sound than the meaning.

"But you should keep it," Gulzar insists. "It gives the song a folklike feeling, of children's games."

Gulzar relishes the language. Though he can elevate his lyrics to an esoteric level with the formalities of Urdu, he seems to prefer the colloquial.

There is a line in the *namak* song that contains the word "*chaunk.*" Over lunch, Gulzar pronounces it several times, savoring the combination of consonants and vowels. *Chaunk* is the mixture of spices added after a dish has been cooked—a blend of garlic, cumin, and chilies fried in oil, then tossed into the food to give it a final burst of flavor.

Today it seems as if they are adding *chaunk* to the music. Returning to the divan after lunch, Vishal and Gulzar discuss the *namak* song again. They are satisfied with the opening stanza and the refrain. Vishal sings another verse then asks Rekha to sing it. She protests that she hasn't come prepared to sing, but gives a brief rendition—husband and wife going back and forth with the tune. Their voices complement each other. Rekha will be the playback singer for the *namak* song. In a few weeks she will record the final version, which will accompany a cabaret dance in the film. After they finish singing, Vishal requests Gulzar to write more verses to complete the song.

"I'll give you plenty of lines to work with," says the lyricist, flipping through his notebook. He then asks about the title song "Omkara," which has already been recorded. Vishal tells him that he has played it for Ajay Devgan and the producer, both of whom like it. He still hopes they will accepts *Omkara* as the title for the film.

"*O Saathi Re* sounds like a television serial," he tells me. "There is one other title that we thought of, *Issak* (a colloquial pronunciation of the word for love)." But clearly he is still pushing for *Omkara* and hopes the music will help resolve that decision.

On our way to the studio, we drive through the back lanes of Pali Hills, taking a shortcut to Juhu. Machine workshops, rubbish heaps, and the clamor of the city surround us. Vishal puts a CD in the car stereo. This is the final recording of the title song.

Sukhwinder Singh, the playback singer, has a strong, masculine voice, accompanied by the folk rhythms and harmonies of the orchestration. As the music fills the car it transports us out of the chaos of Mumbai traffic and into the lyrical landscape of rural U.P. "*Dham Dham, Dharam Dhariya rey!* . . . *Omkara! Hey Omkara!*"

Rajju and Langda.

DEV SAAB'S DURBAR

PALI HILLS is one of the few places in Mumbai where you can climb above sea level, except in a high-rise building. Five minutes' walk up the Zig Zag Road from Gulzar's house is a walled enclosure and the gate of Navketan Studios.

The reception area is lined with posters from Dev Anand's films, including *Guide, Haré Raama Haré Krishna,* and *Ishq, Ishq, Ishq.* Before I have a chance to study them, Suneil Anand comes downstairs to meet me. We were classmates in school and he looks much the same as I remember him from thirty years ago, slim and animated. He keeps himself fit with martial arts, which he studies under a Chinese teacher. A few years back Suneil starred in a martial arts film of his own, titled *Master.*

Navketan Studios has two large auditoriums, re-creating the acoustics of a cinema hall, where dubbing and mixing is done. In the first of these a technician is working on the soundtrack of a film. All of the audio effects can be added in the studio and on one side of the auditorium is a wooden staircase, leading up to a false door that opens and closes. On the other side is a stone staircase, with another door. In the middle of the auditorium are three different surfaces—asphalt, dirt, and concrete—depending on what the scene requires.

In the second auditorium the final cut of Subhash Ghai's film *Kisna: The Warrior Poet* is being mixed. The film stars Viveik Oberoi. Suneil doesn't enter the studio but one of the technicians takes me inside, after we remove our shoes. In the center of the darkened auditorium lies a bank of consoles, where the sound engineers are at work. To one side are overstuffed armchairs, where the director and his assistants are viewing the final cut. We enter during a climactic scene, in which the hero rises out of the smoke, sword in hand. The sound is extremely loud, reverberations circling around us, passing from one speaker to the next. The technician points with his finger to indicate the surround-sound effects. It's like being inside a tornado.

Suneil waits outside on the stairs. He has avoided going into the auditorium and when I ask him why, he explains, "It's part of the protocol of the studio. For a director, the final cut of a film is a private thing until it is officially released." While the shooting of a film is often a spectacle, postproduction is an almost personal process of creation. Unlike in Hollywood, directors generally get to make the final cut, despite pressure from producers and distributors to shape a film according to their perception of the market.

After seeing the studios, I am taken upstairs to meet Dev Anand. His penthouse office has an enormous, L-shaped sofa in one corner. At the center sits Dev Saab, while the rest of the sofa is covered with files, scripts, clippings, photographs, and publicity brochures for his latest film, *Mr Prime Minister.* Cordial and courtly, Dev Saab speaks in a soft, urbane accent. Film magazines often refer to him as "Debonair Dev" or "The Evergreen Dev Anand" because he refuses to act his age. He is dressed in baggy corduroy trousers, a red sweater draped over his shoulders, and loosely knotted shoes. Even at eighty-one, there is a dapper quality about him that sets him apart from many other stars of his generation.

Dev Saab apologizes for the stacks of paper as one of his assistants pushes aside some files for me to sit. On a chair across the room is a giant teddy bear. Half a dozen people are in the room, including an aspiring actor who has come to see Dev Saab, along with her father and other family members. We sit in a circle, as if Dev Saab were giving an audience.

In the feudal world of the Bollywood film industry, many of the big stars and producers still hold court, much like emperors at a durbar. Between shootings, they meet and greet their colleagues, actors, technical personnel, anyone who might approach them for a job, a favor, or an interview. Part business, part social occasion, the etiquette and forms of address are carefully calibrated. A star like Dev Anand may not insist on people touching his feet, but there is a ritual to his reception. Most people refer to him as Dev Saab, an honorific used for senior filmmakers. It elevates an individual beyond the more simple "*ji*" or "sir" that others merit. "Saab" is a version of "sahib," stripped of its colonial antecedents.

Almost as soon as I sit down, Dev Saab launches into a brief narration of his new film. Most of it was shot in Bachao, a small town in Gujarat, flattened by an earthquake in 2001. *Mr Prime Minister* is political satire of seismic proportions—"An Earthquake of a Film, to Shake up the Country," as the brochures describe it. Dev Anand even performs a rap song as the title track of the movie.

"I hope to release it at Cannes, and in America," he says. "I also want to have the premiere in Bachao itself. I think there will be a lot of interest in *Mr Prime Minister* because it's about democracy. I have great expectations for this film."

We are interrupted briefly, as tea and biscuits are served. Dev Saab points to a wad of paper inside a plastic folder on the sofa beside him.

"I've just finished my autobiography, only a few chapters left. I started this book on the night the United States began bombing Iraq. We were in New York [filming his 2003 project, *Love at Times Square*]. I walked outside the Waldorf-Astoria hotel. There's a clock above the entrance. All my life, time has moved forward for me. But at that moment it seemed to stop. I realized that I had to write my story. . . . It has an optimistic ending. I am an optimist."

He pauses for a moment, pointing at the manuscript.

"The problem is that my life goes on. I'll have to keep adding chapters. In 1943, I left Lahore and came to Bombay on the Frontier Mail. I had just graduated from college and I wanted to become an actor. My first break was in 1945. Partition, 1947, never should have happened. Since then I've seen things deteriorate. This new film is very close to my own experience, my vision of how the country has fared and the disaster of coalition politics."

One of Dev Saab's earliest and most enduring hits was *Guide,* a film that showcased his romantic élan. A Hollywood version of this film was also made but it disappeared without a trace, while *Guide* is one of the classics of Hindi cinema. Dev Saab describes how the film came into being.

"The writer Pearl Buck came to India and wanted to do a film with me. She gave me a book in which the main character was a woman but I wasn't interested. I wanted to be the star. Then I found a novel, *The Guide,* by R. K. Narayan, and I sent it to her. We made one version of the film in English and an entirely different version in Hindi because the audiences here wouldn't have accepted the English version." *Guide* was directed by Dev Anand's brother, Vijay Anand.

"For many years I made my name as an actor. Then I decided that I wanted to write and direct my own films. The director is the one who has control in his hands. The first film I directed was *Prem Pujari* (The Worshipper of Love).

"Telling a story is one of the greatest things in life. I love fiction. Writing. Novels. I used to read a lot of Somerset Maugham.

One time in London I was attending a play, and during the intermission I saw a man who looked familiar. I went up to him and said, 'I'm sorry to disturb you but are you Somerset Maugham?' He nodded and I was like a schoolboy. I got a piece of paper and asked him for his autograph."

Dev Saab is always looking for stories and often finds them in unpredictable places.

"One night I was watching the Grammy Awards and Norah Jones won four awards. When I learned that she was Ravi Shankar's daughter from an American girlfriend, I thought, What a wonderful story. A girl who becomes a successful musician, the child of a love affair. I sat down and wrote a script for a film and tried to find backing in the U.S. When Pandit Ravi Shankar heard about this he got upset but I told him it wasn't his story . . .

"I still get excited making a film. There will always be that excitement. With each film I have matured but with each film I also grow younger. When I release *Mr Prime Minister* I will have completed sixty years in cinema."

A few months later, when I return to Dev Saab's durbar, the seats in the penthouse are still piled with papers. Dev Saab sits where he always does, a pullover draped across his shoulders. As I come in, he greets me with a handshake and introduces a marketing consultant. They are discussing an advertising campaign for *Mr Prime Minister.* Mock-ups for two posters have been propped on top of a sofa. Dev Saab narrates the story briefly again and the consultant calls it "mind-blowing."

Dev Saab has just returned from Kathmandu, where he was given an award by the king of Nepal. On the wall is a framed picture of him speaking with the king. Dev Saab is holding the king by his arm in an affectionate gesture.

"Look at that!" he says, laughing. "It was a scandal. Nobody is allowed to touch the king but I didn't know this and I caught hold of his arm. He didn't take offense."

Dev Saab gets to his feet, leaning back from the waist in a heroic stance—youthful, brash, and insolent.

"It was a fabulous occasion. The king has invited me back to make my next film. I knew his father, King Mahendra. When I went there to make *Haré Raama Haré Krishna* he supported me. I could place my cameras anywhere I wanted.

"I've always been a star. Never a character actor, always a star," he tells me. "My next film, *Beauty Queen,* will be made in Nepal. The king has given me permission to go wherever I want. They say it's possible to drive to Lhasa. I want to do it. They say it's tough—four days driving—but filmmaking is an adventure. You have to be fearless."

As he waves toward the pictures of himself and the king of Nepal, Dev Saab embodies Bollywood royalty. We are his courtiers and this is his exclusive audience hall—his *diwan-e-khas.* With an appropriate show of deference, the consultant gets to his feet. "Dev Saab, I'll take your leave . . ."

After he departs, a young TV producer is ushered in. Nervously, she explains that her show features film stars and she wants to do a program about Dev Anand. He smiles and shakes his head.

"I'm afraid I'm so busy right now . . ."

The woman persists.

"How long is your show?" Dev Saab asks.

"Half an hour."

"Oh, impossible. How could you fit my life into half an hour?" He laughs and shakes his head.

There is an awkward pause as his refusal sinks in and the producer shifts nervously in her seat.

"Sir, on a personal level. I just want to say I'm a huge fan . . . and my parents are great fans. Do you think you could give me your autograph?"

Dev Saab makes a regal gesture and the woman leans forward with her notebook.

After she leaves, we discuss the autobiography. Several books have been written about Dev Saab but none of them are authorized by him. He wants to tell his own story. Pointing at the posters of *Mr Prime Minister,* he tells me, "This is my most mature work." But it's certainly not his last. He has already started casting for *Beauty Queen* and we are interrupted by a young woman who has come to audition for the role of a beauty pageant contestant. The idea of Miss India on the road from Kathmandu to Lhasa may snap the suspenders of disbelief, but with Dev Anand anything is possible.

GUNSLINGERS

NOW THAT *Omkara* has gone into preproduction, the center of operations has shifted to a rented office, in a part of northern Mumbai called Four Bungalows. Any sign of gracious single-story structures has long since disappeared beneath apartment buildings and shopping centers. The production office is an unmarked row house, pinched between a line of similar middle-class lodgings. A few doors down is a sign that reads ACTING CLASSES GOING ON, but other than this there is no hint of Bollywood.

The ground-floor reception area opens into a room where the assistant directors work. Abhishek introduces me to the first and second ADs—Ajit Ahuja and Lara Bhalla, as well as continuity supervisor Debashree Mukherjee and Abhik Sarkar, who is the still photographer. All of them are in their twenties or early thirties. Cinematographer Tassaduq Hussain is also in the office. When he learns that I am writing a book he warns me, "You know, this isn't like other film productions."

"More organized?" I ask.

He nods with a noncommittal smile.

Ajit has just returned from a recce to find suitable locations. He hooks up his digital camera to a laptop and flips through the pictures quickly. From time to time the others make him stop, asking to see a building or landscape in more detail. The first series of shots were all taken in the town of Wai, near the location site where art director Samir Chanda is building the set for Omkara's village. Ideally, they want to keep most of the shooting in this vicinity. Ajit has taken a series of street scenes, archways, and riverbank scenes inside the town, with sloping stone steps and temples on either side.

"I like this place," he says.

Tassaduq seems less convinced, though he is intrigued by a brick gateway that frames a narrow street. One of the challenges is to make Maharashtra look like Uttar Pradesh. There are plenty of similarities but subtle differences, too—species of trees, billboards in Marathi rather than Hindi. A more serious issue are the hills around Wai. Most of U.P. is flat and the landscape will look incongruous.

"This can be Bhaisaab's house."

A luxurious bungalow with pillared verandas.

"Kesu's balcony."

A half-finished construction with a tin roof.

"Here's the night shot, down this street, where Kesu drives off on his motorcycle."

"This is the hospital," Ajit explains. "The rooms are damn sad, *yaar. Yahan to dar lagta hai.*" (This was scary.)

He shows us a picture of an emergency room that looks like a morgue. We move on to a sugar factory.

"This is totally U.P.," Abhishek says.

"A top view of this would be kick-ass."

Bullock carts loaded with sugarcane and tractors pulling trailers are lined up at the factory gate.

"Nice colors," Tassaduq adds.

We flip to another street, this time in the town of Satara, not far from Wai.

"I was thinking of this as the party headquarters."

"Too hep. *Is ko down-market bana sakhte hain.*" (We can make this down-market.)

"We'll have to cheat as an option."

"The mountains are still a problem."

"This palm tree just fucks it up." There aren't palm trees like this in U.P.

Ajit shifts to another location, which is actually in U.P., near the city of Allahabad. A temple on an island in the middle of a river appears on the laptop screen. It's spectacular, a crumbling turret of earth surmounted with a tiny shrine.

"This location will make the film. Nobody has ever seen it before."

After the still photographs are finished, Ajit attaches a videocam to the TV. We retrace many of the scenes we were shown before, but this time on video.

Ajit shows us a school that he suggests can be turned into a police station. The handheld camera moves along an open veranda, past gray stone walls and doorways painted red. It has the feel of a police station.

"This looks totally U.P."

"We can use this. Good."

The moving camera stops at a doorway.

"This can be the interrogation cell."

The door opens and a classroom full of children peer out at the camera, eyes wide with curiosity.

Ajit laughs. "The teacher was hiding."

The most interesting interior is a derelict dance hall, with rows and rows of chairs facing an empty stage. The building has the seedy feel of a small-town auditorium. Ceiling fans are suspended above.

We jump abruptly to a street scene again, as the video keeps running. A sign reads NEW ENGLISH MEDIUM SCHOOL. A wedding procession fills the street, the band in glittering uniforms, trombones blaring, a trumpeter facing the camera, the groom on a white horse. It could easily be a shot from the film itself, Omi and Dolly's wedding procession.

As soon as the TV is switched off and the curtains are pulled aside, there's a knock on the door. Lara puts her head inside and announces: "The weapons have arrived."

Everyone blinks, trying to figure out what she means. Minutes later, two men enter carrying canvas satchels. One of them is wearing a red baseball cap, his shirttails untucked. They take the weapons out of the bags and put them on the table, ten handguns—automatic pistols and revolvers.

The presence of the guns makes everyone self-conscious. Abhishek picks up one of the automatics and weighs it in his hand. Each of us then reaches for a weapon, as Lara asks the arms suppliers, "Are these real?"

"Of course," says the man in the baseball cap. He cocks a pistol and pulls the trigger with a convincing click.

"Where are the rifles? You promised us rifles, too."

The men shake their heads. "We can bring them tomorrow but we have to get police permission."

Though I had assumed the guns were quality imitations, holding one of the revolvers in my hand I can see they are real. The smell of oil and gunpowder is unmistakable; they've recently been fired. Though the arms suppliers are licensed to carry firearms, it still feels as if these are somehow linked to Mumbai's criminal underworld.

By now the mood in the room has changed and everyone begins playing with the pistols, pointing them at one another and fooling around, spinning the chambers on the revolvers, aiming at the television screen.

"*Arrey,* Chaubey, careful. It might be loaded, *yaar*!"

"This one is Omi's." A black automatic .357 Magnum.

"This is Kesu's." A smaller .32, compact.

"Definitely Langda's." An Italian automatic with a chrome barrel.

"He has a rifle, doesn't he?"

"Yes, but this will be kept in his waistband."

"Boys and guns," says Debashree, who has joined the group. Even Tassaduq has a gun in his hand and there's an edgy craziness about the moment.

"My parents never let me play with guns when I was a kid," says Ajit, brandishing Omi's pistol.

"A good thing," says Debashree.

"That's why I love them now," he says, pretending to fire, then blowing across the end of the barrel.

"But we need a rifle, with a telescopic sight."

The weapons suppliers assure them it will be possible.

"A .303?"

"No, that won't take a scope. It will be a .315."

"But it has to look good."

Once again, the arms suppliers assure us that the guns are authentic. Until now the story of U.P. gangsters has been just that, a fiction, but with the arrival of the weapons it seems more true to life. Holding Omi's automatic in my hand, I am surprised by how heavy it is. The textured grip is rough against my palm and the trigger has a curved solidity, a lethal tongue of steel. Pointing the pistol at a television antenna on one of the neighboring rooftops, I have to remind myself—this is just a film.

POSTER ARTIST

"I ALWAYS DREAMED of making a film, but it's an expensive medium, so I started painting as a sideline."

Maqbool Fida Husain laughs softly, acknowledging that it's not a bad sideline. He is one of the few contemporary Indian painters to have achieved the celebrity of a film star. His works sell for crores of rupees and he remains active at the age of eighty-nine. We meet at ColorArt Studio in Mahim, a commercial firm that prints high-quality billboards and other artwork, mostly for the advertising industry. Husain is dressed in a rumpled shirt and trousers that match his white mane and beard. Draped around his neck is a black scarf of crinkled silk that looks like a whimsical brushstroke, an artist's signature. His only other accessory is a pair of tinted spectacles with round frames that give him an owlish expression. As always, he is barefoot. It's one of his trademarks, whether he is traveling abroad, entering the lobby of a five-star hotel, or working in a studio.

M. F. Husain is a controversial artist and his work crosses political and religious boundaries. His larger-than-life murals of Indira Gandhi dominate the walls of Delhi's international airport and his nude images of Hindu goddesses have raised the ire of right-wing zealots. At the same time the big screen has always been a part of his imagination.

"When I first arrived in Bombay, I was unknown and I started painting film posters. We used to be paid four annas per square foot." (Four annas was equal to one-fourth of a rupee.)

Poster artists are still hired by producers, distributors, and cinema owners to paint billboards and posters to advertise their films. None of Husain's film posters have survived, though he has a photograph of one of the giant billboards he painted at the Minerva Cinema, advertising P. C. Barua's *Zindagi* (Life) starring K. L. Saigal.

"P. C. Barua was the Godard of Indian cinema," Husain asserts with muted authority. He speaks just above a whisper, his accent cosmopolitan.

I ask whether painting film posters at an early age influenced his later work.

"Yes, of course. It gave me the confidence to handle a large canvas!" he says, gesturing broadly with one hand, as if he were painting a curved line that begins above his head and circles down to his feet.

Husain has made three films himself, beginning with a black-and-white short commissioned by the government in 1966. It was called *Through the Eyes of a Painter,* though Husain is quick to say that wasn't his choice of title. He refers to it instead as *A Visual Equation.*

"When I screened it for the film board, they rejected it," he said. "They said it was juvenile. Made no sense. So I took it back and sent the film to the Berlin Film Festival, where it was awarded a Golden Bear."

In 2000, Husain made *Gaja Gamini.* The title is taken from a classical Sanskrit expression that describes a woman whose walk is as beautiful as an elephant's gait. *Gaja Gamini* is a tribute to actor Madhuri Dixit. Husain admits to being infatuated with her and most of the film revolves around her dancing form. He has also produced an oversize coffee-table book on the film, combining stills with reproductions of his painting. The film failed to attract an audience, though it has a large cast of stars, including Madhuri Dixit, Shabana Azmi, Naseeruddin Shah, and Shah Rukh Khan. Husain appears in the film at several points, sketching the image of a horse on a brick wall and painting a tiger on the flank of a live elephant.

"Editing the film was the most satisfying process," says Husain. "A film is made on the editing table."

He lists some of the filmmakers he admires—Federico Fellini, Jean-Luc Godard, and Roberto Rossellini, whom he met years ago when the Italian director visited India. Asked about the films Salvador Dalí made with Luis Buñuel, Husain shakes his head.

"Dalí was a painter who started with ideas rather than images," he says. "I prefer images to ideas. I don't want people to read my paintings. I want them to look at them. People always want to know the meaning . . ."

He throws up his hands in a gesture of frustration. There is a playful, chiding manner to his speech, as if he does not want to be taken too seriously, while at the same time hinting at something more profound.

"Do you want to see what I'm working on now?" he asks suddenly. Without waiting for an answer he is on his feet and leading me out of the office and down a hallway to an unmarked door. Inside is a huge studio with thirty-foot ceilings. On one side is a large-format printing machine used for reproducing digital images the size of billboards. Against the opposite wall is a partially unfurled roll of canvas twelve feet in width and about thirty feet long with at least another fifty feet still on the roll.

"I'm working on a mural for Yash Chopra's new studio, on the history of Indian cinema. It's going to be huge. We'll blow it up to more than twenty feet high," he says, waving a hand toward the ceiling. "You see, it begins with Dadasaheb Phalke, the father of Indian film, and carries through all of the eras until the present."

The images on the canvas are copied from famous photographs and movie stills, including one of the early silent heroines, Sulochana. Husain has provided captions in his painting, including Sulochana's real name (Ruby Mayer) in parentheses. There is also Zubeida ("The Spitfire of Sex") and a drunken Meena Kumari from *Sahib Bibi aur Ghulam* (Master, Mistress and Servant), as well as Prithviraj Kapoor in *Sikandar* (Alexander the Great). Husain has also included the first film he saw—*Savkari Pash,* by Baburao Painter. Two of the artist's assistants unroll a preliminary sketch, done with black ink on a roll of translucent tracing paper. These images will be transferred to the canvas, like a film projected onto a screen.

Husain says he hopes to finish the mural in another month. He never works slowly and once held a show where he painted a dozen canvases simultaneously in a gallery.

"I want to have a lot of color in this mural. Reds and blues." He is like a director in the studio, surrounded by his unit. Looking at the unfinished painting, it isn't difficult to picture Husain as a young man, freshly arrived in Mumbai in the 1930s, painting film posters for a living. The mural, with its huge faces and lettering in Hindi and English, has the quality of a giant poster that scrolls out in both directions. As Husain explains, "It's like the medium of film itself, a continuous painting."

SUN-N-SAND

"IF YOU LOOK up the definition of acting, it means to *do* something," Naseeruddin Shah explains. "It doesn't mean to imitate or pretend. You must act as if you are doing it for yourself, as yourself."

Naseer goes on to describe an exercise in which actors perform everyday tasks—putting in an earring, shaving—but without the actual objects they would use. He mimes the actions.

"It's very difficult when you try to remember how to go through the motions, whereas you usually do it without thinking."

Saif Ali Khan leans forward intently. He must play a character with a limp—Langda Tyagi. Saif asks what kind of limp he should use. Naseer gets out of his chair and demonstrates a couple of alternatives.

"Your body has memory," he says, meaning an actor draws on recollections of injuries or ailments to create these in a character. But Langda's limp is caused by a clubfoot.

"He has lived with it all his life," Naseer explains. "It mustn't look as if he recently pulled a muscle or hurt himself. Instead it is a lifelong limp."

Shifting his weight, he walks five steps with the heel raised and the ankle turned inward.

Saif gets up and tries it a couple of times as the rest of the cast watches. Vishal hasn't said anything so far but now he interjects.

"Naseerbhai, the way you did it first, I like that. Show us again."

Naseer grins. "This time it will cost you money." But he gets up and demonstrates the limp once more.

Saif follows his lead.

"It will take practice. You're all experienced actors. I don't need to tell you this. Usually, I practice alone in the bathroom. All of us are bathroom actors." Naseer pauses for the punch line. "And the performances we give in front of a mirror are always better than in front of the camera."

The others laugh but Saif persists. "Acting means communicating something of yourself."

Naseer shakes his head. "No. It's not about communicating. It's about doing it yourself, as yourself, not for anyone else. Forget about the audience."

Concluding his lesson on method acting, Naseer adds a word of caution. "You become your character but at the end of the day when the director says 'Pack up,' you get in your car and drive away. You stop being your character—otherwise you go mad. Imagine if you had to be Othello or Desdemona twenty-four hours a day. They'd have to take you to the *pagal khaana*—the insane asylum!"

Seven PM. It's been a long day for everyone else, but Naseer has just arrived. He was originally scheduled to lead a three-day workshop for the actors, but this had to be curtailed to a reading of the script. For the cast of *Maqbool,* Naseer conducted a week-long workshop before shooting commenced, but with so many stars in this production it is impossible to schedule more than an afternoon. The original idea of the workshop was to familiarize the actors with the script and introduce them to the colloquial idiom of the dialogue—U.P. slang, the crude nuances of back-water thugs and gangsters.

Naseeruddin Shah is known as an actor's actor. He is widely regarded as one of the most accomplished stars in Bollywood. His career began in art films during the 1970s but later he made a successful transition to commercial cinema, moving from the roles of a serious and dedicated social worker in *Manthan* (The Churning) to a loopy international villain in *Chaahat.* He has even acted in a couple of Hollywood productions, taking on the part of Captain Nemo to Sean Connery's Allan Quatermain in *The League of Extraordinary Gentlemen.* Naseer continues to play major roles in films like *Monsoon Wedding* and *Iqbal.*

Vishal, Abhishek, Ajit, and Kumarji have been in the top-floor suite at Sun-N-Sand Hotel since noon. After that each actor makes his or her entrance. The first to show up is Ajay Devgan. Out of costume he hardly looks the part of a violent gangster. Ajay's hair is fashionably tinted with rusty brown highlights. He wears a gray T-shirt and jeans. His face is angular, reminiscent of a young Al Pacino.

Deepak Dobriyal is the next to arrive, entering so quietly nobody notices at first, until Vishal calls out, greeting him with his character's name, "*Arrey,* Rajju. How are you? Have you put on weight?"

Deepak has been instructed to gain five kilos for his role. He still looks lean and hungry, though Vishal insists his face is fuller.

"Have you quit smoking, like the doctor told you?"

Deepak nods self-consciously.

Viveik Oberoi comes in a few minutes later, dressed in black, an open-collared shirt with embroidered patterns, loose sleeves. A popular pinup for teenage girls, he is mentioned in all the gossip columns—a *desi* Brad Pitt, whose love life is followed with as much interest as his films. During the reading Viveik wears glasses. Though he has acted with Ajay in several other films, the last film I saw him in was *Kisna: The Warrior Poet,* in which he plays the title role. In *Omkara* he takes on the role of Kesu, a college leader and Omi's lieutenant.

Half an hour later, Kareena Kapoor makes her entrance, sporting the casual chic of a star: black sweater, pink top, jeans, and Nike sneakers. Of all the stars, she has the ultimate Bollywood pedigree, a fourth-generation actor of the Kapoor clan—"the Corleones of Bollywood," as they call themselves. The great-granddaughter of Prithviraj Kapoor, granddaughter of Raj Kapoor, daughter of Randhir Kapoor. Kareena and her sister, Karisma, are the first women in their family to act in films, breaking the male monopoly. She has her family's high cheekbones, fair complexion, and pale eyes.

These are celebrities at the peak of success, faces you see whenever you open a newspaper or magazine, icons of youth, beauty, style, and attitude. Bollywood's stars are constantly scrutinized by the press, their lives dissected in the tabloids, rumors portrayed as facts. As much as they hunger for performances on the screen, audiences in India have an insatiable appetite for gossip within the industry, following the love affairs, divorces, legal troubles, and personal tragedies of the stars.

Soon after Kareena arrives, Dolly Ahluwalia comes in, having driven straight from the airport. In addition to playing the part of Auntyji—a political leader who gives Omkara a party ticket for the election—Dollyji is also the film's costume designer.

She has brought two silver waistbands to show Kareena and Vishal. These are elaborately worked girdles with filigree and inlay. In Shakespeare's play, a handkerchief embroidered with strawberries becomes the catalyst for Othello's jealousy. In the screenplay this has been changed to a silver waistband that Omkara gives Dolly. Langda's wife, Indu, steals it and passes it on to her husband, setting in motion suspicions of infidelity. Dollyji holds the waistbands up to herself and models them. Vishal selects the more elaborate one, a tangled web of silver chains.

Punam Sawhney, the executive producer, has prepared folders for each of the stars, with contact information and a tentative shooting schedule. There are also pictures of their accessories. Ajay's folder has a photo of a Tata SUV, a 9 mm pistol, a double-barreled shotgun, and a Nokia mobile phone. All black.

The folders contain a brief note to the stars:

1. This is largely an outdoor shoot, so we would like to take every possible health precaution. Please inform Punam about the following: a) specific allergies, b) blood group.

2. As this is a synch-sound film, we would appreciate it if all mobile phones are switched off during shooting hours.

3. Do let us know if there are any doubts or queries for us. We'd be more than happy to help you with anything we can.

Most of the concerns have to do with where the shootings are going to take place and where the stars will be staying. Ajay complains about traffic in Pune and says it will take an hour and a half to reach some of the locations. Can they stay in Lonavalla instead? Kumarji gets on the phone immediately and asks someone to book a block of rooms at a hotel in Lonavalla. While we wait for Saif and Naseer to arrive, a medley of ringtones interrupt conversations, most of the calls ignored.

Sun-N-Sand is a Bollywood landmark. One of the first luxury hotels to cater to the film industry, it opened in the 1970s. Though there are many grander and more luxurious hotels in Mumbai now, Sun-N-Sand still attracts a filmi crowd. Below us is the swimming pool, a turquoise amoeba surrounded by tiles. Beyond this is a line of coconut palms and sand, then waves. Ajay and Vishal stand in the shade of a beach umbrella, discussing the location shootings in Lucknow and Allahabad.

Inside the suite, Ajit and Abhishek huddle over shooting schedules, penciling in corrections, as if doing an elaborate crossword puzzle. Ajit rubs his eyes and yawns. When I ask how much sleep he's getting he shakes his head.

"Right now I'm getting enough. The problem is I've started dreaming about the film," he says. "Then I wake up worrying about what we've forgotten. The other night, I realized we hadn't organized fireworks for Omi's wedding."

Debashree tells me that she is writing about the making of the film for a media research group in Delhi. She recently completed a degree in film studies at Jamia Milia Islamia university in Delhi and is undecided about whether she should pursue a career in film scholarship or filmmaking.

Throughout the afternoon people come and go. Tassaduq drops by briefly. Robin arrives, handshakes all around. Rahul Nanda also shows up. He's a marketing consultant—a thoughtful, bookish man who looks out of place in the gathering. Rahul explains that marketing budgets for Hindi films are absurdly low.

"In Hollywood, they spend $15 million to promote a film. Here it's no more than 30 lakhs" (about $67,500).

Rahul has yet to hear the script all the way through and during the reading he is given a seat directly facing the circle of actors and treated with special attention—the marketing guru in whose hands the fate of the film lies.

Though Vishal has already narrated the story to each of the cast members, this is the first time he is seeing them together. I can tell that he and Abhishek are studying the actors. Before the reading starts, Ajit places a videocam discreetly on a shelf, pointed in their direction. Ajay looks bored. Kareena is quietly composed, chatting with Dollyji. Viveik seems the most at ease. When someone suggests we hear the songs that have been recorded, he is immediately into it, drumming on the table, moving to the rhythm. We listen to the title song, "Omkara," and the "*beedi* song," which Kesu will sing with Billo. After that, both versions of Omi's lullaby.

Lunch is ordered as we continue to wait, hotel staff furtively eyeing the stars as they come and go with trolleys of food. Ajay signs a room-service bill as if it were an autograph then takes an apple and bites into it.

There is no explanation given for why we're waiting, except for the occasional mention of Saif and Naseer. At one point, Vishal takes off his shoes and lies down on the couch.

Of all the actors in the room, Dollyji is the only one who has been in a Shakespeare play. She once played Desdemona in a National School of Drama production.

"In 1989," she tells me, "with M. K. Raina," one of the legends of the Indian stage. Dolly has moved between theater and films for most of her career. She also designed costumes for Richard Attenborough's *Gandhi* and Shekhar Kapur's *Bandit Queen.* Dollyji has a role in Vishal's *The Blue Umbrella,* in which she does a hilarious seduction scene.

When Dolly played Desdemona in the NSD production of *Othello,* she also designed the costumes. "I had Othello dressed in a sheepskin cloak. And I wore a gown edged in fur. The cut of the costumes was European but the fabric was Indian—luxurious, embroidered pattern." She smiles at the memory. "I love doing period costumes."

Finally, around 3:30 it is decided that the reading will begin, without Saif and Naseer. Chairs are moved into a circle. The actors face one another, opening their copies of the script. Vishal explains that he will read the minor parts and Abhishek will read the narrative sections. He asks Dollyji to read Indu's and Billo's parts. (Konkona, who plays Indu, has a throat infection and is busy with the release of a new film. Billo's part hasn't been cast yet.)

At this point Ajay refuses to read his lines. He wants to listen. As the hero, it's his prerogative.

"If I have to read the dialogue it will take me ten minutes for each line," he explains.

After an awkward moment, Vishal agrees to read Omkara's lines. Abhishek, who sits on the floor, leaning back against a sofa, begins: "Scene One. Exterior. Arid countryside. Day. Fade in . . ."

The first exchange is between Langda and Rajju. Each person reads his or her part softly, no histrionics, though they seem to be getting to know their characters. Viveik obviously enjoys the rough idiom of the dialogue. For the first few minutes, Kareena has no lines but when she does eventually speak, her voice tempers the crude vocabulary of the gangsters with a muted tenderness.

Half an hour into the reading Saif arrives, wearing a Tusker Lager T-shirt that shows off his biceps. He quickly finds his place in the script and delivers his dialogue in an undertone, violence and bitterness in his words. This is the first time any of them are reading the script aloud, yet they seem comfortable with the language. To help the actors with the dialect, Vishal has given each of them a CD on which he has recorded their lines. They've done their homework. Earlier, the conversations were almost entirely in English, but the actors slip easily into colloquial Hindi, with only minor hesitations. Kareena isn't sure of a particular word and Vishal prompts her but she reads the rest with perfect fluency.

As the reading progresses, momentum begins to build and the voices add another layer to the story, which has already gone through a dozen drafts. The reading is an exploration of the roles and rhythms of the script. At the beginning Vishal told them it would be very casual and they should interrupt with any questions, but after a few initial queries the reading flows smoothly. Dollyji moves back and forth between her own role and the other two women. Vishal reads Bhaisaab's lines—"*Dubara aaney ki zaroorat nahin . . .*"—echoing the jailed gangster in Meerut.

There is some laughter, particularly when Rajju has a line about his "moped having a puncture" and later in the scene with Langda on the bridge, both of them drunk. Neither actor overdoes it but their inebriation comes through in the words.

Halfway through the script Vishal announces an interval and tea is ordered along with a fresh packet of India Kings. None of the major characters in the film smokes, since the censors have recently forbidden the use of tobacco in Hindi films. (Amitabh Bachchan has been sued for appearing on a billboard with a cigar in his mouth.) There is only one scene in which Rajju blows smoke in Billo's face, which leads to a fight. Vishal feels it will pass the censors because it shows smoking in a negative light. There is a question whether any of the characters will chew *gutka* tobacco. Plenty of alcohol flows in the story and it would be unrealistic without tobacco. The language in the film may raise questions, too, but Ajay seems to think it won't be a problem. Though nobody mentions it, Saif's mother, Sharmila Tagore, chairs the censor board.

The interval is short and Vishal calls everyone back together, not wanting to break the mood. They carry on with the wedding scenes, Omkara's jealousy mounting as the preparations for his marriage are under way. Indu and Dolly have an emotional exchange—unable to understand Omkara's angry accusations. Langda conspires with Rajju. Love and passion curdle with jealousy and suspicion.

We reach the final, horrific scene. After suffocating Dolly with a pillow, Omkara sings the lullaby. Vishal hums a few lines as Abhishek narrates the final sequence, Rajju's death, and Omkara's suicide. A pistol to the head and then to the heart. Boom!

> This time OMI shoots. Blood splashes out on the wall. He falls on the bed and lands next to DOLLY almost in an embrace.
>
> We stay with the newlyweds for a little while.
>
> Fade to black.

After the reading is over, Ajay interjects with a suggestion. He wants to be sure the audience knows that Omkara understands his mistake. In the script, his character points his pistol at Kesu then turns it on himself, with a cutaway shot in between. Ajay feels they shouldn't cut away. The understanding of Iago's deception and Desdemona's innocence must be clear in his eyes, the unbearable tragedy and truth.

"If you cut away it won't be as strong," he insists.

Vishal explains that the way it's written will be more dramatic. One moment the pistol is aimed at Kesu. The next moment we see Omkara pointing it at himself. It's a minor detail, probably two seconds of screen time, the sort of question that would arise during editing. Vishal concedes that they can try both ways when they shoot it.

"We can work it out in performance."

The rest of the script meets with everyone's approval. None of the other actors has any questions. We disperse to different corners of the suite or onto the terrace. Robin begins chatting with Saif, telling him that Langda is the best role in the film. Saif nods thoughtfully, admitting he wasn't sure about playing a villain. But he seems well suited for the role, a stubble beard and angular profile. The only incongruity is his hairstyle, fashionably long and combed back from his forehead.

Though he has been acting in films for almost a decade, Saif is finally making a name for himself. His early films didn't excite audiences, but recent roles in *Dil Chahta Hai* and *Parineeta* have made him one of the hottest names in Bollywood. Saif's mother, Sharmila Tagore, is a star of the seventies—one of the most beautiful women to grace the Hindi screen. His father, Nawab Mansur Ali Khan, is the erstwhile ruler of Pataudi, a former principality south of Delhi. Tiger Pataudi, as he is known, once captained the Indian cricket team. His marriage to Sharmila brought together two obsessions in India—cricket and cinema. Educated at Winchester Public School in England, Saif doesn't wear his royalty on his sleeve but he does have the cultivated manners of a postmodern nawab.

On the other side of the terrace, Deepak stands by himself, staring up at a jet taking off over the sea, the sound of its engines muffled. Unlike the others he is more comfortable speaking Hindi than English. Deepak is originally from a small town in the Himalayas called Pauri. He played minor parts in Vishal's other films. Playing Rajju is clearly Deepak's big break. He shows no outward excitement but knows that this could launch his career.

The sun is going down over Juhu Beach, loose strands of clouds tinted gold and red. A breeze tosses the palm trees. Crowds of people are walking on the sand, taking the evening air. From the rooftop, the stars lean forward and stare down at the beach.

"This is Bombay!" Saif announces appreciatively, spreading his arms wide toward the sea.

The clusters of sightseers don't realize they are being watched by Ajay Devgan, Kareena Kapoor, Saif Ali Khan, and Viveik Oberoi. The rooftop terrace provides an island of privacy in a city that lives for glimpses of these stars.

As the sky darkens the neon sign at Sun-N-Sand comes on. It's almost 7:00. Inside the suite there are voices. Someone has arrived.

Naseerbhai is here.

Viveik Oberoi, Ajay Devgan, and Saif Ali Khan off camera.

SUNSET BOLLYWOOD

I WASN'T SURE if Madhur Bhandarkar would arrive with a bodyguard, for he was carrying a price on his head. According to the newspapers, Preeti Jaiin, a disgruntled actress, paid one of the underworld dons to have Bhandarkar killed. Fortunately, the conspiracy was exposed before the murder could be carried out. Gangster-turned-politician Arun Gawli is also under investigation for the *supari* (betel nut—slang for having someone bumped off). Other gangsters like Abu Salem have had film industry connections, dating movie stars and providing under-the-table investments. Even as Bollywood directors exploit the criminal underworld as a subject, Mumbai's mafia is attracted to the glamour and wealth of cinema. A number of filmmakers have had an unhealthy connection with gangsters for many years, though this has improved considerably now that the government has implemented reforms to clean up the black money invested in Bollywood films. Nevertheless, threats of extortion continue.

Bhandarkar's notoriety is far less interesting than his films. His recent hit, released in 2005, was *Page 3,* a satirical take on the celebrity whirl of Mumbai. This film was one of the big surprises of the year, a critical and commercial success.

At Madhur's suggestion we meet at the Marriott in Juhu, which could easily be one of the sets for *Page 3*. Late on a Sunday morning, most people have come here to be seen. In the lobby, a jazz trio plays indeterminate tunes with more enthusiasm than necessary. An artificial lagoon surrounded by cabanas and palm trees stretches out toward the sea. The Marriott lobby is so huge we need to locate each other by mobile phone before trekking across to the coffee shop. Clean shaven and casually groomed, Bhandarkar has an impetuous but friendly manner.

We are joined by Mukesh Tyagi, an aspiring actor who has a bit part in *Page 3* and a larger role in Bhandarkar's next film, *Corporate.* Madhur orders a vegetarian club sandwich and the interview begins, more on his initiative than mine.

"The first film I made was *Trishakti,* a potboiler," he recalls. "It took three years to complete. I made it according to others' whims and fancies. The producers wanted commercial cinema. Bollywood masala. A tried-and-tested formula. It was not what I wanted to make but I listened to the producers. *Trishakti* came and went without a whimper."

He speaks in short bursts, waiting for me to finish taking notes, using clichés without hesitation.

"Breaking into films is a Himalayan task," he says, "especially for someone like me. I come from an ordinary, middle-class family. I don't have a film star for a father."

Like many other young directors, his mentor is Ram Gopal Varma. Bhandarkar worked with him on *Rangeela.* Though he has branched out on his own, Bhandarkar still has his office in the same building as Varma's production company, The Factory.

"After *Trishakti* flopped, I was one year jobless. Then a friend met me and said let's have a drink. He took me to a dance bar. I'd never been before. Women were dancing. I was intrigued. Why were men throwing money at these girls? They were dancing without revealing—no skin showing."

Chandni Bar is Bhandarkar's take on this unique Mumbai phenomenon, a raw, disturbing film that leads us inside the lives of bar girls.

"I spent six months researching this film and writing the script," Bhandarkar recounts. "Initially the girls were very hesitant to talk. But later they invited me into the makeup room. I got to know everyone, the owners, the waiters, the doormen, the drivers. Everyone connected to the beer bars."

Tabu, who starred in *Maqbool,* had the lead role in *Chandni Bar,* playing a Muslim girl who escapes the riots in her hometown only to be forced into dancing at a bar in Mumbai. Her transformation from hesitant disgust to the confident moves of a professional dancer is the strongest part of the film.

Chandni Bar was made before the recent controversy over the closing of dance bars. It may even have contributed, in a small measure, to their demise by bringing this subculture into the public conscience. Bhandarkar includes a number of winks and nods at cinema, from a cut-out of the actor Rajnikanth pasted on the door of the makeup room, to the word "Hero" scrawled in lipstick on the wall.

Though Bhandarkar made his reputation as a serious and innovative director with *Chandni Bar,* nobody was prepared for the success of *Page 3*.

"When I was making it, people said, 'What's wrong with Mr. Bhandarkar? Has he gone mad? What is this title?' "

Taking a large bite of his sandwich, spilling mushrooms onto his plate, he leans back and chews with satisfaction.

"I had the last laugh," he says. "The pundits now talk of *Page 3* as a 'lucky mascot.' It broke the spell and after that many films succeeded. Bhandarkar has become a brand."

His self-confidence is endearing, even when he speaks of himself in the third person. Madhur is openly proud of his achievements, someone who has struggled up the industry escalator and made a name for himself. What seems to please him most is that *Page 3* was a success not only in the urban market but also in small towns and rural theaters.

"I think what appealed to audiences in places like Dehradun or Jhansi is that they never expected the metro city and superrich to have this ugly underbelly. It was very shocking for them."

The film also cuts between high-society party scenes and the derisive gossip of the drivers waiting outside.

"More than anyone it is the drivers who know everything about their employers. If we believe that our drivers say nice things about us, we live in a fool's paradise."

Page 3 was also able to present the perspective of a society reporter who wants to be a serious journalist, a role that Konkona Sen Sharma imbues with an earnest persistence that contrasts the hollow posturing of the very rich.

Cocky but savvy, and nobody's fool, Bhandarkar knows what he's doing. He makes his films on low budgets and keeps a relaxed atmosphere on the sets. As one of the characters in *Chandni Bar* might say, "*Zyada tension nahin lena.*" (Don't take too much tension.)

"I want to make my actors feel comfortable. I'm always joking. One-liners. Pulling their legs. That way they don't give filmi performances. More natural, spontaneous."

Mukesh Tyagi, who has been listening quietly until now, agrees. "On the set, it may seem like chaos, but Madhur is always in command."

Bhandarkar is about to begin shooting his next film in a couple of days. *Corporate* takes aim at major industrialists and their political connections.

"It's not a film about the Ambanis or Thapars. It is fiction. I can't be judgmental in my films. But I want my audience to leave on a thinking note."

Pushing his plate aside, he says, "My movies are experimental."

Dismissing other films as "masala" or "candy floss," he admits to using those same ingredients to create something provocative.

After being serious for a moment, Bhandarkar begins teasing Mukesh, calling him a turncoat. Aside from being an actor, Tyagi is head of business development for Essar Power Limited. He is a corporate insider whom Bhandarkar has cast in his film. Many of the actors he uses are not professionals.

Corporate will be finished in a month and a half, he predicts. The director does not reveal much of the plot but as he says, "It will have the Bhandarkar stamp!"

A few weeks later, I'm on the set of *Corporate.* The shooting takes place near In Orbit Mall, one of the many new air-conditioned oases of wealth and consumption that have cropped up in Mumbai over the last decade. The only signs of filmmaking are electric cables snaking their way upstairs. The art director has created a corporate boardroom on the roof of the building, complete with wood-paneled walls and large windows overlooking a city skyline.

As the shot is being set up, we sit in a couple of plastic chairs. From time to time Madhur shouts instructions, but most of the work is left to his assistants. The atmosphere is relaxed but efficient. At the same time, Bhandarkar keeps an attentive eye on everything. "Shooting is actually the most boring and frustrating part of making a film. You spend so much time setting up a shot, planning every detail. Then you wonder if the audience will care or will they walk out in the middle of the scene," he confides. Yet Bhandarkar seems to relish his work. "I want to wake up every day to do something I enjoy," he says.

Once the camera is set up, the actors are called from their air-conditioned dressing rooms nearby.

"Ready, sir!"

"Fans off!"

CORPORATE

SCENE 37 / SHOT 2 / TAKE 2

Five business executives sit around a boardroom table, staring at a flat-screen TV on the wall. Learning from a news report that a multicrore deal has fallen through, they react with despair and dismay. The camera crane glides in over the table, catching their expressions.

The executives are four men and one woman—played by Kay Kay Menon, Rajat Kapoor, Harsh Chhaya, Mukesh Tyagi, and Bipasha Basu. The men are in dark suits, Bipasha in tailored white. She is diminutive but severely professional. The last film I saw Kay Kay Menon in was *Sarkar,* in which he played the violent, psychotic son of an urban warlord. Rajat Kapoor was a dissolute maharajah in *Kisna* and a smarmy pedophile in *Monsoon Wedding.* Here both men look clean-cut—Harvard MBAs. Bipasha Basu is beautiful in a detached, distant sort of way.

"Oi, Hero!" Bhandarkar beckons to one of the unit boys carrying glasses of lime juice on a tray. During the course of the shooting, we are constantly offered refreshments—water, cold drinks, juice, tea.

The assistant directors are all in their twenties—not much younger than Bhandarkar himself. A production assistant named Swati introduces herself. She has just graduated from college in Columbus, Ohio, and is working on her first film.

"Very smart and energetic," Bhandarkar tells me, pointing at her. Swati has a degree in media technology and communications.

"Americans don't know anything about Bollywood," she says, telling me how she put together a presentation for a college class with clips from recent Hindi films. "They loved it," she says. But a few minutes later, after Bhandarkar excuses himself, Swati asks under her breath, "Do you actually like Hindi films?"

When I admit to having watched *Bunty aur Babli,* she rolls

her eyes. "You really have to not take things seriously if you enjoyed that film."

Swati is working for Precept Picture Company, which is producing *Corporate.* Watching the shot being set up, this bright young girl from Columbus, Ohio, seems bewildered.

"It's so chaotic and confusing," she says. "I think in Hollywood it must be more organized." Someone hands her a list of props that are needed, and she excuses herself.

Later, between takes, Bhandarkar throws himself into a chair beside me and asks, "Have you seen *Sunset Boulevard*? A great film. One of my favorites. I'd love to remake it in Hindi." Then with a mischievous smile he suggests, "Maybe I'll call it *Sunset Bollywood.*"

ITEM NUMBERS

MID-DECEMBER. Only a month remains until the *Omkara* shooting begins. Seated in a high-back office chair, Vishal looks more like a corporate CEO than a filmmaker. His fingers, which earlier were picking at the keys of a harmonium, are drumming impatiently on the faux-teak surface of his desk. Abhishek, Ajit, and Tassaduq sit in front of him. Countless details need to be decided before the first frame can be exposed. Unlike the earlier scriptwriting sessions, when there was time for walks in the hills, now Vishal and his team are trying to tie up all of the loose ends, questions, and crises before filming commences.

As first AD, Ajit has a list of items to be resolved.

"We need a final draft of the script by December 26."

Abhishek nods. No problem; there are only a few last-minute changes to be entered.

"We need to lock the actors' dates very soon, especially Kareena and Saif."

Kumarji will call their secretaries and fix things up. Most of the stars have multiple commitments that need to be juggled—other films, sponsorships, shows. Rather than agents, Bollywood actors have secretaries who handle their commitments and negotiate with producers. Kumarji is Ajay's secretary, and like many others who represent the stars, he is an influential player in the industry. Much of the haggling over fees and adjusting of dates is controlled by the stars' secretaries, some of whom receive a commission while others are paid salaries. They often have to soothe their actors' egos, but if a secretary becomes disgruntled it can jeopardize a film as easily as a temperamental lead.

The shooting schedule has to be finely tuned to make sure that everyone will be in the same place at the same time, but there will also be a need for improvisation.

"*Hum ko* creatively sort out *karna padega,*" Abhishek says in Hinglish—a statement that could be a motto for the industry. (We'll have to sort things out creatively.)

Most of the discussion is practical and to the point, though much of what will take place remains uncertain—locations, dates, travel arrangements. Vishal moves things along like a chairman with a long agenda.

"What about the action director?"

"Jai Singh is locked."

"Choreographer?"

"What about Saroj Khan?"

"She'll have to be controlled. We don't want her to take over."

"She won't. How can she take over? I'm the director."

But Vishal suggests another choreographer, who can handle the livelier, more robust quality of Billo's songs.

Tassaduq remains silent, until the question of the film processing is raised, in particular the DI work (digital intermediate technology allows cameramen and directors to manipulate and enhance the images they have shot). Before the production begins Tassaduq needs to do a series of test negatives. He is methodical and precise, explaining his requirements. The camera will have to be hired at least a week before filming begins.

"I'll also need some of the costumes for the look we're trying to create." The actors aren't necessary, just their clothes. "We'll have to shoot them against a gray wall—overexpose and underexpose."

In the middle of this discussion the door opens and Kumarji steps in. As always, he is carrying two mobile phones, fielding calls in mid-sentence. Eventually, after all of the items on Ajit's list have been covered, we move up to the roof for a cigarette break. Immediately, each person begins calling choreographers, processing studios, and stars' secretaries. Four separate conversations are going on at once. By the time each India King has been smoked down to the filter most of the decisions have been made.

After the break we shift to another office, with a TV. Honey Trehan, assistant director in charge of casting, has just returned from U.P., where he has been auditioning minor character actors. Vishal wants them to have an authentic look and accent. Honey's camcorder is hooked up to the television and he flicks the remote control.

An overweight, rheumy-eyed man is first. He delivers his dialogue in a polite but menacing manner. After this, he does a scene as if he were drunk, replying to Honey's voice off camera. Most of it is convincing. A series of faces follow, brief clips of potential gangsters, including a man with paan-stained lips and another who has very dark features, crossed eyes, and a white stubble beard.

"Bang on! He looks dangerous!" Vishal approves.

One of the other roles they are casting is Dolly's father, a brief but important part. Honey and Vishal discuss which of the actors would look most like Kareena's father.

In some cases we only see the actors in fast-forward. Vishal tells Honey to pause briefly a couple of times, faces frozen on the screen. One man is asked to introduce himself. He says he is an acting teacher in Lucknow and recites his phone number for the camera. Though Honey doesn't say very much about the actors, it's obvious which ones he prefers, giving them more time on-screen before pressing the fast-forward button. He suggests that one or two actors come to Mumbai for a screen test.

Though each actor is trying to present himself as a threatening character, part of the U.P. underworld, their eagerness for the roles comes through in the auditions. Some are given only a second or two. Even those with extended auditions are cut short without hesitation.

One of Honey's assignments has been to find a chorus of women who will sing at the wedding. He has filmed four groups. The clips are arranged in order, from the most sophisticated to the most rustic. The first group is too polished, though it contains some interesting faces. All of them are sitting on the ground. One of the women is beating a drum. Their voices have a raw, abrasive tone. When the second group comes on, Vishal claps his hands immediately.

"*Arrey, ek dum gaonwalley hain!*" he says, delighted. (They're definitely villagers!)

Though we watch the other two groups briefly, his mind is made up. He chooses group two. "Done! Final! Final!"

After the video clips are over, Amita Mangat—Kumarji's daughter, who assists with production—hands Vishal a DVD of the recent hit *No Entry.* At first it isn't clear why we are going to watch the film, but soon it becomes apparent that Bipasha Basu's performance is the focus of attention. Though she has agreed to do the part of Billo, Vishal still has reservations. Bipasha is an actor who usually gets typecast as a seductress and her roles often test the limits of India's censorship codes. In *No Entry* she plays a cabaret dancer.

No Entry is a mainstream Bollywood film, a lighthearted comedy—some might call it masala popcorn. Though it is far removed from *Omkara* in substance and style, the filmmakers know that audiences have responded well to *No Entry* and its stars.

"Have you seen the film?" Vishal asks Amita.

"Yes, twice."

"When does Bipasha appear?"

"After about twenty minutes."

We fast-forward until we reach a nightclub scene in which she does an item number, as a pole dancer. Item numbers are songs inserted into a film, primarily to titillate the audience. They often have nothing to do with the story but everything to do with the actor being a hot item in Bollywood's eyes. Having last seen Bipasha dressed as a company executive during the shooting of *Corporate,* I barely recognize her as a bar girl. Her face is beautiful and she seems comfortable moving to the music, but the team still has its doubts. Vishal leans forward studying her acting, the delivery of her lines.

"We'll ask her to read the part," he says, "and if she can't do it, I'll have to tell her."

Though Bipasha Basu has the celebrity and sex appeal, there is still a question about whether she can take on the role of a gangster's moll.

Billo sings the *beedi* song in *Omkara.*

BANDIT QUEEN

CRIMINALS HAVE always been featured in Hindi films, from the crooks and cutthroats that Fearless Nadia crushed beneath her patent-leather boots, to the international smugglers and black marketeers Dev Anand outsmarted. Over the years there has been a gradual evolution of the screen villain with evil characters who venture beyond the ordinary stereotypes of small-time dacoits (bandits), goondas (goons), and thugs. A few of Bollywood's baddies have gone over the top, like the ultimate menace to humanity Mogambo, played by Amrish Puri in Shekhar Kapur's *Mr India.* Kapur has also directed India's first revenge film with a female lead.

Bandit Queen broke many of the rules of Hindi cinema, giving the lead role to a woman and putting a gun in her hands. The film is based on the life of a female dacoit in U.P. Phoolan Devi was already a legend before Shekhar Kapur made a film about her life—a low-caste woman who was raped and tortured as a girl and fell in love with a dacoit named Vikram Mallah. After his death, she took over leadership of his gang and sought revenge. Though Phoolan Devi's name means "flower goddess," she was an embittered victim of violence who led the Behmai massacre, a brutal attack on high-caste villagers. *Bandit Queen* depicts the ruthless violence of dacoits, stripping away the romantic legends surrounding Phoolan Devi and revealing the corrupt relationship of criminal power and caste politics. The film is as raw as the eroded landscapes of the Chambal ravines where Phoolan Devi eluded the police until she finally surrendered. Jailed for her crimes, Phoolan Devi underwent a transformation, and was ultimately elected to parliament.

Bandit Queen created controversy in India but became an international success. Featuring music by Nusrat Fateh Ali Khan, Pakistan's qawwali sensation, Kapur's film is the antithesis of Bollywood masala. It helped set an alternative tone for contemporary gangster films that discard the traditional formula of good versus evil. Films like *Satya* and *Maqbool* owe a certain debt to *Bandit Queen* for its unflinching vision of violence and the moral ambiguities of a film without a discernable hero.

Shekhar Kapur is a difficult man to locate. Aside from the ordinarily peripatetic lifestyle of a Bollywood director he has taken on assignments around the globe, jet-setting from London to Los Angeles to Toronto. While reports in the press indicate that he has "returned to India," that hardly means he is likely to be in a certain place at a certain time.

I finally track him down at an address in Juhu. The flat where Kapur is holding court is virtually empty and the filmmaker sits on the floor, reclining against a bolster cushion. Two assistants are discussing accounts with him and he is trying to untangle credit card payments.

Before joining the film world, Kapur went to London to study accountancy, a career that he soon gave up for the glamour of Mumbai. For several years he worked as an actor and model before turning to directing. He comes from a family of filmmakers and is a nephew of Dev Anand. Shekhar's first big hit was *Mr India,* with memorable characters like Amrish Puri's Mogambo and Sridevi's Hawa Hawaii, who appears in possibly the most outrageous song sequence in Hindi cinema—a cabaret number that defies every convention of choreography or continuity.

"Actually, *Mr India* was a flawed script," Kapur says, explaining that "the central problem in the story wasn't particularly compelling. In the beginning it didn't do very well at the box office. Even now people remember incidents or moments from the film rather than the story itself."

With rumpled hair and beard, Kapur has an unhurried look. He speaks in a low voice that disguises the intensity of his words. With his assistants he can be convivial and combative at the same time. We talk about the story behind a film, the need to draw viewers into the narrative.

"The audience wants to know: What is the problem? Why am I watching this?"

Yet he's not a director who panders to his viewers. "*Bandit Queen* was a film without a third act," Kapur explains. "I did it intentionally. I wanted the audience to leave the film feeling unhappy."

Part of the challenge with *Bandit Queen* was that Phoolan Devi was still alive when it was made. The script, written by Mala Sen, was based on Phoolan Devi's prison diaries, but Kapur only met her after he'd made the film.

"She said to me, 'I knew you'd made *Mr India,* and I thought there would be songs and dances in this film.'"

Later there was a controversy and court cases filed against Kapur for distorting the facts, but Phoolan Devi did appear with him at a press conference demanding that the censors approve *Bandit Queen* without making any cuts. A few years later she was assassinated by a man who claimed he was taking revenge for the Behmai massacre. Mysteriously, the killer escaped and disappeared.

Kapur is currently involved in *The Golden Age*, a remake of *Elizabeth*, the film that took him to the Oscars and made his name as one of the few Bollywood directors who has successfully gone to Hollywood. He seems ambivalent about the idea of sequels. His real passion, at the moment, is an idea he has been nurturing for years, a futuristic film with an apocalyptic premise. The title, *Pani*, means water. The story is set in Mumbai twenty years in the future, when the divisions between rich and poor have become even more acute.

"There is the upper world and the lower world," Kapur narrates. In the high-rise buildings there is plenty of water but down below it has run out. "The upper world has everything you can imagine. Paradise. When we first see it, there are naked women swimming in blue pools of water."

Down below are water rats. "These are children who live in the pipes that have run dry. They sneak up to the upper world and steal water."

Kapur's vision of the environmental disaster that awaits Mumbai is not too far removed from reality. The city struggles to survive on limited reservoirs of fresh water and only the very rich have enough for their needs. In the slums of the city, a bucket of water a day is often all that a family survives on.

The script for *Pani* still has to be written. At the same time Kapur has offers to direct other films, including a screen version of William Dalrymple's bestseller *White Mughals*. Other projects have tempted him but Kapur has turned them down. "I was supposed to direct *Phantom of the Opera*," he says, but he couldn't see eye to eye with Andrew Lloyd Webber.

In a recent interview in *Time* magazine, Kapur is quoted as saying that he would like to see Hindi cinema produce its own superheroes. *Mr India* experimented with this idea—a character who turns invisible and defeats the forces of evil. *Krrish,* an upcoming film starring Hrithik Roshan, is about a superhero. We discuss the possibilities of making the equivalent of an Indian *Batman* or *Superman.* The idea seems to intrigue Kapur. When I leave, he shakes hands and delivers the filmmaker's mantra: "Let's keep talking."

GOING FOR TAKE

THE FIRST SHOT of most big Bollywood productions is celebrated with a *mahurat* ceremony. These are often elaborate events, with as much glitz and glamour as a multi-star stage show. Astrologers are consulted for an auspicious date to ensure success. A senior actor or politician is asked to bring down the clapper, while priests chant hymns and champagne flows. The camera and sound equipment is garlanded with flowers and daubed with sandalwood paste and vermilion. Extravagant receptions are held, where all of the cast and well-wishers assemble to launch the production. In many cases a *mahurat* is as much a marketing tool as a religious rite—a means of catching the media's attention.

When I ask Vishal if he is going to have a *mahurat* for *Omkara* he shakes his head emphatically, saying, "I don't go in for that sort of thing."

Nevertheless, when the time arrives, Kumarji has arranged for a priest to perform a small *mahurat.* It takes place on a small bridge over a stagnant stream in the middle of rural Maharashtra, two kilometers down a potholed road beyond the village of Takave. The Brahmin priest arrives in chaste white cotton and sets up his accoutrements just behind the camera and sound equipment.

Sanskrit verses are chanted, an image of Ganesh—the remover of obstacles—is garlanded, vermilion tilaks are applied to foreheads, and a coconut is broken. None of the cast or crew participate in the puja but cashew *barfi* is distributed as *prasad*, a sacrament that sweetens everyone's tongue.

There is a large crew for the shoot, at least fifty men wearing Kumarji's company logo on their blue shirts—Big Screen Entertainment. The total unit is about 360 people. It's also a family affair. Kumarji's mother, wife, and children attend the *mahurat*. Rekha and Aasmaan are present, as are Punam Sawhney and sound designer K. J. Singh's children. The financiers have come down from Mumbai—Raman Maroo and his nephew Ketan Maroo, who own Shemaroo, the largest DVD and VCD distribution company in India. They have put up more than half of the money for the film and arrive to witness the first shot and felicitate the producer and director.

The camera is scheduled to roll at two o'clock in the afternoon but technicians have been setting up since eight in the morning. Everyone breaks for lunch before the *mahurat* shot is taken. For two days, the unit has been camped out at the Dukes Retreat, a resort hotel in the hill station of Khandala, about an hour's drive from the location. There is plenty of anxiety and restless energy, but the main concern is whether Saif has cut his hair. Until the night before, Vishal was still trying to persuade him. Earlier, during the script reading, he arrived with a fashionably shaggy mop but Vishal wants a more clippered look. Frantic SMS messages have gone back and forth. There are whispers that Saif's Italian girlfriend is telling him not to get his hair cut. The star isn't sure if he should take the plunge. He is only willing to have his own hairdresser do the job.

But Saif arrives on location, suitably shorn to within a centimeter of his scalp. Villainous but ruggedly handsome, he strides down the dusty footpath to the bridge, followed by an assistant carrying an umbrella. Dolly Ahluwalia accompanies him with a garment bag containing costumes. One of the first things Saif does is take off his shirt and ask for coconut oil. Though it's mid-January, the sun is burning hot and there is hardly any shade.

The weapons handler is summoned to show Saif his rifle, a well-worn .303, with a battered wooden stock.

Saif approves, laughing. "It looks as if it was pinched from a policeman."

He hefts the rifle to his shoulder, takes aim at a distant tree, and works the bolt action. Dummy bullets are also produced and a cartridge case that is immediately rejected.

"Too organized," Saif tells Dollyji.

Langda's costume consists of heavy boots, green trousers tied at the ankles with twine, a short green kurta over which he wears a woolen vest. With tobacco-stained teeth, Saif looks menacing, very different from his romantic persona in *Parineeta* or his hip cosmopolitan swagger in *Salaam Namaste.*

The bridge where the first shot takes place is about three feet wide. Wooden platforms have been erected on either side to give the crew more room to maneuver. Even then it is crowded. Ajit Ahuja, as first AD, is wired with a microphone. He orders everyone off the bridge except those required for the shot. Tassaduq is seated on a wooden crate with the camera almost in his lap. Several reflectors have been positioned on either side but the sun is so bright they seem unnecessary. One of the assistants holds a bottle of Johnnie Walker Black Label and measures out the whiskey to the right level. The gangsters have finished off a third of the bottle. Deepak Dobriyal is waiting to one side, dressed in a loose shirt and bell-bottoms. Unlike Langda, Rajju has long hair and Deepak had to grow it out for the role.

The first shot is primarily Rajju's scene, a difficult one for an actor to begin with. He is in tears. His engagement to Dolly has been broken off. She is going to marry Omkara. The challenge of starting on such an emotional note is enormous. A lot is at stake in this scene. Vishal could easily have chosen a quieter moment in the script, something simple to start filming. Instead, he forces his actors to take a risk.

As Vishal explains, "I always want the first shot to be a scene in which there are only two characters, but with emotion. I also like to begin somewhere in the middle of my script."

"Silence, please! Lock sound!" Ajit's voice calls out.

There are several cries in response, from security personnel—known as sound arresters—stationed at different points around the location. They keep the crew and curious bystanders silent.

"Quiet, please. Going for take!"

Vishal signals for sound, camera, and action.

"Okay, rolling!"

It's so silent the clapper can be heard a hundred meters away.

"Scene thirty-seven, shot one, take one."

Langda delivers the first dialogue, goading Rajju, who bursts out with a line about his moped having a puncture, which got the biggest laugh during the script reading. But from his perspective there is no humor. Rajju is distraught. He gets to his feet and threatens to jump in the water.

With everyone silent, except for the actors, I am suddenly aware of other sounds. Two river terns fly past, a high-pitched piping. Bleating goats are grazing nearby. A fish breaks the surface of the water like an exclamation point. A breeze ruffles the furred casing on the microphones.

Vishal orders "Cut" as Rajju gets ready to jump, swaying drunkenly. There is an audible mumble of voices as the technicians prepare for a second take. About a hundred villagers have gathered to watch the shooting from a hill nearby. Once again, Ajit calls for silence as the actors reposition themselves. This time, as soon as the camera starts, a black cow appears on the hill behind the bridge and begins to make its way down, letting out a loud mooing noise. This may be more background noise than Vishal wants but he lets the scene play out until the moment when Rajju threatens to jump.

On the third take, crows are calling but Rajju's anguished cries rise above the ambient sounds, wounded and pathetic. This time, when Vishal calls "Cut" he indicates he is satisfied with the shot. Everyone applauds, from the financiers to the grips. A bugler, hired by Kumarji, gives a festive trill of celebration.

Ajit announces, "Set up change." The same scene will be shot from the opposite angle. Though the actors must hold the tension, everyone else seems enormously relieved. An ecstatic Kumarji comes across the bridge and embraces Vishal. There are handshakes all around as the technicians begin to shift the camera and wiring. Abhishek and Vishal take a look at the shot on a video replay. All of the spectators who have been standing on one side of the bridge must move to the other, accompanied by backslapping and congratulations. *Omkara* has begun with a successful shot.

Earlier Vishal had been guarded and uneasy. Now he seems suddenly relaxed, playfully tousling his son's hair, grinning at Rekha.

"*Kamaal kiya, Deepak ney,*" he says. "*Yeh to film uda key ley jaiega!*" (What a job Deepak has done! He'll fly away with this film.)

Raman Maroo presents Vishal and Kumarji with gifts. While the crew and actors set up for the next shot everyone else searches for shade. There are no trees but half a dozen beach umbrellas have been erected over clusters of plastic chairs. When I ask K. J. Singh how much of a problem the breeze causes for sound recording, he shakes his head.

"We have close-in mics attached to the actors. In fact their voices are coming in so loud we'll probably have to tone it down. The booms are only there as backup."

K.J.'s long hair is tied back in a bushy ponytail and his head is covered with an embroidered skullcap. He looks a bit like a Rastafarian. K.J. is officially listed as sound designer, while Subhash Sahu is in charge of location sound.

"I'll be doing most of the work in postproduction," says K.J. "I've worked with Vishal from the first film music he did, in

Maachis." K.J. is now busy with other projects, handling the sound for composer A. R. Rahman's concert tours to places like Hong Kong and London. Once again, I am reminded that Vishal and his team have their roots in music. For them, the texture of a soundtrack is as vital as the visual images. Asked about the cow that mooed during the second shot, K.J. smiles with pleasure.

"We got all that. Whether we use it or not will depend on continuity." K.J. excuses himself to go back to the bridge. Synch-sound adds an element of unpredictability. Fortunately, the location is out of reach of any wireless networks so there are no intrusive ringtones.

After the first two shots are completed, the crew sets up for the second part of the scene, when Rajju jumps into the water and Saif has to rescue him. The drop from the bridge is about twelve feet. A rope with a rock attached to one end is used to test the depth—about eight feet of water at the deepest point. The river is a stagnant green color, with slime on the surface. Though Saif will use a stunt double, Deepak has insisted on doing the shot himself.

"Can you swim?" Vishal asks.

Deepak nods with a hesitant smile.

The first person to jump in the river is a young man hired from the village nearby. He plunges from the bridge so that Tassaduq can time the shot and get the right angle. An assistant cameraman checks everything with a tape measure.

Again, a chorus of voices call for silence. Rajju sways precariously then jumps, crying out Dolly's name. When he hits the water, he goes under briefly and comes up floundering, crying for help. Vishal lets him pretend to drown for five or ten seconds, but when the shot is over Deepak takes a few easy strokes and climbs onto the side of the bridge. Waiting above is a wardrobe assistant with a towel and a dry set of clothes. Deepak will have to jump into the water once again.

On the riverbank, Robin Bhatt and Ketan Maroo are seated together, leaning into the shade. Ketan is a tall, cautious man, dressed in a casual brown shirt with a gold chain around his neck. As we watch the camera being set up, Robin points out how the angle has been changed to show little of the surrounding hills. Tassaduq will cheat the shot, to make the landscape appear as flat as possible, so it looks more like U.P.

"Filmmaking is all about cheating," Robin jokes.

Ketan explains that he first heard of the project in October, when Kumarji approached him with the idea. He felt that an adaptation of *Othello* would have a broad appeal, attracting viewers outside of India. Asked what convinces him to invest in a film, he says, "The producer and director must be passionate about a script."

He then laughs and says that he has often been approached by people who have slick proposals, packaged and ready. But these are usually opportunists, more interested in making money than in completing a film.

"They come to us with a glossy portfolio full of pictures of stars. When you ask, 'Is Rani Mukherjee actually committed to this film?' they say, 'No, but I have written the script with only her in mind.' Later, if you say, 'Why not try Amisha Patel?' they're quite ready to switch."

Robin repeats, "Filmmaking is all about cheating."

Ketan agrees but he also believes he can spot a genuine project. Though he doesn't mention the money invested in *Omkara,* enormous risks are involved. Sinking crores of rupees into a film that starts on a dusty riverbank in the middle of nowhere seems a dangerous gamble.

A little later, Kumarji joins Ketan and Robin. He tells a story about a film he was involved with several years ago. "In one scene a helicopter had to land in a field. As this was being shot, an elderly woman who lived nearby came and started berating us. She claimed that the sound of the helicopter had frightened her horse and it injured itself. She was going to call the police and stop our shooting. The woman was shouting and threatening to take us to court. After a while, I got a bottle of wine and gave it to her. She took it happily, went off and got drunk, letting us complete our shooting."

Robin follows this up with a story about a man who took money from him because he claimed that his fields had been destroyed in a shooting. A week later the real owner surfaced and demanded to be paid.

Kumarji's own story illustrates how a passion for film can lead to success. Again, Robin is the person who tells me this story.

"About twenty years ago we were making a film with Jeetendra and Vinod Khanna," he says. "I was working as an assistant director. We were shooting in Himachal, near Manali—outside a village called Sundernagar. As we were getting ready for the shoot, we noticed this boy in khaki shorts and white shirt. He was constantly hanging around. In his hand he had a notebook. One day we asked him, what's in the notebook? He said, 'I've written a story for a film.' We told him to show it to us and he had written everything down, with roles for Amitabh Bachchan and Vinod Khanna. Anyway, we were there in the middle of nowhere, a village with a farmhouse as the set. Someone would ask, 'Where can we get something to drink? Where can we get cigarettes? Chicken tikka?' This boy was always able to bring it for us, whatever we wanted. Even though there was security to keep people away, somehow he was always able to sneak in to watch the shooting. Halfway through, there was an accident and the farmhouse burned down. We had to pack up and go back to Bombay. A year later, when we returned to finish the film, this same boy was there. After the shooting was completed, he left home and ran away with us to Bombay.

"At first he got a job on a couple of films as a unit boy, carrying tea. Soon he was assisting the production manager. Around this time he became friendly with Veeru Devgan and remained close to him. Years later, when Ajay became a star, Veeru Devgan suggested that Kumarji become his secretary. Now he handles all of Ajay's business affairs, his production and distribution company. And here he is producing his own film. *Kahan sey kahan pahunch gaya!*" (From where to where has he traveled!)

Watching Kumarji controlling an army of unit boys, grips, and technicians in their Big Screen Entertainment uniforms, the truckloads of equipment, the makeup vans, the stars, it's hard to imagine that young boy twenty years ago, carrying a dog-eared notebook with a scribbled story, the improbable dream—now presiding over his own *mahurat.*

Vishal Bhardwaj, Abhishek Chaubey, and Kumar Mangat.

RAJKAMAL STUDIOS

THOUGH HINDI MOVIES enjoy the broadest distribution in India, the total number of films made in regional languages like Tamil, Telugu, Kannada, Malayalam, Punjabi, and Bengali is far greater. Linguistic loyalties and provincial chauvinism encourage filmmakers to produce films in competing languages and dialects. For instance, Assamese, Bhojpuri, and Garhwali films target limited but enthusiastic audiences, who may understand Hindi but prefer to watch a film in their mother tongue. Even in Mumbai, the center of the Hindi film industry, Marathi-language films have a long history and continue to be produced, though Bollywood attracts more glamour and larger budgets.

Mumbai is the capital of Maharashtra, and areas of the city like Dadar and Parel were settled by textile workers from rural areas of the state. After the mills shut down, following strikes in the 1980s, there was massive unemployment and a restive population that wanted to claim its share of the city's wealth and assert a Marathi identity. This has fueled Bal Thackeray's Shiv Sena, a populist right-wing militia that opposes everything from Muslims to Valentine's Day.

At the Bharatmata (Mother India) Cinema in Parel a Marathi movie is playing, *Kalubai Chya Navane Changbhale.* My taxi driver loosely translates the title as "Kalubhai's Husband Is a Good Man." The poster has a defiant image of a man carrying a large trident. Clearly, the film is meant to appeal to Marathi chauvinists, who support the Shiv Sena.

Not far from the Bharatmata Cinema lies Rajkamal Studios, founded in 1942 by one of the legends of Indian film, V. Shantaram. He began his career in Marathi cinema but branched out into Hindi films and succeeded in finding an audience throughout the country. Rajkamal Studios is preserved as a monument to the legacy of V. Shantaram, though it is seldom used for filmmaking now. Unlike most historic studios in Mumbai, which are in a crumbling state of disrepair, Rajkamal remains much the same as it must have looked in the 1950s and 1960s. The grounds are immaculately groomed, with a small park at the entrance and an extensive library on filmmaking.

Chandrakant Patil has worked at Rajkamal Studios for thirty-six years. A gray-haired man with glasses that settle halfway down his nose, he greets me in the reception area, where the glass doors are etched with the studio's emblem, a woman rising out of a lotus.

"V. Shantaramji was a great man," Patil recalls. "An all-rounder. He did everything in his films—writing, producing, directing, acting, editing, distribution. Everything happened under one roof. A shooting took place over there and the film was developed over here. Nothing was sent outside. V. Shantaram even had his own laundry washed inside the studio. It all happened here, from pin to elephant!"—Patil's favorite expression.

A display case runs the length of one wall, about forty feet of dark wood cabinets filled with all of the awards, medals, and trophies that V. Shantaram received. It includes the Padma Vibhushan—India's highest civilian award—and the Dadasaaheb Phalke Award for a lifetime achievement in filmmaking. Next to this is the Samuel Goldwyn International Film Award and a Golden Bear from the Berlin Film Festival.

Rajkamal Studios produced a number of films with a social message like *Dahej,* which portrayed the evils of dowry, and one of V. Shantaram's biggest hits, *Do Ankhen Bara Haath* (Two Eyes, Twelve Hands), which was about prison reform.

"V. Shantaram was a perfectionist," says Patil, gesturing toward the array of trophies. "He did everything himself . . . from pin to elephant!"

Several portraits of V. Shantaram adorn the walls, including a black-and-white photograph showing him glancing over his shoulder with directorial intensity. He wears his trademark white hat, a version of a Gandhi cap, though slightly larger and perched at a rakish angle.

His son, Kiran Shantaram, is chairman of the V. Shantaram Motion Picture Foundation. He has also produced a couple of Marathi films and was appointed sheriff of Mumbai for two terms.

Explaining the differences between Hindi and Marathi cinema, Kiran Shantaram says that Marathi films are shown tax free in the state, which helps draw crowds. There are also generous grants from the state government for films in Marathi. But beyond a difference in language, there is a separation of sensibilities between Hindi and Marathi films, which tend to be more conservative.

"I'll tell you a story," he says. "My father made the first color film in Marathi called *Pinjra* [Cage], which was very successful. He later remade this film in Hindi and it was a flop. I always used to go to the releases of his films to watch the audience reaction. There is a scene in *Pinjra* where a woman tries to seduce a schoolteacher. She pretends that her leg is hurt and he agrees to put some medicine on it. When she lifts the hem of her sari up to her knee there was great excitement in the cinema hall. People were whistling and clapping. Later, in the Hindi version, my father used exactly the same shot. I went to see the release in Kanpur

[U.P.] and a police inspector was standing behind me. He was supposed to be in charge of security. When this scene came he passed a comment, '*Kya paagal hai? Sari aur uncha kar!*' [Are you mad? Raise the sari higher!] That gives you a hint of the differences between Marathi- and Hindi-speaking audiences."

Kiran Shantaram is intent on maintaining his father's legacy, even though filmmaking has changed dramatically from the era of the 1950s and 1960s. He points to the white cap on his head.

"This is my father's hat I'm wearing."

THE BRICK KILN

THOUGH MOST of *Omkara* is being filmed in Maharashtra, Vishal wants certain sequences to be shot in U.P. to provide a visual signature of the state where the story is set. Few images are more distinctive than the brick kilns of Uttar Pradesh—towering chimneys that rise above rectangular trenches in which raw bricks are fired.

Forty-five minutes' drive from Lucknow, the capital of U.P., our car turns off the highway onto an eroded strip of asphalt that soon becomes a dusty, unpaved lane. We bounce along between fields of yellow mustard and arhar lentils, ripening in the winter sun. There are several kilns in the area and we head toward the tallest chimney, painted with stripes of red and white, an emblem of a crescent moon and star on top. It looks like a minaret without a mosque. A dozen khaki-clad constables block our way, along with one of the sound arresters in a gray safari suit. From here we walk to the location, where a team of mules is being positioned near the brick kiln. This is the hideout of a gangster named Surinder Captaan. Omkara and Langda have come to negotiate with him about a political rival.

Security is tight—at least two hundred policemen armed with .315 rifles, Sten guns, and pistols, as well as bamboo staves. There are also thirty private guards, dressed in black with bulletproof vests. Their company name, Federal, is printed across their chests. In addition to these bodyguards there are the ubiquitous men in gray—the sound arresters, who also help with crowd control. Throngs of villagers are held back four hundred meters from the kiln, though they keep creeping closer and have to be chased off several times by the police.

Yesterday there was a mob scene at Lucknow University where the crew was shooting with Kareena, and the lobby of the hotel where the stars are staying was swarming with fans. Vishal admits that until the last minute he wasn't sure if he would be able to get the shots he wanted at the university. The timing of the shooting coincided with a political rally and this added to tensions. Student leaders were upset that the film depicts gangsters on their campus and attacked some of the unit's vehicles. The Lucknow edition of the *Hindustan Times* features pictures of Kesu's election posters, with Viveik Oberoi's photograph, which were plastered on the university walls. The newspaper article plays up the irony of campus politics spilling over from film into reality.

Kesu arrives at the brick kiln on his motorcycle, a red Royal Enfield that makes a deep throbbing sound. During this shot, he pulls up in front of Omkara and Langda, waving a mobile phone. The phone contains compromising MMS images of the rival politician having sex with a prostitute, which will be used as blackmail. When this is shown to Surinder Captaan, he flings the phone on the ground. Later, he taunts Omkara about his affair with Dolly, which leads to a fight between the two gangs. In the shooting schedule, the entire encounter is broken up into dozens of shots that don't follow the sequence of the script. All of this will be filmed over a period of three days.

It's hard to tell who are the actors and who are the employees at the brick kiln. The caretaker is a stooped man in a sooty turban and dhoti, who carries a hooked iron rod to open and close the vents and flues. Heat rises through the ground as if we are standing on a live volcano. The only place to escape the sun is the shadow of the brick kiln's chimney, which moves steadily throughout the afternoon like a sundial, so that we must reposition our chairs every ten minutes. After the motorcycle scene, filming moves to a small shack on top of the kiln, where the caretaker lives with a flock of chickens that are pecking at the ground.

Surinder Captaan, played by Maanav Kaushik, is dressed in a stained dhoti and loose sweater. Maanav has a week's stubble on his chin and looks threateningly dissolute, even when he puts on a Nike baseball cap and Ray-Ban dark glasses between takes. He and his wife are writers, producing scripts for film and television.

Maanav talks about the challenges of being a writer in Mumbai. "People are always saying there aren't enough writers with good stories but the biggest problem is that producers and directors don't want to listen to new ideas. For an unknown writer without connections it would be impossible to break in. Even for me, it's hard to get anyone's attention. They never seem to want the script you narrate. Tell them a story and they'll say, 'No, *yaar,* we want a comedy instead.' "

Opposite the caretaker's shack is a hand pump. An elderly woman is being positioned for the next shot, in which Omkara helps fill a brass water vessel and lifts it onto her head. The old woman wears a long-sleeved blouse and a pale green sari embroidered with folk motifs. As costume designer, Dolly Ahluwalia has created a gritty, rustic look. Rather than dressing characters up she often has to dress them down. Even the mules that appear in the background of one scene arrived that morning decked out with bells and colorful regalia.

"The owner had decorated them for the shooting and I had to tell him to undress them," Dollyji says.

The brick kiln looks like an anthill, crew members moving about industriously to set up the shot. Omi, Langda, and Kesu are seated on a charpai—a string cot—placed in the sun, eating a meal out of brass trays. With them is Kichlu, a member of

Surinder Captaan's gang. As they finish eating, Maanav comes out of the hut and begins taunting Omi.

Ajay rises and tells Viveik to pour water from a brass lota for him to wash his hands and rinse his mouth. Spitting out the water Omkara advances toward Surinder Captaan. When Devgan wants to look threatening, he locks his eyes on his opponent. Though he isn't a large man, the way he moves is enough to frighten someone twice his size. Shoulders straight, arms loose, a dangerous swagger in his stride, he looks as if he is going to lunge forward at any moment. Instead he walks right past Surinder Captaan and pumps water into the old woman's jar.

"Cut. Excellent."

Removing his headphones, Vishal goes across to the video monitor to check the shot. I can see him smiling as he repeats the dialogue under his breath. The camera setup is then changed and reaction shots are taken of Kichlu, Langda, and Kesu. After this, the point of view is turned around to get a shot of Surinder Captaan emerging from the hut.

From this angle, the fields and mango trees beyond the brick kiln are visible, as well as the crowds of spectators. Over the microphone, Ajit asks them to move, politely at first and then with greater insistence as the spectators remain where they are. The police begin raising their lathis and the crowd disperses, though still not far enough to be out of the shot. It takes twenty minutes before the area is finally cleared. Maanav has already delivered his dialogue a dozen times for the earlier shots but now the camera is focused entirely on him. The first take goes smoothly until a policeman walks across, waving his stick at the crowd and ruining the shot.

"Cut!"

Maanav repeats the scene without hesitation but this time there is the sound of a tractor in the distance.

"Cut!"

The third time a mobile phone begins to ring.

"Cut!"

By now Maanav has lost his rhythm. The dialogue, which is in dialect, is difficult to pronounce. After fifteen flawless deliveries, he fumbles his lines.

Vishal tells him to relax, coming forward to reassure the actor, but the momentum of the scene has been broken. Only after another five takes is it finally completed.

Inside the caretaker's shack the stars are seated in a circle along with Ketan Maroo and Kumarji, who have flown in from Mumbai to keep an eye on the shooting. Saif's hair has begun to grow out slightly since the first shot two weeks ago. He is still dressed in military green. Viveik has on a more fashionable plaid shirt and red sleeveless sweater. Ajay wears a rust-colored shirt, black trousers, and a red scarf. They are talking cricket.

India and Pakistan are playing their third test match in Karachi today and Ajay calls out for someone to tell them the score. "*Abhey, pata karo score kya hai!*" A Murphy transistor radio hangs from the rafters of the hut, but it is one of the props. The brick kiln has no television. Ketan Maroo checks the score on his mobile phone: 272 runs for the loss of 2 wickets. The conversation turns to India's batsmen, who are facing problems against the Pakistani bowlers.

"It must be like acting," Ajay says. "You have to keep your concentration."

They discuss how technology has changed the game of cricket dramatically, with instant replay and computerized graphics that display every turn of the ball. Saif tells about the time his grandfather, Iftikhar Ali Khan Pataudi, played test cricket for England in 1932, in the Ashes series against Australia at Sydney.

"This was before independence," he explains. "I still have a picture of the scoreboard. Pataudi 102."

Saif's father, Mansur Ali Khan "Tiger" Pataudi, captained the Indian team in the 1960s. Saif talks about the spirit of the game, which has been lost, the sportsmanship displayed by earlier cricket players, long before there was instant replay. He tells about fielders who called batters back, even after an umpire gave them out, admitting that they hadn't cleanly taken a catch.

There is a competitive etiquette to acting, too. Ajay is clearly the hero of the film, but Saif and Viveik are intent on giving strong performances. Even in the camaraderie of the shooting, one can sense a friendly rivalry.

Earlier, during the shooting of the motorcycle scene, Ajay came over to Vishal and quietly mentioned that Viveik's gesture, waving the mobile phone, was "totally out of character."

Vishal nodded but when he and Abhishek replayed the scene on the video monitor, they decided the gesture was okay. On the second take, Vishal let Viveik perform the scene exactly the same way. It was a minor, perhaps insignificant, moment in which the hero asserted his position, though he didn't offer his criticism directly. Good sportsmanship on the pitch as well as on the set is governed by subtle, unwritten codes of conduct.

Today's Bollywood stars are more athletic than their predecessors, with greater emphasis on sculpted physiques and healthier lifestyles. Saif's personal trainer, Satyajit Chourasia, is visiting and tells me he has come to the location to help "pump up" the actor for his fight scene.

Powerfully built, with tattooed biceps and a shaved scalp, Satya has a shy, defensive smile. He also has a long list of Bollywood clients, from Aamir Khan and Hrithik Roshan to Esha Deol and Rani Mukherjee. His gym is called the Barbarian Power Gym in honor of Schwarzenegger's film *Conan the Barbarian.* Satya is a devotee of "Ahhnold," as he pronounces his idol's name, and he is determined to change the physical culture of Bollywood.

"The earlier film heroes were influenced by the *akadas* [wrestling clubs]," he says, mentioning action stars from the 1960s and 1970s, like Dara Singh and Dharmendra, for whom bulk was as important as brawn. Though these actors practiced body building they were not as tautly muscled as Saif, who has trained with Satya for five years. Barbarian Power Gym is equipped with all of the latest machines and Satya has developed his own regimen of diet and workouts, so that when the stars take off their shirts, they show off their pecs, lats, and abs.

Like so many Bollywood biographies, Satya's story begins in a small town, Nagpur, where he opened his first gym. Coming to Mumbai, he hung around the sets at Film City, hoping for a break.

"One day, Aamir Khan noticed my biceps and asked me how he could develop his own," Satya recounts. "Aamir told me to open a gym in Bombay." He is now expanding and hopes to have one hundred Barbarian gyms in another five to seven years.

When we break for lunch, everyone moves into the shade of a nearby mango grove. Food is served out of tiffin carriers brought from the hotel, a dozen dishes from butter chicken to fried okra, along with rice and bread. Saif and Ajay quiz Satya on which are the healthier foods to eat, though the menu doesn't lend itself to a low-carb diet.

A separate area has been set up by the caterers to feed crew and security. While we serve ourselves, the crowds begin to close in. The army of policemen, whose job it is to keep them away, are busy eating. Eventually, we are ringed by several thousand men, pointing and jostling, ogling the stars. Too late, the security guards try to move them back but the crowd resists. They demand that Ajay and Saif wave to them; only then will they retreat. The actors comply and grudgingly the crowd moves back a few steps. There is a thin line between adulation and aggression. Compared to the polite clusters of villagers in Maharashtra, crowds in U.P. are unruly and restive.

Three small-town gangsters never had as much police protection as Omkara, Langda, and Kesu. As the actors return to the brick kiln they are ringed by bodyguards, constables, and security.

After lunch, the family of a senior police official from Lucknow arrives to observe the shooting. The women are dressed up, as if for a wedding. Chairs are brought as they watch a couple of shots, then request a photograph with the stars. Ajay and Viveik oblige, posing with the women, who stare unsmiling at the camera. As soon as the photograph is taken the visitors depart. A little later, while Viveik and I are talking, a flash goes off behind my shoulder. Immediately security moves in to deal with the intruder, a journalist from one of the Lucknow papers. The film is stripped from his camera and he is hustled off the set.

After a full day on location our hair and clothes are thick with dust and ash. Vishal gives me a ride back to the hotel in his car, along with Rekha and Aasmaan, who looks tired, having spent the day working as clapper boy. Though Vishal has been on location since seven this morning, he is still running on adrenalin and has a tennis game scheduled in the evening. Pleased with the progress of the film, he is already thinking about his next project.

Rekha suggests adapting Ayn Rand's *The Fountainhead*. Immediately, Vishal agrees, excited by the idea.

"*The Fountainhead* is one of my favorite novels," he says. "The main character is an architect. The way he approaches his work, as a perfectionist, you can never look at a building the same way again."

Entering the outskirts of Lucknow, the traffic grows thicker, swarms of bicycles weaving through a blue haze of smog. Vishal takes out his phone and calls Ronnie Screwvala, head of UTV, which produced *The Blue Umbrella*.

"Ronnie, I want to make *The Fountainhead* . . ."

Ten minutes later, when the conversation ends, Vishal tells us that Ronnie has read the novel three times. He too thinks it will make a terrific film. As we reach the heart of Lucknow, circling a roundabout and passing through the historic bazaar of Hazrat Ganj, we discuss how the main character in *The Fountainhead* could be a filmmaker instead of an architect. His movies will reflect his own highly individualistic vision. Teasing Vishal, I say he should be careful not to turn it into an autobiographical film.

"But I'm not a perfectionist," he protests.

Lucknow is the capital of U.P. and also the historical and cultural center of Avadh, famous for its nawabs and begums—the Muslim aristocracy. There's an old joke about the excessive politeness of Lucknow, in which two nawabs cross paths and insist that the other go first—"*paheley aap*" (after you)—a stalemate of manners that leads to inaction. Lucknow is also known for its Urdu poetry and elocution.

On the wall of my hotel room is a picture of Wajid Ali Shah, one of Lucknow's former nawabs, but there are reminders of Bollywood as well. The Lux soap in the bathroom has a picture of Kareena on the wrapper and in the minibar is a bag of Lay's potato chips with an image of Saif holding a globe in his arms. Switching on the TV, I see ads with Ajay promoting Tata Indicom. A few minutes later Irfan Khan—the hero of *Maqbool*—is pitching Hutch mobile phones. In the bizarre juxtaposition of advertising and cinema, Othello and Macbeth endorse competing telecom companies. But it is Saif, heir to the throne of Pataudi, a nawab-in-waiting, who advertises potato crisps with a Latin flavor, that makes it seem entirely surreal.

The second day of shooting at the brick kiln is devoted to the fight scene between Omkara and Surinder Captaan. This follows immediately after the confrontation at the water pump, when Surinder Captaan pulls a gun on his rival. Though the actors use stunt doubles for parts of the sequence, they must perform the scenes leading up to the fight, as well as close-up shots.

Fight director Jai Singh looks like a wrestling coach, with the shoulders and neck of an ox. He sits in a chair, holding a swagger stick, as his team of stuntmen rehearse the scene. They have cleared an area away from the camera and eight of them limber up and get ready to fight. At a signal from the fight master, they rush at one another, throwing punches and grappling. All six of them fall to the ground, grunting and groaning, pretending to be shot and dying in agony.

Waving his stick, Jai Singh breaks up the fight and tells one of the stuntmen to fall in a different direction. With a hand as big as a wicketkeeper's glove, he grabs hold of another team member and demonstrates how he wants him hurled to the ground. Remarkably, no one has been injured, though each of the rehearsals looks like a fight to the death. A group of policemen watch with amusement as the fighters roll about in a cloud of brick dust. By the end of it the stuntmen are covered with dirt and straw.

Being the son of legendary action director Veeru Devgan, Ajay has participated in more than his share of fight scenes over the years. Before the shot, Vishal and Ajay consult with Jai Singh, blocking the action and placing markers on the ground to make sure the fight remains within the camera's field of vision. Surinder Captaan is given a pistol, hidden under his sweater. One of the stunt doubles holds a rifle but most of this fight is hand-to-hand combat with blows from bamboo staves. These have been split at the ends to make extra sound. Though an audio track of the fight is recorded, most of this sequence will be set to music, *Omkara*'s title song.

Watching the action with me is Vikram Gaikwad, who is in charge of makeup. Today he is on the set to create injuries and wounds sustained in the fight. Vikram is also responsible for the overall appearance of the actors.

"In each case we had to make the stars look less refined," he says, "more like criminals."

Vikram tells how they had to work on Saif to transform him into Langda Tyagi, changing the suave, cosmopolitan nawab into a U.P. hoodlum.

"When he said he didn't want to cut his hair, I agreed to make a wig for him. We had it ready, but I told him it would be better if he simply cut his hair. In the end he submitted and agreed."

Putting on the wig and makeup would have involved hours of work each day and the latex and other materials aren't suited to India's climate. Though an expert in prosthetic makeup, Vikram says, "I always suggest that actors wear less makeup. But most of them are insecure about their appearance, which is why they don't want to look natural."

Several days ago they shot a scene in which Dolly wakes up in the middle of the night and opens the door for Omi.

"When Kareena arrived for the shot I told Vishal it didn't look right. No woman wears so much makeup to bed. Vishal spoke to her. She submitted and wiped it off."

Gaikwad runs a school for makeup in Pune. On his mobile phone he shows me a photograph of the actor Arjun Rampal being transformed into a seventy-year-old character.

"It's not just about making his hair gray. We have to flesh out his face, add lines and sagging skin."

In addition to working on films, Gaikwad has a team that specializes in bridal makeup. "Every woman wants to look fair on her wedding day," he says, "and every actress wants to look fair on-screen. Some of them put on so much makeup you could take it off with a spoon."

At this point, we are told to be silent as we watch the fight begin. Once again, Ajay assumes his menacing persona. There is little need for any makeup, though one of Vikram's assistants touches up the shadows around Omkara's eyes, dark wells that sink into his skull. As the camera rolls, Ajay shoves Kichlu toward Surinder Captaan, then springs forward. The first few seconds of the scene start well but Maanav takes a moment too long to draw his pistol. Vishal asks them to repeat the action immediately, not wanting to break the tension. Within minutes the actors are back in position and once again the fight begins. This time the pistol comes out smoothly, a flash of steel. Omkara grabs Surinder Captaan in a vicious embrace, pining his arms to his sides and butting him with his head.

"We've brought our own blood," Vikram tells me. Though he sometimes uses synthetic blood manufactured abroad, it is more expensive and Gaikwad prefers mixing food coloring with water and cornstarch to get the right consistency. "It all depends where the wound is and what weapon is used. If you cut your finger with a razor blade, it bleeds one way. If you get stabbed in the stomach with a sword, gunshots, a punch in the mouth—in each case the blood is slightly different."

He describes in gruesome detail how he creates bullet wounds.

"Sometimes the shot blows out the back of the skull. Other times it's just a small hole in the middle of the forehead with a single drop of blood." He gestures with his finger, tracing the trickle between his eyes and down his nose. He explains how blood changes color within minutes of being exposed to the air. "It grows darker and gradually turns black. I've studied all kinds of cuts, bruises, and burns. If you look at photographs of burn victims, at first the skin is red, then it begins to blister. By the third day it looks like an omelet."

While he is telling me this, the stuntmen and actors carry on with their fight, a whirlwind of dust and fury, groans and cries of anger and pain. Three separate cameras film the action from different angles.

The fight goes on for hours, extending over a day and a half, though each take is no more than sixty seconds. The skirmish is fragmented, blows interrupted, injuries added, bullet holes healed with the wipe of a makeup sponge then painted or glued on again, fresh blood pumped into old wounds, repeated gunshots, characters falling, getting up, then falling once again on cue. Later all of this will be pieced together to create a convincing montage of violence but here at the brick kiln, amid the clouds of dust, it seems as if a discontinuous riot has broken loose.

Between shots, Viveik puts on protective padding for his knees and shins, hiding it under his trousers. Two of the stuntmen flip him onto the ground and pretend to kick him, while a third raises a bamboo lathi to deliver a fatal blow. At the last minute, Viveik improvises his own choreography, reaching over and picking up a metal bucket that lies near the hand pump. Leaping to his feet, he slams the bucket into the faces of two of the men, then knocks down the third with a vicious karate kick.

Dolly Ahluwalia is watching from the sidelines, along with Vikram, who shakes his head and mumbles under his breath, "How can one person beat up so many villains?"

"Why are you asking that?" Dollyji says, in mock astonishment. "He's a hero."

"But . . ."

She grins. "Come on, *yaar.* No buts . . . This is Bollywood!"

Kesu fighting at the brick kiln.

HOW TO HANDLE ACTORS

BEING AN INDIAN of American origin has its advantages and disadvantages in Hindi films. My cousin, Tom Alter, got his first break in Ramanand Sagar's *Charas* (Hashish) more than thirty years ago, long before the expression Bollywood came into vogue. He has seen the industry change from the 1970s, when directors like Hrishikesh Mukherjee, Shakti Samanta, and Manmohan Desai reigned; when Rajesh Khanna was still a superstar; Dharmendra and Hema Malini were everyone's favorite screen couple; and before Amitabh Bachchan had fully made his name. Tom has acted under the direction of V. Shantaram, Raj Kapoor, Chetan Anand, Manoj Kumar, and Satyajit Ray, as well as a host of lesser-known filmmakers. He has witnessed the advent of video and the decline of cinema in the 1980s, when story and song gave way to violence and disco. Tom has seen the coming of television and worked on the small screen in a number of popular serials. He has also acted in regional cinema—Bengali, Assamese, Telugu, Tamil, and Kumaoni films. Hindi is his first language, as much as English, and Tom has studied Urdu for years. The son and grandson of American missionaries who first came to India in 1916, Tom converted to Hindi cinema in 1972, when he enrolled as a student at the Film and Television Institute of India in Pune. In January 2006, I returned with him to visit the institute, where he has been invited to teach monthly workshops for acting students.

The institute's campus evokes a lot of cinema history. Originally Prabhat Studios, it was used by many of the great directors of the 1930s and 1940s, particularly V. Shantaram. Many stars began their careers at Prabhat Studios, actors like Guru Dutt, Waheeda Rehman, and Dev Anand. Legend has it that the massive, barnlike structure of Studio 1 was used for shooting the famous opening scenes in *Kaagaz Ke Phool* (Paper Flowers), where an aging actor returns to the studio in which he made his name and wooed his costar.

A village set for a student production has been constructed on the studio floor—but the way the light streams through the double doors seems exactly the same as in Guru Dutt's black-and-white classic. Lamps and wiring gather dust in the corners and there are two metal staircases Guru Dutt climbs, to look down on his memories of filmmaking and fame. Most studios are similar—a cavernous void—but Prabhat's atmosphere seems to match the setting in *Kaagaz Ke Phool.* One can almost see the actors' youthful silhouettes reliving their doomed romance. Guru Dutt's own life mirrored the tragedy of his film, when he drank himself to death after Waheeda Rehman left him.

The institute produced a number of accomplished actors in the late 1960s and early 1970s—among them, Shatrughan Sinha, Jaya Bhaduri, Shabana Azmi, Naseeruddin Shah, and Om Puri. Behind Studio 1, Tom points out the old annex where these actors learned their craft from professor Roshan Taneja.

The institute's acting course was closed down in 1976 and only reopened two years ago. Tom and other alumni have been invited back to give short courses and workshops. The campus has many memories for Tom—"the best two years of my life," he says as we pass a playing field where students are practicing cricket. On ahead stands the Wisdom Tree, a spreading mango, its roots surrounded by a circular platform. Nearby, the institute cinema is screening Orson Welles's *Citizen Kane* and in the theater across the way, students are rehearsing a Hindi translation of Maxim Gorky's *Lower Depths.* A black-and-white mural on one wall depicts images from Indian films and includes a portrait of the radical Bengali filmmaker Ritwik Ghatak.

The institute has a well-used, shopworn feel about it. A rusty camera crane stands next to Studio 1. Brick walls are painted different shades of gray, background for a shot. In front of a dormitory labeled GENTS HOSTEL, a car drives past with students inside, holding a reflector and aiming a camera. Tom leads me into "the jungle," an overgrown section of the campus. With the right camera angles it could be a remote forest. On ahead is Shantaram Pool, named after the director who built it as a set. A small temple is tucked inside the matted dreadlocks of a banyan tree. The city of Pune encroaches only as a frame of rooftops outside the boundary walls. Every inch of this campus has been photographed hundreds of times and the detritus of filmmaking litters the grounds—a pile of painted bricks, old wires coiled up like snakes in the underbrush.

On this visit to the institute, Tom conducts a workshop for the second-year directing course titled "How to Handle Actors." Nine students attend, four women and five men. The discussion is mostly question and answer. Someone asks about child actors. "Don't you think we corrupt them by using them in films?" Some questions are a single word, others ramble on about the idiosyncrasies of actors like Daniel Day-Lewis or Uttam Kumar—as much a bull session as a class.

"Ask yourself, what do you want from your actors?" Tom says. "In my humble opinion, out of more than two hundred films I've done, only five percent of the directors went as deeply into the character as I wanted . . . When an actor takes a stand, he or she may well be right. Give him a chance . . . if you let an actor go, sometimes you get amazing results."

Tom has grown a white goatee for a recent production of *Maulana Azad,* an Urdu play in which he gives a solo performance. He has flown into Pune for less than forty-eight hours and has to go on to be the compere for a stage show in Delhi. Though he lives in Mumbai, Tom constantly travels from one assignment to the next—shootings, plays, and celebrity events. His comments to the student directors are interspersed with stories from his own experience.

"Sometimes, you must be careful what you say. A director will tell an actor something and it can ruin a performance, sometimes a career."

He recalls a shot he did with Raj Kapoor and Rajesh Khanna, for Hrishikesh Mukherjee—"a director I admire greatly. Hrishida told me, 'Tom, you are standing between two legendary actors, both known for being melodramatic. You should deliver your lines without emotion . . .' Following these directions was a mistake for me because it was unnatural. It took me years to get over that piece of direction."

Tom explains how an accomplished actor like Pankaj Kapoor can rescue a mediocre script by finding humor in the driest dialogue. He tells about famous actors who were difficult to work with, like the comedian Mehmood who used to order his directors to "go sit down, I'll do it myself." Or Dilip Kumar who insisted on sixteen retakes of a reaction shot in which he simply nods his head.

"Ego is a very necessary thing in filmmaking but the color you give your ego is what matters," Tom muses.

The discussion goes on for two hours. At the end Tom cautions the directors to treat actors with sensitivity. "It all comes down to, what is an actor creating with? Himself or herself . . . the most fragile thing."

Afterward, I speak with Sourav, one of the directing students. "Usually, I'd be in bed right now," he says, though he has roused himself for the 9:00 AM workshop. Sourav explains how the course is structured. First-year students are introduced to all facets of filmmaking, then in the second year they begin concentrating on direction or other disciplines. Much of their work is done in teams—director, cinematographer, and sound engineer. Among other exercises, they are assigned to shoot a documentary, an ad film, an action sequence, a dramatic scene, and a song.

"But we often work on our own ideas," Sourav says, suggesting there is a tendency to subvert the curriculum. "Some teams will make an action sequence without any action, or they'll do a song that has no music, only sounds."

As we talk, a group of first-year students are standing nearby, having their first opportunity to handle a cine camera. They gather round, as if it were a new toy, peering through the viewfinder and adjusting the tripod. The institute provides students with the equipment they require, including a limited quota of raw stock.

Following the workshop, Tom is scheduled to dub a student film in which he has a role. An acting student named Anurag plays the part of a young man dying in an emergency room. Scenes of doctors using defibrillators are intercut with shots of Anurag and Tom facing off across a chessboard.

The sound studio is like an aquarium in which the actors sit on one side of a glass barrier, staring at a projected image of their scene. Sailesh, the director, sits inside the recording booth next to a sound console and a computer on which Gyanesh, the audio engineer, controls the recording. Even with advanced technology, it comes down to actors matching words to the movement of their lips, a kind of reverse ventriloquism.

Only ten or twelve lines need to be dubbed but the process is painstakingly slow. First they view the pilot with the original sound—full of static and hard to follow. Then they rehearse their lines while the scene is replayed. Finally, after the shot has been projected six or eight times, they are ready for an audio take.

Forty-five minutes are spent dubbing five lines, as Sailesh and Gyanesh direct the actors.

"Tom, sir, a bit more aggressive."

"Out of synch."

"One *paisa* late . . ."

Because of the poor quality of most sound recordings, the majority of Hindi films are dubbed. For the hours an actor spends in front of the camera, an equal amount of time is required in the dubbing studio.

Earlier, Tom had told me there is a rift between students in the acting course and those in other disciplines. In a sense, the barriers between actors and technicians reflect a division within the industry as a whole. While the directors and crew see themselves as trained professionals who master the complex technology of filmmaking, actors are often considered unprofessional, insecure. For this reason, Tom has purposely scheduled a workshop in which the directing students collaborate with actors.

Three second-year acting students begin with an improv. Sudhir, Megh, and Faisal play a famous singer, his assistant, and a fan who comes to see the singer in his dressing room. Afterward, the directors offer a critique.

"There wasn't enough commitment to the characters."

"At a certain point you got stuck."

"I was surprised you didn't go in that direction."

Tom tells the group that when he was a student at the institute, his favorite part of the acting course was improvisation. Now he and Rasika step out of the room to prepare for a scene together.

Rasika enters and quietly sits down in a chair, fumbling with her sweater. A minute later, Tom comes in and stands a short distance away. At first there is no conversation, then a brief exchange about bus numbers, timings, and destinations. We learn that it is 5:00 AM, at a bus stop in Mumbai. Tom begins pacing, then suddenly blurts out, "Do you get along with your father?" Rasika takes a couple of steps back and doesn't answer. The improv continues with Tom breaking down in tears. He weeps into his hands and asks, "Would you throw your own father out of the house?" The directing students watch with fascination and some discomfort as Tom pushes the limits of his character's distress.

After the improv is over there is complete silence, as the two actors collect themselves. The first few comments are polite, a murmured compliment, a question about the setting. But after a couple of minutes one of the directing students begins criticizing Rasika's performance. He feels she hasn't responded as fully as she might have done. Tom comes to her defense, saying the predictable response would have been more sympathy for a distraught stranger but instead it's interesting that Rasika held back.

The directing student isn't dissuaded. "I couldn't understand why she didn't say more to comfort him. She was being insensitive."

"Do you mean the character or the actor?"

"The actor."

"But that was the character," Faisal tries to explain.

Rasika now grows defensive. Folding her arms and crouching forward in her chair, she explains how she prepared for the improv. Her character has her own problems, she says. Here is a strange man having an emotional breakdown at a bus stop at five in the morning. She isn't going to put her arms around him.

"Still, it was fucking insensitive . . ."

The directing student's harsh response catches everyone off guard. Whether he wants to provoke Rasika or is just trying to be brutally honest, it's hard to tell.

"Shall I repeat what I said or did you hear me?" Rasika replies, as if she is ready to spit on him.

At this point Tom intervenes. He stands up and speaks for a few minutes about the difference between actors and the characters they play. He also repeats what he said about directors needing to show understanding and sensitivity. Slowly the tension in the classroom subsides but an undercurrent of hostility remains between directors and actors, a tension that will probably never be resolved.

CYPRA

BEYOND THE TOWN of Wai is a small settlement called Dhom. Half a kilometer farther on lies Cypra, Omkara's village, a full-scale set constructed specifically for the film. This isn't Othello's Cyprus, but the location does overlook a blue reservoir that could be the Mediterranean. More than fifty structures have been built on several acres of land, from tiny thatch huts to an imposing *haveli*—the country house where Omkara lives. A tall, arched gateway to the village is made of bricks and plaster, with emblems of two fish on either side. If it weren't for the sound arresters in their gray safari suits and the makeup vans parked nearby, you'd never know this was a set. Unlike in U.P., there aren't any crowds, though an enterprising villager has set up a tea shop to serve the few curious bystanders craning their necks to catch a glimpse of the shooting. No armed policemen are needed to cordon off the set.

Even inside the gate, I keep feeling as if it's an existing village occupied by the film crew. Electric cables, switch boxes, and a camera crane betray a movie set, but there is still a disconcerting slippage of reality. The village is complete, with a Hanuman temple flying vermilion pennants and a mosque with green domes and minarets. In the main square, a *shamiana* tent is being erected for a song-and-dance performance. All of this is a tribute to the genius of Samir Chanda, production designer and art director for the film. The level of detail he has achieved includes everything from rusting farm equipment to tiny saplings taking root in cracks in the walls, all meticulously reproduced. Dew on the leaves of artificial plants has been created with drops of clear resin and there are TV antennae made from the rims of old bicycle wheels. Stuck in one of the thorny acacia trees, growing next to the village, is a colored tissue-paper kite. This is installation art on a grand scale, with an added sense of impermanence. After the shooting ends all of these structures will be dismantled, leaving nothing behind.

Punam Sawhney greets us as we enter the village and shows us around, pointing out her office, disguised as a modest, mud-walled home. Inside are a couple of computers where assistants crouch over shooting schedules and call sheets. There are also a dining hall, changing rooms, and toilets hidden within the mud walls of the village. Crossing a threshing floor, we have to pick our way over electric wires and a collection of lights and reflectors. On a field outside stands a giant, clear plastic ball, like a huge soap bubble, used to create the impression of moonlight.

Most big-budget Bollywood productions feature elaborate sets, but very few films re-create an entire village. For two and a half hours of screen time, three months have been spent laying out the rutted streets and building the mud-walled homes, then reducing them to a well-aged, lived-in condition. Omkara's *haveli* is the largest building, rising three stories above the other homes, with rain-streaked walls of dull orange and green, screened parapets, and pillared verandas. Omkara and Dolly's bedroom is on the top floor, a spacious, romantic suite with a four-poster bed, a swinging couch, and stained-glass windows.

Next to the *haveli,* on a slightly lower elevation, is Langda's home. Inside a courtyard grows a sacred *tulsi* (basil) plant, decorated with marigolds and sticks of burning incense. Tucked within a tiny alcove lies a comb and a tin of talcum powder. A baby's picture hangs on the wall next to a frayed tapestry of swans. One section of the veranda is an outdoor kitchen, lined with brass and copper pots. A charpai cot is covered with a printed quilt, on which rests a straw basket. Everything looks as if it were part of someone's home, but when you try to move the basket it is fixed to the bed, glued in place like all of the other props.

Today the shooting begins at Langda's home. The courtyard doorway opens onto a view of the reservoir. A swing hangs from the wooden lintel. Kareena Kapoor, as Dolly, is seated on the swing, wearing a white silk outfit decorated with sequins. Konkona Sen, as Langda's wife, Indu, looks more suited to the setting, wearing a blue cotton sari. She is making cakes of cow dung with her hands and pressing these against the courtyard wall to dry. On the other side of the doorway stands Viveik Oberoi, as Kesu. He has come to ask Dolly to intervene with Omkara on his behalf. As Indu's son, Golu, runs back and forth with a toy wheel on a stick, Dolly swings carelessly in the doorway. The contrast between her and Indu is striking—a young girl in love and a housewife caught up in the drudgery of daily chores.

The cow-dung cakes that Konkona forms and flattens with her hands are real manure, produced by cows and oxen tethered on the set. In villages throughout India, dung cakes are used as fuel. Once dried they are stacked in piles to supplement a scarce supply of firewood. Dolly teases Indu, asking how she coaxes gifts out of her husband. Indu responds sarcastically, saying she massages Langda's lame leg. Kesu interrupts to ask the favor of Dolly, who makes him promise that he will do something for her in return.

Between each take the personal assistants for the stars step in with umbrellas to provide shade. For this role in particular, Kareena's complexion must remain as fair and unblemished as in her BoroPlus ad. Viveik, whose character's nickname, Firangi, means "foreigner," also has to avoid sunburn to maintain a contrast with Omkara's dark features.

Every time the camera stops, the cow-dung cakes have to be peeled off the wall and remixed with water to keep them moist. Konkona holds her hands away from herself between each take, nose wrinkling. For over an hour, her hands are immersed in dung, like a potter molding clay. Only on the fourth take of the final setup does she let out a cry of disgust, dropping the manure on the ground. A worm has emerged from the dung.

Tactfully, Vishal decides he doesn't need any more takes and the actors retreat to the veranda, except for Indu's son. He has to run his wheeled toy back and forth over the courtyard bricks so the rattling sound can be recorded. When silence is called, the only ambient noise is the buzzing of a fly, attracted by the cow dung.

"It was a maggot," says Konkona, shuddering after she has washed her hands with disinfectant and lit a cigarette to calm herself. "The worst part is the smell. If cow dung is dry it's all right, but they keep adding water to make it gooey."

Trying to be reassuring, Viveik explains that cow dung is one of the cleanest fuels, burning with an even heat and giving off very little smoke. He also describes how it is mixed with mud plaster to keep away insects, a natural pesticide. Konkona seems unconvinced on the merits of cow dung, but when asked why she decided to accept this role, she immediately puts on a more positive face.

"I've never done anything like this before. It's completely different. I gave up another film for this role."

She has played a middle-class housewife in *Mr. and Mrs. Iyer,* a society reporter in *Page 3,* an orphan of the 1984 riots in *Amu,* and a schizophrenic in *15 Park Avenue.* But the long-suffering wife of a U.P. gangster hasn't been part of her résumé until now.

For her, one of the most difficult aspects of the role is the dialogue. Though she has acted in several Hindi films, Konkona admits that language is a problem.

"I'm Bengali. My Hindi isn't perfect and the dialect is tough. The other actors are more comfortable with it. The first time I had to give my lines my mouth went dry."

Konkona joined the unit a couple of days back. She has inherited her mother's good looks. One of the most glamorous beauties of Bengali cinema, Aparna Sen has successfully made the transition from actor to director. She helped launch Konkona's career with *Mr. and Mrs. Iyer* and also directed her in *15 Park Avenue.* Recently, Konkona directed a short film for the Kala Ghoda Arts Festival in Mumbai. In an industry dominated by men, women directors are a rare exception.

After making a call on her mobile phone, Kareena joins us. In her white costume, she has a pale, ethereal beauty. More than any of the actors she has the stamp of a star, that unapproachable look of self-possession. I ask her why she chose to play the part of Desdemona.

"After I saw *Maqbool* I wanted to work with Vishal. And have you seen *The Blue Umbrella*? Wonderful . . ." Kareena's face lights up beneath a patina of makeup, a look of genuine delight. "When I heard the narration, I was completely convinced."

Though she is one of the most sought-after female actors in Bollywood, this film is different from the usual multi-star vehicles that get released each week. Even for an established star, there is a need to find roles that propel her further. In Shakespeare's play, the women have relatively minor parts. Desdemona is a distillation of pale beauty and little more. Only in an early scene, where she defies her father and chooses Othello, is there any real depth to her character.

"Vishal has given the women larger parts in the script," Kareena says. "More sensitive and complex roles." The interaction between her character and Indu is a relationship that carries none of the aggression and bitterness of their men.

When lunch is called, Viveik retreats to his makeup van. After the heat outside, the air-conditioning is a pleasant change. There are sofas with white upholstery and a black leather armchair for the star. One wall of the trailer is filled with audio and video equipment, as well as a TV screen.

Collapsing into his chair, hands clasped behind his head, Viveik seems more at ease away from the camera. His phone has ringtones of dogs howling and roosters crowing, but he ignores them.

"I'm hungry," he says. "I've always been a foodie. In Bombay I love to eat things like *pao bhaji* from vendors on the street. Sometimes I just stop my car and get out to have something to eat. My friends get worried . . . but if you're cool about it, the crowds are pretty cool. Hey man, I'm here to eat, chill out. You sign an autograph and they leave you alone. In big hotels, like the Marriott, I know all of the chefs. I call them up and tell them I'm coming and they make things you won't find on the menu."

Before serving lunch, Viveik's assistant hands him an apron.

"They want me to wear this thing to protect my costume," he says, tossing it aside. "I hate putting it on."

As we eat, he talks about his spiritual guru in Rishikesh and his plans to take a pilgrimage to Lake Mansarovar and Mount Kailash in Tibet. He also tells about the two years he spent in America, studying at New York University.

"I loved it," he says. "While I was in New York, I worked a lot of jobs—everything from $6 an hour to $500. Whatever money my father sent me, I put in the bank and didn't use it. I wanted to support myself."

Now that he makes much more than that, he spends a portion of his earnings on charities, paying the medical expenses of children with heart defects. After the tsunami in 2004, Viveik raised money for relief operations. His celebrity status helped bring in donations but it eventually backfired, when Jayalalitha, the chief minister of Tamil Nadu state (herself a former film actor), accused Viveik of self-promotion. Despite the negative publicity, his voice conveys an earnest concern for whatever work he does, whether it be altruism or acting.

The films he's most proud of are *Company, Yuva,* and *Saathiya.* In the first two, he worked with Ajay Devgan. The actors complement each other. Viveik projects a youthful, edgy innocence. Ajay, on the other hand, has a more mature, hardened profile. Jaded shadows darken Ajay's eyes as if he's seen too much of the world. There is a positive and negative energy between the two actors, well suited to *Omkara*—the volatile personal chemistry of Cassio and Othello.

Cut to:

SCENE 56. EXTERIOR. OMI'S HOUSE. TERRACE. EVENING.

[The sun is just beginning to set. **KESU** sits opposite **DOLLY** and strums a guitar.]

KESU (singing):

I just called . . . to say . . . I love you . . .

[**DOLLY** follows him. **KESU** corrects her pronunciation and notes. All of a sudden, **KESU** turns and looks out toward the road. He sees **OMI**'s car heading toward the house. He panics.]

This scene follows immediately after Dolly on the swing with Kesu and Indu. Though it occupies only eight lines in the script, there is much more to the scene than the briefly sketched action, and it takes a whole afternoon to film.

Earlier, there was some debate as to whether the actors would lip-synch this song, but Vishal has decided to let Viveik and Kareena sing it themselves. Hitesh Sonik has come down from Mumbai to help Viveik with the guitar, which he has been practicing for a couple of months. Originally, the song was going to be Bryan Adams's "(Everything I Do) I Do It for You," but Vishal has changed it to Stevie Wonder's "I Just Called to Say I Love You."

Sitting on the balcony of Omi's *haveli,* Vishal looks tired. He has been working since dawn and it's now three o'clock. Yesterday, they kept shooting until 11:00 PM.

"Filmmaking is a kind of madness not everybody can handle," he says. "Shooting is really the toughest part. The creative side comes in postproduction, when you have it all on film and you can sit down and put it together."

Ajit comes over and tells Vishal, "Ready, sir." The stars have been called and the camera is set up on the terrace. A line of laundry hangs to one side. In the background is an unpaved road, beyond this the reservoir.

Kesu and Dolly lean against the parapet on the terrace. He is strumming the guitar and she holds a piece of paper with the lyrics in her hand. Dolly has asked Kesu to teach her the love song, so that she can sing it for Omkara. He prompts her, finishing with the line "I love you from the bottom of my heart." Dolly then sings with some hesitation. Neither actor has a musical voice but it sounds natural, even if Kareena hits a few wrong notes.

Dialogue has been added to the scene. Kesu tells Dolly she has mispronounced the word "bottom." She enunciates it clearly, emphasizing the last syllable. Kesu wants her to sing with an American accent, putting the stress on the first syllable and stretching the vowel—"*baa*tum" instead of "bot*tom.*" They sing it again, together, playfully. Though the song is meant for Omi, there is more than just a hint of affection between Kesu and Dolly.

"I just called to say I love you . . ." With each successive take the two of them become more relaxed. Every time the camera is moved, Viveik and Kareena retreat to the shade of the *haveli.* After filming from three different angles on the terrace, Tassaduq mounts the camera on a crane and sets up from the opposite direction. He and one of his assistants are perched thirty feet off the ground. The crane looks like a steel giraffe, though the upholstery on the seats is faux tiger skin.

As sunset approaches, everyone begins to rush before the light is gone. Props and equipment have to be moved out of frame. Batteries in the sound equipment have to be replaced. The actors quickly reposition themselves. Just as the ambient sounds on a set become more apparent when there is a call for silence, the last minutes of daylight heighten our awareness of the shadows that are suddenly lengthening, the amber glow and sharpening contrasts.

". . . from the *baa*tum of my heart." As soon as the song ends, Kesu looks over his shoulder and sees a black SUV driving along the road. Realizing it is Omkara, he runs to escape. Dolly calls after him but Kesu leaps from the terrace saying Omi will skin him alive if he finds him at the *haveli.* Dolly then turns to watch her lover driving into the village. Kareena's pale features, bronzed by the setting sun, break into an innocent smile of anticipation.

Kesu and Dolly, with Indu making cow-dung cakes.

JAVED AKHTAR

I FAIL TO see the point," Javed Akhtar says emphatically. "*Sholay* can't be improved upon. Why would anyone want to remake that film? There can be only one *Sholay*! It's like the Taj Mahal! Even if you could, why would anyone build another Taj Mahal?"

As cowriter of arguably the most successful Hindi film—certainly the most influential—Javed Akhtar has a vested interest in preserving the sanctity of *Sholay* (Embers). But his reaction to the news that Ram Gopal Varma is planning to remake the film seems more visceral, a genuine sense of disbelief and outrage.

"There are other films that can be remade, like *Don,* which would benefit from a larger budget. My son [Farhan Akhtar] is going to remake *Don* . . . but *Sholay,* it's impossible."

Film journalists are already calling the proposed remake *Ram Gopal Varma's Sholay,* as if the classic has been usurped. There has been a recent flurry of Bollywood remakes, including *Devdas, Bluff Master,* and *Umrao Jaan.*

Sitting in the living room of his flat, overlooking Juhu Beach, Javed Akhtar has just turned sixty. His birthday was one of Mumbai's high-profile events that spilled out of the society columns and splashed onto the front pages of newspapers. Javed and his wife, actor Shabana Azmi, are one of Bollywood's celebrity couples. At the peak of his career, he has good reason to be confident, even arrogant. When most colleagues of his generation have quietly retreated to the sidelines, Javed has made the transition from storywriter and scriptwriter to lyricist. His songs are sought after by the biggest names in the industry, from Yash Chopra and Subhash Ghai to Ashutosh Gowariker and Ketan Mehta.

I begin by asking him, "What makes a good story?"

Javed thinks for a moment before leaning back.

"All over the world, not just here, but in Hollywood or Europe, the requirement for a story is paradoxical . . . Everyone wants a totally new story that has come before."

He goes on to explain that film producers want something fresh and different but they are afraid to venture away from familiar, tested formulas and plotlines that have succeeded already.

"Historically, in India, storytelling comes out of a tradition of the epics like the Ram Lila, or Nautanki theater, performances that would go on all night. In these there was always a combination of story and song. Urban theater followed the same tradition. Urdu/Parsi theater combined dramatic narratives with songs. It's very, very Indian. Narrating a story with songs is totally part of our culture. Films followed this tradition.

"Hollywood films, I would say, are closer in structure to a short story, whereas Hindi cinema is more like a novel, or a saga. It gives you the whole spectrum of human emotions and experiences . . . Unfortunately, too often the stories for films are overburdened . . . A good story should create a frame through which we see the world."

Javed and his collaborator, Salim Khan, elevated scriptwriting from a subsidiary element to an essential part in the filmmaking process. Even then, Javed always narrated the story before handing over a bound script.

"I prefer it that way because I can convey the drama and intensity of the story . . . It's like listening to a speech rather than reading an article."

According to an old joke in Hollywood, every writer must be able to tell his story in thirty seconds, just in case he finds himself in an elevator with the head of 20th Century Fox. But Bollywood allows for more time. As Javed says, "I require at least three hours to narrate a story."

The partnership of Salim and Javed scripted some of the most memorable films of the 1970s and early 1980s. By this time the duo had become powerful enough to demand a percentage of profits and insist that directors not deviate from their plots, neither of which had ever been done by writers before. But in 1992 Javed decided to quit.

"I could give you a lot of different reasons why I stopped writing scripts, but the truth is that I had lost the urge or the hunger to write. I was also afraid of writing bad stories. It was better to quit before I humiliated myself."

After his collaboration with Salim ended, Javed turned to poetry and reinvented himself as a lyricist. In an earlier interview he has said that to be a lyricist, one doesn't have to be a great poet. The requirement is versatility. Javed elaborates.

"By versatility I mean that you must be able to write in different styles and voices. Here in India, every film has songs, so poets are required. Earlier there were at least ten good poets working in the industry. Now there are really only two: Gulzar and myself. As a lyricist, you must understand the ethos of a story and its characters. The intellectual level. The milieu. For one film you must be able to write a *bhajan,* a devotional hymn, and for another a cabaret number. You must have the flexibility to adjust to the period as well. In *The Rising* I had to write lyrics in nineteenth-century language, whereas in *Dil Chahta Hai* (Do Your Thing) it was a totally contemporary setting. *Lagaan* (Land Tax) is set in a part of U.P. called Awaad, where I grew up, and I used the language of that region, Awaadi. I knew it because it was spoken in my family."

Another reason for versatility is that lyrics must be written to fit the music.

"The tunes come first," he explains. "And I must be able to write according to the composition, especially if it doesn't follow a standard format."

The room we sit in is tastefully decorated, with floors of polished Kota stone—a rich mustard color. On the walls are works of art, including several paintings by M. F. Husain. One is a picture of an English hunter in a pith helmet with a rifle, posing over a dead tiger, his Victorian memsahib at his side. The inscription reads TAMING OF THE SHREW—SHABANA. M. F. HUSAIN.

Outside the picture window of the living room, a storm is coming in across the Arabian Sea, rain clouds massing on the horizon, palm trees tossed by the wind. Waves scroll in and the water turns the color of a sepia photograph. Seeing the ocean ruffled by the storm, I am reminded of one of Javed's most famous songs, "Saagar Kinare" (At the Sea's Edge), set to music by Rahul Dev Burman and sung by Lata Mangeshkar and Kishore Kumar. Javed's lyrics echo the waves of the ocean, as two lovers compare their passion to the forces of nature.

THE BEAST WITH TWO BACKS

FEBRUARY 20. Now that the unit has moved to the village set, most of the shooting follows the chronology of the script. A rhythm and momentum begins to build and the actors know what is coming next, unlike the first twenty days of the schedule, with different locations, thousands of kilometers apart.

"It's always best if it's sequential," Abhishek explains. "But for us it was a logistical problem because, with this film, we had so little time for preproduction. The village set was still being built while we were shooting elsewhere."

Though it meant a lot of travel and juggling of actors' dates, the schedule seems to have worked to their advantage.

"All of the big scenes are behind us now," Abhishek says with some relief. "Lucknow was crazy. We didn't think we'd be able to pull it off. But it worked. While we were shooting at the university we didn't even realize there was a student protest going on, until the last shot when someone said, 'Hurry up, we have to get out of here.' And of course, the temple scene near Allahabad was humongous . . . five thousand people, actors arriving by chopper. Now it's so much easier, we can control the entire set."

For the past week, however, the unit has been working extra hours and everyone is worn down. The heat has also added to the exhaustion. By ten o'clock in the morning it's uncomfortable, even with fans, and the crew is looking forward to night shoots, which begin tomorrow.

The scene that follows Kesu and Dolly singing on the terrace is Omi's arrival in the village. For these shots the camera is set up on the edge of Cypra, next to a ruined temple. Kites are flying in the air, one pink and another white, sailing and jinking overhead. Honey Trehan directs the background action, a pair of oxen being led across a strip of wasteland, a man pushing a bicycle overloaded with cotton quilts. A herd of goats refuse to cooperate and are finally shooed off the set.

Having seen Omkara returning home, Kesu jumps onto his motorcycle and escapes. Omkara and Langda catch a glimpse of him driving past on a parallel lane. Omi's suspicions are aroused. In Shakespeare the characters ride ships from Venice; here we have a Royal Enfield Bullet and a Tata Safari SUV. The shot requires careful timing and coordination of both vehicles and the camera trolley. The lane that Kesu passes through is higher than the main street of the village. Tassaduq follows Kesu, then swoops down to catch the SUV coming to a stop. On the first take, Kesu passes by too slowly. The next time he races past. As Omi sees him, he gets Langda to brake. In the dialogue that follows Langda tries to tell Omi that it couldn't have been Kesu, while at the same time feeding his suspicions.

Ajay is dressed in black for this scene, including dark glasses. Between takes, a cigarette dangles from his lips. Saif wears olive drab, as always. As their car pulls up in front of the camera, children scatter. Women seated in front of a doorway are winnowing wheat.

While we're waiting for the camera tracks to be laid someone mentions that Saif is in a bad mood. Like everyone else, he's suffering from lack of sleep. A little later, when I ask him how he is, he shakes his head.

"Not good. I'm feeling very low today, depressed. Missing my kids," he says. "What kind of life is this? You're away from home all the time. It's like being a sailor."

For all the celebrity and excitement of stardom, there is a constant tension between the demands of an actor's personal and professional life. Though each of the stars will get a break from time to time, they are on location for almost two months, living out of a hotel, waiting in their makeup vans to be called for the next shot. The tedium and drudgery of acting gets on their nerves. Yet when a shot is called, they must respond with a convincing performance.

Not only the actors but everyone from the director to the grips and gaffers must maintain their concentration. Between each take, crew members gather in front of the fans, which are turned off whenever the shooting begins because of the noise. One of the men who handles the sound boom sits in the shade holding a microphone in his lap. It is covered with a furry casing to muffle the sound of any breeze. With a distracted look on his face the sound technician strokes the microphone as if it were a Persian cat.

After shooting from both sides, focusing first on Ajay, then on Saif, the camera is positioned directly in front of the SUV, tracks laid out on the road. As the car comes to a stop, Tassaduq is pushed forward to film the two characters directly through the windscreen. Five feet behind the camera is a row of plastic chairs in which Kumarji and his family are sitting to watch the scene. Saif reverses the SUV, then drives forward about twenty meters, coming to a sudden halt in a cloud of dust. This time, however, he brakes a second too late and collides with the camera tracks. There is a loud crash as he derails the trolley. Everyone in the unit jumps forward anxiously. Fortunately, it is a minor accident and no one is hurt.

As the grips rescue the camera and help Tassaduq off his seat, Saif gets out of the SUV, joking, "I'm okay. I'm okay." Ajay stays where he is and remains in character, glaring through his shades.

At the end of this scene, Langda pulls out a mobile phone to call Mental, his henchman. Improvising his lines, he tells Mental to send him a text message, "an SM," as he puts it. Watching on the video assist, Abhishek and Ajit crack up. It's an inside joke—Kumarji always says "SM" instead of "SMS." In the shot that follows, Omi grabs Langda by the chin, trying get the truth out of him. There is a sudden aggression in the scene but when it finishes, Saif looks into the camera and makes a goofy face, clowning out of character. Two minutes later, when Vishal announces "Pack up" there is relief on the set. Everyone is looking forward to twelve hours of sleep.

More than any of the other actors, Saif has taken hold of his character and made Langda into a personality of his own. At several points during the shooting, he improvises on the script, adding interpretations that Vishal and Abhishek haven't anticipated. Iago is the most compelling role in Shakespeare's play and Langda is the insidious catalyst of tragedy in *Omkara.* At the same time, Saif has added an unpredictable, twisted humor to the role.

In many ways this is closer to Shakespeare's Iago than the brooding baritone in Verdi's opera or the sullen conspirator in Orson Welles's *Othello.* As Saif plays Langda, he becomes a demonic figure with an almost human face.

At points this poses problems for Vishal. In one of the scenes between Langda and Indu, the script suggests that she is trying to seduce him while he shows little interest in making love. When shooting this scene, Saif changed his character's role and added a sexual tension, a fierce arousal that wasn't there before.

"He became like a beast," Vishal says with a laugh. "Saif did some interesting things. He took the cummerbund and put it around his head."

The silver girdle covers his face like a bizarre sex toy. Both Vishal and Abhishek liked what they saw but it meant changing other parts of the script, revising dialogue. Saif's performance also reminds them of Shakespeare's phrase "the beast with two backs." Translating the language of Shakespeare into Hindi slang, they choose the expression "*juggalbandi*" which literally means a duet, "back and forth," a term that describes two musicians playing together. On a cruder level, it suggests a coital embrace.

After dark, Cypra takes on a different character. The hillside behind the village is lit up with floodlights that sharpen the silhouettes of the rooftops. Bare bulbs glimmer inside the huts but the gateway and lanes lie in shadow, unlit passages leading into the central square, illuminated for Billo's performance. Strings of colored lights hang from the balconies, winking and swirling. The stage has been erected under a brightly printed cotton canopy. At the back is a banner in Hindi that reads BILLO CHAMANBAHAR & ORCHESTRA.

It's nine o'clock but the show hasn't started. Now that filming has shifted to a night schedule, everyone is in a more relaxed mood. Temperatures are cooler and the party lights add a festive atmosphere. The dance sequence also offers a change of pace.

Kumarji sits in the first row of seats, having his shoulders massaged by an assistant. Though the stress of being a producer must weigh on him, he seems untroubled when he tells me the film has already gone over budget and will now cost more than twenty crore.

"This set itself cost two crore," he says, "and twenty or thirty lakhs to maintain."

Earlier Kumarji had joked about the first film he produced. "It was a flop. We lost two crore." He shrugs it off as if it were a minor bet on a hand of cards. The cost of everything has gone up since he made that film. "Madhuri Dixit cost me twenty-one lakhs. Kareena is taking two-point-three crore. The salaries I pay the crew have risen ten times what they used to be. Every day it costs a lakh to hire each camera."

Kumarji seems to enjoy the numbers, as if making a film were a simple matter of arithmetic. Seated next to him is his daughter, Amita, who has ambitions of becoming an actor. Though she hasn't been offered any roles yet, Kumarji recently arranged a photo shoot so that she could compile a portfolio. On the screen of her mobile phone, Amita scrolls through a dozen pictures of herself.

As we speak, setting and lighting technicians are adding the final touches for Billo's performance. Bipasha Basu, who plays Billo, has arrived on the set for the first time today. She waits backstage, having her hair combed by a stylist. Bipasha will perform two of the songs Vishal has composed, but first she has a scene with Viveik.

Stretched out on a bed, Kesu strokes Billo's arm as she puts on lipstick and arranges her hair. Because this scene takes place inside a confined space, only the director and cameraman are able to watch directly what is happening. The rest of us huddle around a video monitor, like voyeurs peering in on the couple's intimate conversation. Kesu tells Billo he loves her. She protests that he must say that to all the girls, teasing him with affectionate abuse. Her language is crude but playful. When Kesu asks her to spend the rest of her life with him, she falls into his arms.

On the video screen, the room looks claustrophobic, dimly lit. After a call for silence, there is only the distant barking of dogs. The actors perform their roles with amorous intensity, Billo leaning over Kesu flirtatiously. He grabs her hard in a passionate embrace and unhooks her blouse. It is a private moment between two lovers and the tightness of the shot seems intrusive, the way their faces fill the screen, their eyes, their lips, the strands of hair that fall across Bipasha's cheek.

Between each take, Abhishek comes out to check the video assist, rewinding the embrace so that the characters pull apart, then fall into each other's arms again—a comical beast with two backs. Afterward, Vishal, Bipasha, and Viveik watch the scene together, leaning forward in their chairs.

Flecks of glitter in Bipasha's makeup light up her features. She has large, almond eyes. Her hair is down over her shoulders and she wears a black chiffon top with a loose red skirt. The last time I saw her she was dressed in a business suit, shooting Madhur Bhandarkar's *Corporate.*

"Completely the opposite of this." Her laugh has a sexy huskiness. "This year I'm doing a number of very different roles. Earlier, when I was making four or five pictures at once, I had to look the same in every film, for continuity. Now I can change completely."

Though she played a seductive danseuse in *No Entry,* the role of Billo is different, a small-town orchestra singer, entertaining an uncouth audience of violent men.

As an actor who often takes on sultry and suggestive roles, Bipasha has to face some of the same indignities as her characters. She describes how she has been mobbed and manhandled by fans.

"I'm scared of going up north, to U.P. or Delhi. Even the police, who are supposed to be there for protection, try to grope you. For the release of *Apaharan* [in which she acts opposite Ajay Devgan] they wanted me to attend a showing at a multiplex in Delhi. I refused. Afterward, Ajay told me it was a good thing I wasn't there, otherwise we would have been ripped apart."

It isn't just men that mob her. She tells about being dragged into the audience by a group of female fans at a stage show in Goa, where she was performing with her boyfriend, John Abraham. He and Bipasha are one of Bollywood's most evident couples, advertising Pepsi and shampoo together. They also feature in the gossip columns of film magazines and Sunday newspaper supplements, where their private lives are picked apart by journalists.

"The problem with fans is they feel they own you," Bipasha complains. "They want to touch you, grab you, tear your clothes. For a man it's bad enough but for a woman it's much worse."

Though the character Billo Chamanbahar is not a Bollywood sex symbol, her audience is no less unruly and demanding. They shout requests and leer at her, a lone female performer surrounded by a crowd of drunken men. The women in the village watch her dance from the balconies, their heads covered out of modesty.

Immediately following the scene between Billo and Kesu, the sound engineers record room tone. Everyone stops where they are and remains motionless, as if observing a minute of silence. Afterward, Subhash Sahu removes his headphones and nods.

"Room tone changes depending on the time of day," he tells me. "It's affected by everything from temperature to humidity."

Even when there is no dialogue in a scene the silences must be recorded. Room tone provides a foundation over which other audio tracks can be laid, whether dialogue or music. At night there are fewer ambient noises. Instead of the moaning of cattle and birdcalls we hear the hum of insects and the soft snoring of an extra who has fallen asleep in one corner of the set. Now that the song sequence is going to start, Subhash can finally relax, because it isn't being shot in synch-sound. With the songs playing over the loudspeakers, there is a party atmosphere on the set.

Meghna Manchanda, who is editing *Omkara,* has also come to watch the shooting. A temporary editing studio has been set up at the hotel in Panchgani, where she has started work on the video material, piecing together rough cuts of the scenes.

Though Meghna has worked on documentaries, this is the first feature film she will edit. She has also done a couple of ad films with Vishal.

"Ad films are totally different," she says. "It's almost automatic. You know the first cut is 1.5 seconds, the next is 1.75 seconds. With a feature film it's driven by the performances."

Asked who her favorite character is in the film, she laughs.

"First I was an Omi fan. Then I became a Rajju fan. Now maybe I'll become a Langda fan . . . It all depends on what I'm editing that day."

She glances over at Saif, who is lounging on the set, waiting for the next shot. Meghna says she was surprised when Vishal offered her the job.

"I was in the middle of editing a film about camel racing in Rajasthan." But this was an opportunity she couldn't pass up. Though she is working only on the video material right now, it will provide a head start for the final editing process. By putting all of the material on DVD, then cutting and pasting it on a computer, the initial scenes begin to take shape even as the rest of the film is still being made.

As the generator shuts down for a moment, the village falls into darkness. Above us, stars appear in the night sky and in the distance we can see the lights of Panchgani on the ridges above the reservoir.

The camera has moved outdoors again and Tassaduq begins by filming a few incidental shots of men carrying ladders and the band tuning up. Vishal's assistant, Shailender, has a brief cameo role. He tests the microphone: "Hello, hello, one, two, three, mic testing . . ." Shailu has played minor roles in *Makdee* and *The Blue Umbrella.*

For the next shot, the camera travels on about twenty meters of track, following Langda as he helps himself to a bottle from the open bar, arranged on a handcart in one corner of the courtyard. There are bottles of whiskey, as well as beer and *desi sharab*—country liquor of a venomous orange hue. Saif walks across to Deepak, who is sitting in the center of the village square. He is still wet from having jumped in the river.

Saif greets him with a bear hug and throws a blanket over his shoulders. There's an interesting contrast to their characters, one powerfully built but lame, the other scrawny yet trying to act tough—"Now, my sick fool Roderigo, whom love hath turn'd almost the wrong side out," as Iago puts it in the play.

During this sequence, Langda gets Kesu drunk. In Shakespeare's play, Iago intentionally plies Cassio with wine after Othello has ordered him to stay sober. When a drunken melee breaks out,

Cassio is relieved of his command. The scene is straight out of Shakespeare. Instead of Venetian troops, however, a group of policemen, politicians, and gangsters have gathered to watch Billo's performance. They are drinking together, an animated tableau of crime and corruption. Following Langda, the camera captures his malicious intentions, set against the revelry of the audience. As he limps across the crowded square, the bottle Saif carries seems full of poison.

SHYAM BENEGAL

STRONG WOMEN are at the center of most Shyam Benegal films, so it isn't surprising that he is adapting *Carmen* for the Hindi screen. Titled *Chamki Chameli* (Sparkling Jasmine), the film tells the story of a woman from a Gypsy community in Rajasthan.

"She is one of the Kalbeliya Gypsies. They are migrant people, known as bards and balladeers. The British listed them as 'criminal tribes.'"

Benegal is basing his film more on the novel by French writer Mérimée than on the opera by Bizet. His heroine is a Gypsy woman who becomes the obsession of an officer in the Border Security Force. Much of the filming will be done in Pushkar, Rajasthan.

The film traces the relationship between the Gypsies of Rajasthan and the Romany people in Europe. Music is one of the cultural links and the songs composed by A. R. Rahman will be a fusion of Indian and flamenco music.

"The music becomes one of the characters," Benegal explains. "My film is operatic but not in a European sense."

Hindi cinema generally uses music as interludes or transitional devices in a film, but as Benegal points out, earlier filmmakers also used it to suggest "the interiority of their characters. Characters were often defined by music in the 1950s and 1960s, which we consider the golden age of Hindi cinema."

Benegal himself has explored cinema history in his films, particularly *Bhumika: The Role,* considered by many to be his masterpiece. It is based on the memoirs of Hansa Wadkar, who starred in Marathi and Hindi films during the 1930s and 1940s. Like Carmen, Wadkar was a strong and passionate woman, who had a series of relationships with different men. She is a performer and a lover who struggles for independence and respect within a male-dominated society. The lead role in *Bhumika* is played by Smita Patil, who invests it with an ardent yet vulnerable passion.

"In *Bhumika* I had several objectives," Benegal points out. "Firstly, I wanted to tell the story of an artiste, an actress, Hansa Wadkar. Secondly, I wanted to tell the story of the film industry in the 1930s and 1940s, the advent of sound. The talkies. Thirdly, I wanted to show the evolving technology of cinema, from black-and-white to Eastmancolor."

The film was photographed by Govind Nihalani and progresses from subtle shades of gray to the rich brilliance of color. The muted shadows of a garden, in which Wadkar hides as a child, gives way to the vivid pink of a rose with which a film hero woos his lover. Visually, the film evokes the textures and tints of different decades, while lingering on subtle images like a gecko clinging to the ceiling.

When I mention that *Bhumika* could be compared to Guru Dutt's *Kaagaz Ke Phool,* Benegal agrees. "*Bhumika* actually contains a tribute to *Kaagaz Ke Phool.* The dinner-and-dancing scene is a bit of a parody. I also used some of the original costumes from *Kaagaz Ke Phool.*"

Asked if the situation and circumstances of Hansa Wadkar's life correspond with the lives of female actors in Bollywood today, Benegal forcefully rejects the idea. "When she was acting, women in the industry were given no respect. She had no standing in society. Today the heroines of Hindi films are sought after in the highest circles. They are even invited to the prime minister's dinner parties. Look at Rani Mukherjee! President Musharraf of Pakistan hosted her. The whole social thing has changed . . . Now they are quite respectable."

Bhumika uses music in an operatic manner, with windup gramophones and the echoed refrains of Wadkar's grandmother singing to her as a child. The classical ragas contrast with the giddy, brightly lit song sequences from her films. Wadkar's own passion comes through in her dancing, as she flirts and flaunts to a filmi beat, or swings through a monsoon shower.

"I like stories about people who have mystery . . . people who can't be completely explained." Benegal pauses to search for a word on which to pin his narratives, then settles for "ambiguity," pronouncing it with satisfaction.

Though he is revered as one of the masters of "art films" or "parallel cinema" (both terms he rejects), Benegal began his career in advertising. *Ankur* (The Seedling), his first feature, is a story of exploitation in rural Andhra Pradesh. The film launched Shabana Azmi's career and made Benegal's reputation as a filmmaker with a social conscience. He has had his detractors as well, for he seldom reduces himself to simple diatribes on poverty or women's rights. There are as many moral shades of gray in his work as there are calibrations on a light meter. When pressed on the issue of promoting a secular message in films he hesitates.

"I prefer the word 'inclusiveness,'" he says. "Film is a medium that includes everyone. Hindi cinema has done a lot for inclusiveness."

Benegal has also faced criticism for technical aspects of his movies. "Some people have said that my films are 'too finished,'" he admits, without any resentment, "because of my background in advertising. But advertising taught me how to communicate, the economy of expression, to tell a story simply but not to simplify."

A film like *Bhumika* shows careful attention to color and visual nuances that most filmmakers brush over. Yet the story and the imagery are anything but commercial in their rendering. *Bhumika* is Bollywood at its best, even if it was made long before the term itself was coined.

MOOD! MOOD! MOOD!

BILLO AND KESU writhe together on a charpai cot, arms and shoulders shuddering in time with the music. Their rhythm and facial expressions suggest orgasmic pleasure, a dance of unrestrained lust. Kesu's shirt is unbuttoned to the waist. Billo's sequined bodice shimmers as her breasts jostle inside the taut fabric. Leaning toward each other, they lip-synch the lyrics, eyes brimming with desire. The two lovers are surrounded by a crowd of drunken men, who lift the cot over their heads until the dancers almost touch the strings of blinking bulbs above.

This isn't a Stevie Wonder song. It's pure Bollywood, explosive energy with a short fuse. Hearing the music, it's impossible to sit still. Even the dour sound arresters, in their gray safari suits, are smiling, elbows and knees twitching to the tempo.

Na gilaaf, na lihaaf, thandi hawa bhi khilaaf, sasuri . . .
Itti sardi hai kisi ka lihaaf lai le . . . ja padosi ke
choolhe se aag lai le.

Neither a cover, nor a quilt, the cold breezes are against me, my mother-in-law . . .
It's so cold I need someone else's quilt . . . go get fire
from a neighbor's hearth.

Gulzar's lyrics seem innocent enough, if it weren't for the hidden meaning in the lines, amplified by the erotic beat of Vishal's music and the throaty sensuality in Sukhwinder's voice. The song picks up on Shakespeare's metaphors of bedding: "'twixt my sheets he has done my office." Borrowing a quilt suggests an illicit affair, as does fire taken from a neighbor's hearth. Calling someone a mother-in-law means you're sleeping with her daughter. But in this song, the words seem less important than the driving rhythm of the music, which conveys unadulterated lust.

Earlier in the evening, a dance improv was held on the stage, allowing minor actors and lead extras to show off their moves. Though the main characters in this scene are Kesu and Billo, plenty is happening in the crowd, which eventually ends up invading the stage. After getting Kesu drunk, Langda and Rajju conspire to start a fight. Unlike most item numbers, a narrative thread runs through the song.

The dance director, Ganesh Acharya, is a large man but remarkably light on his feet. Everyone in the unit calls him Masterji. Demonstrating a dance step, he mimes the action of flying a kite and deftly turns it into a seductive gesture. Masterji barely moves but even the slightest shimmy of his shoulders or the roll of his hips conveys a carnal sensuality in synch with the throbbing music. His assistant, a young woman about a third his size, leaps from the stage into Masterji's arms. He spins her around and gently drops her on her feet. Putting his cheek against her breasts he slides down to her navel in a lascivious maneuver.

Now it is Viveik's turn to repeat the choreography with Bipasha. They rehearse the scene several times, with and without the music. At one point, Masterji himself plays the role of the woman and Viveik nuzzles against his chest and belly. Though the movements are overtly sexual, nobody seems at all self-conscious. While Viveik practices on his own, the female assistant demonstrates Bipasha's steps, moving with her like a shadow, leaning back in an attitude of erotic abandonment.

Bipasha's outfit is kitsch couture. The skimpy fabric of her backless blouse is covered with red, blue, purple, and orange sequins. Her dopatta is also a shimmering scarf of tiny mirrors, not a veil of modesty but a banner of seduction. Her matching skirt, a pleated cascade of sequins, looks as if it is electrified. On her wrists she wears glass bangles that clink and sparkle. Her bare feet have been reddened with henna and bells adorn her ankles.

Billo Chamanbahar is heir to a tradition that can be traced back to the classical Kathak dancers of north India and Nautanki performances—a kind of folk burlesque. Under the British, she would have been referred to as a "nautch girl," providing entertainment for dissolute nawabs. The choreography of Hindi film dances is linked to this tradition, a blend of art and eroticism. The style of performance is influenced by the repertoire of *tawaifs* or courtesans: elaborate gestures of greeting, protestations of innocence, the coy lifting of a veil.

For the song picturization, as it is known in Bollywood, Masterji takes over the direction, though Vishal remains on the set and asserts control at several points. Calling out instructions, the dance director starts and stops the music by whistling into the microphone. Masterji exhorts the crowd, "More josh! More mood!" After a while he just shouts, "Mood! Mood! Mood!"

Like a master of ceremonies at an orgy, he revs up the audience, using the microphone as a throttle. One of the unit describes Masterji as "hard-core commercial," though he seems to appreciate the rustic folk quality of the song. As he coaches Viveik for another portion of the dance, Masterji has him drinking from a bottle, while swinging around a lamppost by one hand. There is also a sequence in which gangsters and policemen form a ring around him, dancing wildly. In addition to pelvic thrusting, Masterji instructs Viveik to flick his shirttails up and down, like a matador with his cape.

Langda and Rajju are in the front row of the audience and join in the dancing. Despite his character's limp, Saif throws himself into the celebration. At first Rajju seems too inebriated to dance, but after Langda coaxes him, he staggers to his feet and struts about in rhythm to the song. Professional dancers from Masterji's troupe are positioned in the crowd to help set the pace for the others. One man holds up a fan of hundred-rupee notes for Billo. Another waves his scarf above his head and performs an antic ballet of arousal, while a third is possessed by epileptic desire.

Tassaduq begins filming by positioning his camera on the stage but soon takes it off the trolley and hoists it onto his shoulder. The camera weighs at least twenty pounds and Tassaduq is assisted by three of his crew. One man holds the cables so they won't get tangled as they weave through the crowd. Another follows directly behind the cinematographer, bracing him with one hand on his back to make sure he doesn't fall. The third carries a screen of blinking lights, adding to the flickering colors on the set. Amid the chaos of the dance, Tassaduq is swallowed up by the crowd. Moving backward and forward, the camera penetrates to the center where Kesu hurls himself about, then shifts quickly to another angle, catching Langda and Rajju whispering on the sidelines. Several times it seems as if Tassaduq is going to stumble and fall, as folding chairs collapse around him and dancers trip over themselves. Somehow he maintains his balance and captures the energy of the dance.

Vishal watches on the video assist and claps when Saif appears, as if he were doing a backstroke through the crowd. Music is blaring over the speakers. Most of the song sequence is not recorded in synch, but at a couple of points Subhash Sahu captures the sound of the crowd cheering, whistling, and thumping their feet.

Around midnight the unit breaks for dinner, though the dancers look as if they could keep partying all night. Tassaduq fills a plate with food and sits outside on a bench under the stars. He seems to be enjoying himself. Even after the call for dinner, he wandered about with a video camera for ten minutes among the dispersing crowd.

"It's wild," he says. "At moments, I'm looking through the

lens, concentrating. Then I realize it's Bipasha Basu . . ." He shakes his head and grins.

Tassaduq has a laid-back manner, despite the fact that this is his first feature film. Though originally from Kashmir, he went to college at Temple University in Philadelphia and did a master's degree at the American Film Institute in Los Angeles, where he's been based for the past ten years. Most of his previous work has been short films, ads, and music videos. Last year, he came to Mumbai to see what opportunities there were in Bollywood. For a while he worked with Ram Gopal Varma's production company, The Factory. Impressed by *Maqbool,* he sent Vishal his showreel. The timing was fortuitous as Vishal was looking for a cinematographer. Tassaduq explains that he was ready to go back to Los Angeles last October when Vishal phoned and offered him the opportunity to work on *Omkara.*

He speaks quietly, thoughtfully. His experiences making music videos have helped with the song picturization. Comparing the song sequence to shooting the rest of the film, he says, "This is a completely different beast. With the dance director, we haven't planned too much. I just use my intuition."

Explaining that he and Vishal decided to use a lot of handheld camerawork for the song, Tassaduq says they wanted to make it "a little more raw. The dance is like waves and I try to give it that feel," moving in and out of the crowd.

He agrees that Hindi film songs and music videos on shows like MTV have much in common. "There's a lot of borrowing back and forth."

When asked about the differences between Hollywood and Bollywood, he takes a bite of food and chews on the question before answering.

"I'd say, the first thing is there's more color in Hindi films. The other thing is the stars." He pauses and shakes his head. "Here they constantly have someone following them around with an umbrella to shade the sun. It gets frustrating sometimes, when it's difficult for me to get a light reading. And between every shot they're combing their hair and having someone touch up their makeup."

But with the stars in *Omkara,* he feels there haven't been serious issues.

"I'd heard horror stories about actors demanding to be shot from certain angles and not made to look too dark, but everyone has been very cooperative. In part, I think it's because they respect Vishal."

The relationship between a cinematographer and an actor can become contentious, particularly when a star doesn't end up looking as glamorous as he or she would like. But as Tassaduq points out, in India this is changing as actors become less insecure about their looks. A film like *Omkara* deglamorizes the stars. As an example, he mentions a scene they shot the night before, of Bipasha singing onstage. She looks stunning in her sequined outfit, gesturing coyly as she lip-synchs the song, but the lights on the stage attracted swarms of mosquitoes and other insects. They could have used bug spray to drive them off, but "we decided to leave them in because it was more authentic." Tassaduq prefers to work with the light and shadow he can create on a set, rather than manipulating the imagery in postproduction.

After dinner, Masterji picks up his microphone and gives a loud wolf whistle to summon the crowd. Music starts up again and we move on to the second verse.

Beedi jalai le jigar se piya . . . jigar ma badi aag hai.
Dhuaan na nikariyo lab se piya . . . je duniya badi ghaag hai.

Light up a *beedi* and smoke with your soul . . . there's a fierce fire in my soul.
Hold the smoke within your lips . . . this world is truly malicious.

Beedis are a cheap cheroot and this song is simply known as the *beedi* song. Gulzar's lyrics seem to taunt the censors, who have outlawed smoking in Indian cinema. According to new codes introduced this year, a film must not show the use of tobacco in a positive light, which leaves plenty of loopholes for creative license. Subverting the rule, *Omkara*'s script has Billo asking one of her patrons to put out his cigarette, though the song she sings uses innuendoes of smoke and embers to suggest romance and passion.

After dinner it takes awhile for the crowd to get back in rhythm and Masterji shouts at them, demanding, "Mood! Mood! Mood!" His personal assistant follows him around, carrying a folding chair, but he only takes the load off his feet a couple of times during the entire evening.

Two of the extras have gone to sleep: a pair of young boys, curled up on a bed, wrapped in blankets. At 2:00 AM there is a chill in the air, as a breeze blows off the reservoir. Some of the extras have sneaked away and the crowd looks thinner. Having shifted to a night schedule recently, everyone is jet-lagged. It's impossible to re-create the energy and excitement that was there before. Instead, Tassaduq focuses on close-up shots of specific gang members, like Vipin Singh. Bearded, with bloodshot eyes and tobacco-stained teeth, he looks dangerous, not the sort of person you would want to meet at 2:00 AM. Vipin is a stage actor from Allahabad and he has worked in Bhojpuri films. As soon as Masterji whistles into his microphone and the music resumes, Vipin gesticulates wildly, circling Bipasha and Viveik like a deranged celebrant at a bacchanal.

Between takes there is an angry shout at the back of the square and a scuffle breaks out. Immediately, all of the extras rush toward the sound to see what is happening. A fight has broken out between members of the setting and lighting crews. Amid the confusion of drunken dancing it's difficult to tell if it's a real fight or not. At first, nobody is exactly sure what has happened but Kumarji's production supervisors quickly break it up. Tension remains as the shooting continues.

Later, around 5:30 AM, when Vishal calls "Pack up," there is the noise of a bottle shattering, shouts of abuse, and the sound of a struggle. Over the heads of the crowd, I can see somebody hitting another person with a stick. This time, it takes ten minutes to break up the fight. Everyone is tired and irritable, wanting to go home to sleep, but the fight on the set is disturbing. Again, it's the same confrontation between setting and lighting crews. After the fight has been stopped, Vishal calls his assistant directors together and they huddle in a circle. He insists that anyone who was involved in the fight should be thrown off the set. Though Vishal doesn't raise his voice, he is clearly angry.

By the next evening, the conflict seems to have been resolved and the dance continues. Tonight Masterji has asked for a larger crowd. Thirty extras have been added to the scene, hired from villages nearby. By 8:00 PM the performance begins again, with Masterji whistling into the microphone and demanding, "Double josh! Full mood!" The music has been cranked up a few notches.

In front of the stage, the dance troupe rehearses its choreography, one of the men pretending to be a woman, his scarf pulled demurely over his head, wagging his hips. Masterji laughs into the microphone. Bipasha hasn't arrived yet. Only men are in the crowd but there is a mood of rampant sexuality, a drunken horniness that erases the lines of gender, as men thrust their hips at one another.

Following Masterji's instructions, Langda grabs Rajju by the neck and pulls him back, mumbling in his ear, as the crowd parts to let them dance. The revelry has reached a crescendo. With more extras, the village square seems ready to explode from celebration into violence. Between shots, Kesu and Rajju practice throwing punches, preparing for their fight.

Throughout all this, Omi's absence can be felt. He is the gang leader, the title character, the lover consumed by jealousy, "the green-eyed monster which doth mock the meat it feeds on." But at this moment he is blissfully in the arms of his beloved. The contrast between the quiet bedroom scenes in which Omi and Dolly make love and the raucous celebrations in the square sets two layers of sensuality against each other. The song will stitch these separate images together. Revelry in the village square will be intercut with shots of Omi and Dolly in the *haveli,* behind which hangs an artificial moon.

Outside, Rajju struts to the music, then blows smoke in Billo's face. Kesu angrily takes the cigarette out of his mouth and throws it aside. Rajju immediately lights up again. Billo begins to cough and Kesu loses his temper. He shoves Rajju, then punches and kicks him wildly, the alcohol adding savagery to his blows. When one of the policemen tries to intervene, Kesu turns on him and breaks his nose, turning the party into a vicious, drunken fight. The dance becomes a brawl.

Kesu, Billo, and Langda dance to the *beedi* song.

GOVIND NIHALANI

PROBABLY NO ONE has directed more riots than Govind Nihalani. His most recent film, *Dev,* focuses on political and police negligence in the face of sectarian bloodshed. It stars Amitabh Bachchan, Om Puri, Kareena Kapoor, and Fardeen Khan. The story is a fictional account of the Gujarat riots of 2002, in which Hindu fundamentalists in the state government encouraged attacks on Muslims by vengeful mobs. It's a subject that Nihalani has explored before in his television serial *Tamas* (Darkness), which depicted the rioting of partition in 1947. Based on a novel by Bhisham Sahni, *Tamas* was made in the shadow of anti-Sikh violence in 1984.

While Nihalani trains his lens on scenes of excruciating horror and bloodshed, at the same time he mesmerizes his audience with the imagery. At points where you want to shut your eyes you simply cannot look away because the pictures are so intensely shown. In this way, Nihalani forces us to watch what we might otherwise choose to ignore. The riot scenes in *Dev* have an operatic intensity that makes the tragedy all the more real.

Seated in his office at Rajkamal Studios, Nihalani is at work on a laptop. A television in the background is showing a cricket match, without the sound. Posters of *Hazaar Chaurasia ki Maa,*

(Mother of 1084), *Thakshak,* and *Dev* are on the wall. Though most of his work expresses anger over social and political injustice, today Govind Nihalani's moral indignation is directed at video piracy, which costs the film industry crores of rupees each year.

"It's a very dirty business. You have to deal with criminals," Nihalani says. "There's no point in paying them off, because you can't go around the city making sure that nobody is showing your film illegally. Even if you catch someone, they'll shut it off for half an hour then start it up again. The week after my film *Thakshak* was released, it was running on two cable channels. It's a little better now, more tightly regulated, but a lot of it is still controlled by the underworld."

While we're talking, a lawyer comes in with contracts to be reviewed, pages and pages of legalities defining the rights to a film, all of which the pirates ignore. It seems to be a losing battle.

"Some people argue that nothing is completely original but then why should we have intellectual property rights?" Brushing a hand over his beard, Nihalani shakes his head in frustration.

Though Nihalani made his reputation with low-budget films like *Aakrosh* (Cry of the Wounded) and *Ardh Satya* (Half Truth), with *Dev* he has been able to broaden his vision with big stars and a larger budget.

What attracts the money?

"It depends. If you have a good story, with a low budget, you can get someone interested. If it's a big budget you must have a star. A male star provokes the maximum response. If I can go to an investor and say, 'Here is the story. X, Y, Z have agreed to be in it,' then there's a very good chance of raising the money."

Nihalani is fascinated by the evolving technology of films and has no problem with issues such as digital special effects or the colorization of old black-and-white films.

"My answer to those who oppose colorization is that you cannot stop technology. It's always changing and developing. If you want to be a purist and see the film in black-and-white, original prints are still available. I don't believe in resisting technology. I just saw *Polar Express.* It's amazing what they have been able to do . . . the facial expressions, the gestures, everything was perfect. The only thing they couldn't get right were the eyes . . .

"Most Hindi filmmakers still look to Hollywood for inspiration. The problem is, the visual effects that they achieve, we have only a third of the money with which to reproduce them. So we have to be inventive. Often it doesn't work . . . Personally, I have been inspired by a lot of European cinematographers, some of whom went on to work in Hollywood."

Digital technologies that allow for dramatic special effects are gradually being adopted by Bollywood filmmakers. The recent superhero film *Krrish* uses some of the same computer gimmickry as *The Matrix.* There is also a whole new genre of so-called "designer films," which have a synthetic gloss, their production values enhanced by digital imagery. Nihalani has written essays about the visual aesthetics in Indian cinema.

"I feel that the look of a film is very important. Each movie has its own visual personality . . . If I read a script or a novel, I can immediately visualize how this film should look."

In *Dev,* Nihalani focused on the color blue—"not a cold blue but instead the blue at the heart of a flame"—the fires that consume a Muslim neighborhood.

Asked what is distinctive about the visual aesthetics of Hindi films he immediately mentions the eyes.

"Our culture has a feel for eyes. There is the whole idea of *nazar*—the look, the glance. If you see tribal art, it emphasizes the eyes, or Kalighat paintings, Jamini Roy. In miniature paintings the eyes are always so beautifully done."

Nihalani uses the actors' eyes in *Dev* to convey the personality of their characters as well as the horror of the riots they witness.

While Amitabh Bachchan and Om Puri stare out at us with the eyes of two policemen who have seen more than their share of violence and evil, Kareena Kapoor's eyes distill a clearer vision, as painfully transparent as shattered glass.

"In cinema the eyes decide how long you can hold the close-up. With so many actors it is the eyes that are mesmerizing. Amitabh Bachchan. Rekha. Ajay Devgan. Their eyes may not be perfect but they hold you in their gaze."

POLITICS

Meerut is ablaze with the election symbols of Bhaisaab's Jankranti (People's Revolutionary) Party—a flaming torch burning against a saffron background. Strings of paper flags flutter overhead and the walls are plastered with political posters. Townspeople line the street to cheer their candidate, waving flags and wearing headbands emblazoned with the party emblem. This is small-town democracy in north India, where electoral symbols take on intense importance for a population that is often illiterate.

Bhaisaab stands in an open jeep, a bald man in a cream-colored kurta with round dark glasses, smiling and folding his hands in greeting. Next to him stands Omkara, all in black. He too smiles, as the procession leads off with a dozen young men on motorcycles—outriders waving party flags. Behind them follows a band in blue uniforms, playing raucous tunes with shrill clarinets. Just in front of them are the gang members dancing, weapons in their hands. Kesu and Langda hold rifles over their heads. Mental and Vipin brandish pistols. It is a parade of power, displaying the nexus of crime and politics, demagoguery and democracy.

Naseeruddin Shah has shaved his head for Bhaisaab's role and it makes him look older than he is, and more dangerous—an evil incarnation of Mahatma Gandhi. His smile is a combination of benign indulgence for his followers, as well as a transparent mask that reveals his cruelty. The same smile fills his election posters. None of this is entirely fiction, for dozens of elected officials in India have criminal cases against them, convicted murderers in state assemblies, who are either out on bail or govern from their jail cells.

Omkara's presence in the jeep signifies his ascendance to power. For the crowds on the street, voters who will elect him to office, the parade confirms that he is Bhaisaab's political protégé.

"Bhaisaab, *zindabad*!" (Long live Bhaisaab!)

Abhishek and Honey coach the crowd, urging them to shout the slogans loudly as the procession begins. Five hundred extras appear in the shot, though curious onlookers along the street double that number. In the hot noonday sun, it takes awhile to build up enthusiasm. Actors in U.P. police uniforms cordon off the street, while Maharashtrian police provide crowd control for the shoot. Once again, there is a sense of dislocation as the town of Wai turns into Meerut. The crowd scene is far less volatile than it was in U.P. Though the stars have security guards to protect them, there are no armed policemen. Wai's shopkeepers carry on with their business. A hawker sells ice cream to both the extras and the onlookers. Above one of the shops is a large sign with Kareena Kapoor advertising Pepsi. The three cameras will have to cheat that shot to keep her image out of the frame. In the film, Desdemona can't be seen endorsing soft drinks.

As the shot is being set up, some of the actors duck into the shade of a dry goods shop, standing next to gunnysacks of turmeric and red chilies—enough masala to set all of Bollywood on fire. The actors are perspiring in their winter uniforms. Nearby, Omi's gang members take a break as well. All of them carry weapons. Sanam Kumar, who plays Mental, tests the safety catch on his pistol, while Vipin jokingly puts a revolver to his temple, pretending to shoot himself.

Avtar Sahani, who plays Senior Superintendent of Police Babulal, is a theater actor and director from Delhi. He has a play currently in production, a Hindi version of a Greek tragedy, based on the mythology of Prometheus and Zeus. With added days in the film's schedule, Avtar has had to abandon his stage production for the shooting of *Omkara.* He admits that he's worried. His play is set to open in another week. Instead of rehearsing with his cast, he's a thousand kilometers away, playing the part of a corrupt police official.

Avtar talks about the economic constraints of theater. While the budget for *Omkara* is 20 crore of rupees, he receives only 1 lakh of rupees as a grant from the government, to put on his play. "I usually try to stretch that money to cover two productions." Renting an auditorium in Delhi costs at least 20,000 rupees. The rest of the money goes for props, costumes, and advertising, leaving Avtar nothing to pay his actors. Theater remains the poor cousin of cinema, but films like *Omkara* draw actors from the stage to the screen.

"Whatever I earn for this film, I put half of it into my plays," Avtar tells me.

While the crowd is being set up for the procession, the stars are waiting in their air-conditioned makeup vans, parked along a side street. In Viveik's van, Vishal and Abhishek are meeting with Ram Mirchandani and Alpana Mishra from UTV, the company that is going to produce *Romanchak.*

It's been decided that Abhishek is going to direct the film that he and Vishal wrote last summer. This will be Abhishek's debut as a director, and Vishal has encouraged him to break out on his own. Once *Omkara* goes into postproduction he will focus on the script and produce a final draft. If all goes well, they should be able to start filming within a year.

Viveik has agreed to play the lead in *Romanchak,* and they discuss casting and dates. Shootings like this provide an opportunity for producers to meet with directors and stars, when everyone is working together on a project. One production feeds into the next. Ram and Alpana have driven down from Mumbai for the day. They want to cast Kareena as the female lead in *Romanchak.* Vishal assures them he will speak to her and try to persuade her to take on the role. He and Abhishek excuse themselves to go and supervise the political procession.

Alpana is UTV's vice president for motion picture production projects. She started her career in advertising and film marketing. UTV, one of the fastest-growing media conglomerates in Mumbai, has expanded its software and television operations into cinema. Their most recent success is the new hit *Rang de Basanti* (Colors of Spring), starring Aamir Khan.

"Everyone is smiling," as Alpana puts it. "We're now planning to produce at least eight films a year."

"Synergy" is one of the catchwords in Bollywood today, complementary layers of making and marketing films. The use of celebrities in advertising is increasing but there's a dearth of star talent, Alpana complains. With a growing demand for star endorsements and fewer big names than there used to be, the industry is stretched.

"Everyone is competing for about twenty stars, which means you can't get dates until a year from now . . . They're doing ad films, stage shows, as well as cinema."

Stars are sometimes even hired to perform at lavish weddings. The demand for celebrities seems insatiable. Bollywood and cricket provide the bulk of the big names for endorsing everything from mobile phones to chocolate bars.

"There's a lot of market research that shows it makes a huge difference if a star endorses a brand," Alpana insists. "People actually believe that Amitabh Bachchan uses a Parker pen and the other products he advertises. It's gotten to the point where models are cribbing because the celebrities are taking all the jobs."

Alpana speaks of product placement almost as if it were a casting decision. FedEx and Coke make cameo appearances in films just like the stars. "Of course there has to be some reason for it to be there."

Meanwhile, the parade scene is now ready to be filmed. Bhaisaab's procession travels about three hundred meters along the street, toward a high brick archway that serves as the western gate for the town of Wai. On the wall next to the arch is a large sign with Amitabh Bachchan's image advertising Chyavanprash, a herbal digestive. But the focus today is on Bhaisaab and his constituents. Banners and flags with the torch symbol riffle in the breeze as the band strikes up and the signal is given for action, relayed by walkie-talkies. One camera is positioned on a crane above the arch, another at an angle to the street, the third halfway along the route. Motorcycles rev up, cheers erupt. Langda and Kesu throw themselves into the dancing, rifles waving over their heads. In addition to the printed symbols, there are actual flaming torches. Firecrackers explode and marigold petals are showered on the politicians as their jeep moves slowly through the cheering crowd. Vishal watches the parade on video monitors and as soon as it is over he gives a thumbs-up. One take and they've captured exactly what he wants.

That evening Naseer and Vishal play tennis at the hotel in Panchgani. Naseer no longer wears a dhoti, but shorts. His mustache has been wiped off. The game provides a welcome distraction from the shooting, a chance for the director and actor to unwind off the set.

Abhik Sarkar, who is taking still photographs for the production, comes by and snaps a few shots. Though he's worked as an assistant director on other films, photography is one of his passions and he's happy to be doing the stills. Like all of the others, Abhik is enthusiastic about the production.

"We've been waiting for this a long time," he says. Abhik obviously has no time for the candy-floss plots of many big-budget Bollywood films that rely on foreign locations and sentimental plots.

"I don't have anything against lighthearted comedies, but don't pretend they're something else," he says, complaining about the intellectual pretenses of some directors.

By comparison, *Omkara* is raw and rooted in rural India. As we're talking, Subhash Sahu joins us and we watch the tennis game. Vishal and Naseer are competitive opponents—a director and actor volleying with the same intensity they bring to the set. Subhash is a 1994 graduate of the Film and Television Institute in Pune. He reminds me that today is the anniversary of *Alam Ara,* the first talkie produced in India. It was released on March 14, 1931. As a sound engineer, Subhash recognizes the significance.

"Seventy-five years ago, Indian cinema got its voice."

Bhaisaab and Omkara at a political rally.

CALL SHEET

SHEMAROO PRESENTS
BIG SCREEN ENTERTAINER
CALL SHEET #45

Bungalow #104, Janki Devi School Lane, MHADA Versova,
Andheri (West) Mumbai 400053

BREAKFAST ON LOCATION 7:30 AM

Dir: Vishal Bhardwaj	CREW CALL	DATE: 15 MARCH '06
Prod: Kumar Mangat	7:00 AM	Shooting Day 44
DoP: Tassaduq Hussain		Precalls: Art, Honey
EP: Inderjit Chadha	SHOOT CALL	Mansi, Security
1 AD: Ajit Ahuja	9:00 AM	**Dep.** 6:30 AM

Sunrise: 6:26 AM Sunset: 6:24 PM Weather: Hot & Sunny

LOCATION: VILLAGE SET, DHOM GAON

UNIT BASE: **Separate Bases for all Depts.; Meal near Temple**

NOTES:
- **CREW PARTY AT CLIFF INN 7:30 PM ONWARDS!!!**
- Quick Ref. Nos. Hotels (02168), Brightland Resort 260700, Ravine 241060/61, Cliff Inn 240944
- Please carry warm clothes for night shoots
- Emergency contact: Sanjeev Prodn (09821712065) Lara DIR (09821447266)
- Restrooms located near Temple

SC. NO.	SET	CH. #	ONE LINE
97	Omi's House	1, 5, 9, 12, 13	Bhaisaab jokes with the gang
92	Temple Area	1, 3, 9	Kesu sets up the tent; Bhaisaab arrives
96	Langda's House	2, 4, 5	Indu consoles Dolly; Langda averts a tricky situation

CH. #	ACTOR	ROLE	DEP.	SET CALL
1	Ajay Devgan	Omi	7:30 AM	9:00 AM
3	Viveik Oberoi	Kesu	7:00 AM	9:00 AM
5	Konkona Sen Sharma	Indu	7:00 AM	9:00 AM
9	Naseeruddin Shah	Bhaisaab	7:15 AM	9:00 AM
13	Sanam Kumar	Mental	7:00 AM	9:00 AM
2	Saif Ali Khan	Langda	1:00 PM	3:00 PM
4	Kareena Kapoor	Dolly	1:00 PM	3:00 PM

Printed out the night before, the call sheet is distributed to cast and crew. It not only outlines the shooting schedule but goes on to list everything required on the set, including a barber and tailor, two Arriflex cameras with Cooke lenses and a manual crane, twenty-four beer bottles, three gas cylinders, a bowl of cashew nuts, Langda's .303 rifle, six donkeys, six cows, two calves, and six goats—altogether more than a hundred props and other items. Instructions for sound, wardrobe, makeup, security, and catering are all listed, as well as a line from the script: "*Yeh to woh Omkara hai hi nahin jiskey liye ham sab chodey aye hain* . . ." (This is not that Omkara for whom I left everything . . .) It's Dolly's line but could apply to the entire unit, who have been working on the film for more than two months.

As soon as Lara Bhalla distributes the printout, the assistants read through it with concentration. The call sheet is a checklist for the next day but also a parallel script that dictates the action, a detailed summary that anticipates all eventualities. Or almost everything . . .

Ajit has fractured his knee. He is propped up in bed with a cast that extends from his thigh to his ankle.

"Injured in the line of duty . . . doing crowd control," Debashree teases him as Ajit goes on to explain.

"Last week we were shooting a railway scene in Satara. I stepped into a hole by mistake. A hairline fracture and some of the ligaments are strained."

With the first assistant director immobilized, the rest of the direction team gathers in his room to organize themselves for the following day. The group has a close working relationship, an easygoing rapport, mixing jokes with logistical details. Most of them were in college together and have worked with one another on other films. Now that Ajit and Honey, who is still recovering from an earlier motorcycle accident, are both hobbled with injuries, there are jokes about three Langdas (lame ones) on the set. Ajit says that whoever shares his room has to put on his shoes for him. Ajit and Lara argue about the remaining schedule. She wants to know what is happening over the next six days and Ajit tells her that he's going to lock up the revised shooting schedule by tomorrow. Another two weeks remain. Questions about actors' dates still have to be resolved. Naseeruddin Shah needs to be persuaded to extend his schedule. Ajay Devgan has insisted that he wants a three-camera setup for the scene in which Omi kills himself. He doesn't want to have to do the final scene more than once. Someone has to call Kumarji to make sure that everything will be in place. In the middle of this, Ajit's phone rings. Konkona is calling. She is on her way down from Mumbai and wants to know the schedule for tomorrow. Ajit reads out her departure and shooting timings from the call sheet. Konkona's character, Indu, appears in the first scene. She must be ready for a set call at 9:00 AM.

SC. NO. 97.

BHAISAAB JOKES WITH THE GANG

This cryptic, one-line summary doesn't begin to describe the complexity of the scene that takes place inside the courtyard of Omkara's house. Wedding preparations are under way and Bhaisaab has come to felicitate the groom. As Omkara is fitted for his marriage outfit, an embroidered *sherwani* coat of white silk, the gang members gather around Bhaisaab, drinking beer and eating salted cashews. Earlier, during the setup, Lara had to announce two or three times, "Crew . . . Please don't eat the prop food!"

Though the shooting is scheduled to begin at 9:00 AM, there is an hour's delay because a bamboo pole has to be erected in the middle of the courtyard. It's a tradition in U.P., Vishal explains, a marriage ritual specific to that region. At the base of the bamboo pole is an arrangement of banana leaves, a mortar and pestle, a large clay pot, a smaller bowl of raw wheat, mango leaves, burning incense, and an oil lamp. None of this was listed on the call sheet and has to be set up at the last minute. When it's finally put in place, Naseer takes his position on the charpai, reclining against a bolster pillow. He is dressed in a raw silk kurta and dhoti, one foot cocked over his other knee. Kesu sits in front of him on a stool. Bodyguards with Stenguns stand to one side. On the other side are the corrupt policemen, including S.S.P. Babulal.

The jokes that Bhaisaab tells are the same ones that Robin Bhatt recounted during the scriptwriting sessions in Mussoorie. These have been worked into the screenplay, part of the casual conversation among the gangsters. As the tailor fusses over the buttons and seams on Omkara's wedding coat, guests arrive at the house and preparations are made for the party. A gas cylinder is carried in, as well as crates of soda. In the foreground, two men string chrysanthemums and marigolds into garlands. Shimmering foil banners hang above the doorways, announcing the "Blessed Wedding."

Despite the festive decorations and the laughter of the guests, Omkara is in a sullen mood. He is convinced that his bride is having an affair and even as he prepares for their wedding, his mind is clouded with doubt. The camera is positioned behind him and catches Omkara in profile, a dark silhouette that frames the rest of the scene.

Between each shot, Ajay Devgan sits apart from the other actors, on a veranda facing the courtyard. Having removed his wedding coat, he is dressed in simple white cotton, a gangster at ease in his home. The dark glasses, black shirt, and pistol have been put aside. But as he lights a cigarette, Ajay still seems possessed by his character. All around him the crew circulates, shifting equipment and props, but Omkara ignores them, tormented by jealousy.

I hesitate to disturb him but when I pull up a chair, Ajay smiles and waves aside my apology. Asked how he maintains the intensity between shots, he shrugs.

"It's not that difficult," he says, though his eyes still convey Omkara's emotions. "I don't try to hold it inside of me . . . otherwise I'd go crazy."

The cigarette smolders in his hand like a slow fuse. He's happy with the progress on the film though he admits to a certain weariness with the shooting.

"It's been over two months now. We're all a bit tired."

But there's no chance of a break.

"I'm off to Bangkok right after this," he says, "to start shooting for another film."

There are no holidays in Bollywood and virtually every day of the year is scheduled. At least with *Omkara,* Ajay doesn't have to juggle dates with other films during most of the shoot. Often, actors will go from a morning schedule on one film to another film in the evening, an exhausting shuttle between one role and the next. Though Ajay usually plays characters who have a dark side, full of angst and anger, he's known for lightening the mood on a set with practical jokes. Other actors have mentioned his generosity and good humor. Though a Bollywood hero holds the highest rank on the set, sometimes even above the director, Ajay seldom asserts his position. He's known to sacrifice his own lines in favor of fellow actors, and unlike others, he doesn't preen in a mirror between shots.

When Ajay is finally called to repeat the shot, he excuses himself, grinds the cigarette beneath his sandal, and takes up his position with the tailor. As soon as the call for silence goes out, an almost imperceptible change occurs. Omkara's face hardens, his shoulders rise, his head tilts slightly as he listens to Bhaisaab's joke.

"For my twenty-fifth wedding anniversary, I took my wife to Timbuktu."

"What will you do on your fiftieth?" Mental asks.

"I'll bring her back again."

While the actors break into laughter, none of the crew cracks a smile. They've heard the punch line a dozen times already.

Kesu follows with a joke of his own, about a man who loses his voice. He goes to a doctor's house and rings the doorbell. The doctor's wife answers. With a hoarse whisper the man asks, "Is the doctor in?" The wife then answers, "No, come inside, quickly."

Again there is uproarious laughter, but the reference to a wife's infidelity strikes a nerve with Omkara, who removes his marriage coat.

"Now I'll tell you a joke," he says.

The others fall silent at the sound of Omi's voice.

"Once there was a man who got married . . ."

Omi steps forward and leans against a pillar in the courtyard, fingering one of the marigold garlands. Everyone waits for him to continue.

"And then?" Babulal asks.

Omi's expression is full of bitterness, one eyebrow raised in mock amusement.

"Nothing. Finished."

After a couple of beats, the gangsters begin to laugh, nervously at first and then with growing hysteria, as if it were the funniest joke they've ever heard. From the opposite side of the courtyard, Indu enters. She doesn't smile as her eyes meet Omi's. Indu has just come from consoling Dolly and knows that something is terribly wrong—love has turned to vengeance.

As usual, this scene is shot from different angles, focusing on Bhaisaab first, then Kesu, and finally Omi. Each time, the gangsters must laugh at the hollow jokes. All of the humor has been wrung from the scene, but still the actors hoot and slap their thighs. Listening to them again and again, there is an ominous echo in their laughter—a comic moment that leads to tragedy. After the final shot, there is an audio take—none of the lines, only the laughter recorded for well over a minute. It's like listening to a laugh track on TV, without the picture.

SC. NO. 92.

KESU SETS UP THE TENT; BHAISAAB ARRIVES

We're moving backward in the script, as Bhaisaab's entourage drives through the village and arrives at the entrance to Omkara's house. Kesu is lashing bamboo poles together to support the colorful canopies and bunting erected for the wedding. He has been demoted to this menial task and mutters angrily to himself. After Bhaisaab goes past him, he shouts at some of the workers, then pulls out a handkerchief to wipe his face. At the same moment, a mobile phone falls from his pocket and the camera zeroes in on it. In a later scene, the phone ends up in Rajju and Langda's hands, another weapon to use against him.

SC. NO. 96.

INDU CONSOLES DOLLY; LANGDA AVERTS A TRICKY SITUATION

This is the scene before Indu enters the courtyard, when she realizes the tension between Omkara and Dolly. It takes place inside the bedroom of Langda's home, where gifts have been collected in preparation for the wedding. The call sheet lists fifteen boxes of sweets, ten baskets of fruit, two jewelry boxes, six saris in transparent wrapping, and Langda's .303 rifle. Except for the last item, all of the props have been prepared by the art department and arranged inside the bedroom. Despite the brightly colored ribbons and wrapping on the wedding gifts, Dolly is in tears.

Kareena arrives for the shooting with her boyfriend, Shahid Kapoor, who has driven down from Mumbai for a visit. He is one of the fresh new faces of Bollywood who was recently signed for several big films, including one in which he will act opposite Kareena. As a star couple, they feature in all of the film magazines and gossip columns. Kareena is in costume—a bright yellow *salwar kameez.* She has turmeric stains on her arms and face from the *haldi* ceremony, an essential part of wedding rituals in north India. The bride is daubed with yellow turmeric paste by a group of unmarried girls to symbolize her purity. During this ceremony songs are sung and blessings offered. The turmeric also cleanses the bride's complexion and makes her skin look fair for her wedding day.

Shahid takes a seat behind the video monitor. Ajit hobbles up onto the roof of Langda's house to watch the scene. Because of the cast on his leg, he has spent most of the day in the production office working on schedules. Over lunch, he and Vishal had a conference with Kumarji to sort out dates. Though Vishal is unhappy with the extended hours of shooting, he reluctantly agrees to "push it" in order to complete the film on schedule. Even today, it has been impossible to follow the timetable on the call sheet. Instead of packing up by 4:00 PM, as they had hoped, the shooting will go on until 7:00.

Meanwhile, Dolly's wedding is turning into a nightmare. During the *haldi* ceremony, which should be a joyous event, the bride breaks down in tears. A hawk has dropped a dead snake into a ritual pot of milk—an evil omen of Langda's poisonous scheme. Omkara angrily asks Dolly where the cummerbund he gave her has gone, accusing her of having an affair with Kesu. The pendulum of Shakespeare's tragedy is set in motion.

Because the scene is being shot inside a bedroom, fading sunlight is not a problem. A bank of arc lights are mounted on a scaffolding and reflectors help illuminate the indoor set. Through the doorway, I can just see Dolly huddled on the bed, with Indu comforting her. Because Dolly has betrayed her father by deciding to marry Omkara, she has no family attending the wedding. Indu and Langda serve as surrogate parents, though Indu doesn't realize what evil her husband has done. During this scene, Dolly begins to mention the cummerbund, which has gone missing, but Langda quickly interrupts her so that Indu doesn't suspect his scheme.

Kareena has glycerin put in her eyes to make the tears flow, for she must weep constantly through a dozen takes. Even the most accomplished method actor would have trouble sustaining a flood of tears for more than an hour. As she lifts her head to look at Indu, Dolly's eyes are streaming. She is distraught after what has happened at the *haldi* ceremony and crying inconsolably because of her lover's accusations.

Indu tries desperately to comfort her and finally gets Dolly to smile briefly through her tears. It is a long scene, full of intense emotion and subtle language. After the third take, Kareena comes out to watch her performance on the video monitor. Her eyes are still streaming with glycerin. Sitting next to Shahid, she blinks away tears as she watches herself sobbing on the screen.

"*Yeh to woh Omkara hai hi nahin jiskey liye ham sab chodey aye hain . . .*" (This is not that Omkara for whom I left everything . . .)

Vishal, Jai Singh, Ajay directing an action sequence.

TIME TO DIE

"WHAT DOES IT take to scare audiences in India?"

Instead of answering my question, Soham Shah leans forward in his chair and begins talking about his love of wildlife. He is understandably cautious, having been accused of flouting conservation laws. Recently, animal rights activists and wildlife advocates have raised alarms about the use of animals in Indian films. The government has enacted strict codes and forced filmmakers to cut scenes in which unauthorized animals appear. Soham explains that wild animals have never really been properly shown in Hindi films.

"They are depicted in a clichéd manner and I wanted to break that cliché," he says. "I've spent a lot of time in national parks and sanctuaries. With this film I wanted to make people appreciate wildlife, especially tigers. I wanted to re-create the ambience of the forest."

He then begins to answer the original question.

"I had seen the film *The Ghost and the Darkness* [about maneating lions in Africa] and I wanted to do something like that. But in India it's not possible to scare people with a tiger for two hours. A film like *Jaws* or *Jurassic Park* won't work here. That's why I chose to add the supernatural. At the same time, I use the tigers' presence as a backdrop for the story. What I wanted to create was the tension you feel while waiting for a tiger to appear. The silences. The experience of nights in the jungle. Unknown sounds."

"Time to Die" is the translation Soham gives for his film's title, *Kaal.* "Your fate."

Though he had originally visualized the entire film being shot inside Corbett National Park, one of India's premier tiger reserves, Soham realized early on that there would be too many restrictions. Instead, he opted for a few dramatic shots in the central grasslands of the park, then used adjacent forests for the rest of the filming.

"While writing the script, I always had the grasslands in my mind. When I realized that we couldn't use live tigers in India, we looked around for other locations to match the landscape in Corbett Park. We looked at Europe but the climate didn't suit us. And in Africa we could have got trained lions but no tigers. Finally, we settled for Thailand. I had sent photographs of the grasslands to my location manager and he found a private farm, about two hours from Bangkok, which had similar scenery."

The tigers and their trainers were flown in from Hollywood.

"These were the same tigers used in *Gladiator* and they were very well trained." Most of the time the cast and crew had no nets to protect them. In one scene the tiger begins gnawing on the seat of a jeep.

"That wasn't scripted," Soham admits with a smile. "The tiger tore the seat right off. The actors themselves were in the jeep. No stunt doubles."

Soham looks like a teenager, though he is twenty-nine. Dressed in T-shirt and jeans, he says another influence for his film was M. Night Shyamalan's *The Sixth Sense.*

"A character that you only realize is dead at the end of the film is an interesting idea. I tried to do something like that with Ajay Devgan's role."

Soham's decision not to include any songs tests the conventions of Hindi films, but the producers decided to include an opening item number with Malaika Arora and Shah Rukh Khan. It has nothing to do with the story. The music and picturization were played on television for several weeks before the film's release and added to the hype of the film, which was also aggressively advertised in the press and on billboards across the country.

Soham began his career in film as a publicist and ad campaign director. He worked as an assistant director on Ram Gopal Varma's *Bhoot* (Ghost). The other film he assisted on was Karan Johar's *Kabhi Khushi Kabhie Gham* (Happiness and Tears). With both directors he formed a strong bond and after a brief apprenticeship, Soham took over the director's chair. *Kaal* could be described as having the characters from a Karan Johar film—rich, spoiled brats driving a Lexus SUV who suddenly find themselves in a Ram Gopal Varma film, an edgy, gritty world of dangerous forest guards and shadowy terrain full of malicious spirits.

The acting in this film is nominal. Lara Dutta and Esha Deol have little to do but stand in an open jeep, wearing short skirts and looking frightened. Viveik Oberoi and John Abraham are given a bit more substance—getting in each other's faces and occasionally wrestling with pythons. Devgan is the only character with any depth, a dark, mysterious figure who seems to be able to tame tigers with his eyes.

THROWING COLOR

MENTAL COMES toward me with a malicious grin, a crazed hit man approaching a soft target. He carries no gun but his right hand is full of red powder (*gulal*) that he smears across the side of my face.

"Happy Holi!"

Two more of Omi's gangsters close in from either side. One has yellow powder, the other blue. Before I know it, my face is masked in color. We embrace. Our hair, our skin, our clothes are dusted rainbow hues. S.S.P. Babulal and his policemen are out of uniform, also painted with color.

Music is blaring from the speakers—"*Kajra Re! Kajra Re!*"—the item number from *Bunty aur Babli.* But this crowd of off-duty cops and gangsters only want to hear the *beedi* song.

"Vishalji, *woh beedi wallah gaana sunao,* please!"

They mimic Babulal's lines from the script. Vishal himself is coated with red *gulal* and other pigments. He sends for a CD of the music and when it arrives, the party explodes. Two weeks have passed since Billo's performance was filmed, but tonight the cast and crew cut loose as if they had never stopped dancing. Arms wave, shoulders vibrate, hips wag and wiggle, feet trip in rhythm to the song. Though the film unit has been working since 7:00 AM and pack up was after dark, by 9:00 PM the revelry is in full swing. Holi is usually celebrated during the day but because of the schedule, the unit can only throw color after dark. At the Cliff Inn hotel in Panchgani there's an open bar outside and tables set up around a poolside dance floor.

For the past three months the cast and crew have lived within this story. It has become a part of them, just as they are part of it—both on and off the set. Everyone in the unit lives the narrative, using the language of the screenplay, reciting the dialogue, humming the songs. In the end, the story may be compressed into a couple of hours, but for the cast and crew it is a much longer span of time hovering between artifice and reality, between set and hotel room, between one take and the next.

The Holi party has been thrown by Ajay Devgan for the entire cast and crew. When he and the other stars arrive, they are greeted with color, faces gently daubed. Saif has both cheeks streaked with red, like an Apache warrior. Kareena, whose tears have finally stopped flowing, gets a green tilak on her forehead and a matching smudge on her nose. Konkona ducks aside but someone manages to leave colored fingerprints on her cheek. Viveik is smeared with vermilion. Out of costume, the stars look less like gangsters and more like college classmates at their fifth reunion. Ajay wears a long-sleeved Ferrari T-shirt and jeans. Viveik has on a red sweatshirt with a Gap logo.

The person who gets the most Holi colors is Kumarji. One of the tea boys respectfully applies a tilak just below his hairline then makes a gesture of touching the producer's feet. Meanwhile, Vipin Singh steals up behind Kumarji and rubs both hands over his face and hair, as if he were giving a psychedelic facial massage. Two or three others join in, until the producer is barely recognizable.

Though the hierarchies within the unit remain intact, Holi is a festival that breaks down barriers and the party loosens things up. The rules and etiquette of the set are eased as grips and gaffers mingle with the stars. Even the sound arresters let down their guard. Vishal and Rekha's son, Aasmaan, has been waiting patiently all day to play Holi. Now he is completely covered in color from his hair to his shoes. He smears a handful of red *gulal* on Vishal's face, while someone else adds streaks of yellow to his hair. When Tassaduq arrives, Saif is the first to apply *gulal,* after which the rest of the crew joins in.

Drawing up a chair, Saif mentions the film *Saudagar.* "Do you remember the Holi scene in which nobody has the courage to put color on Dilip Kumar? Then suddenly someone comes up behind him and smears his face. It turns out to be Raaj Kumar." He looks across at Ajay, tempted to do the same, but thinks better of it.

Countless Hindi films include Holi sequences, exploiting the vibrancy of the colors, as well as the accompanying revelry. More than any other festival in India, Holi lends itself to cinema. The throwing of color, unleashed passions, intoxication, dancing, and drumming—a celebration scripted for Bollywood. In essence, Holi is a festival of spring, welcoming the arrival of equinoctial rains. Its mythology is also connected to the destruction of the female demon Holika, and the triumph of good over evil. But more than this, Holi is a ritual of Eros, in which the rules of society are unleashed and love is given free rein.

Nowhere is Holi celebrated with more enthusiasm than in U.P., where it often degenerates into chaotic revelry and violence. Though it has a joyous side, there is also a dangerous element to Holi that keeps most women indoors. At the crew party, however, it's all in good humor. While the dancers are almost entirely male, Viveik gets Kareena to join them for a few minutes, as well as Konkona and some of the other women in the unit. Meanwhile, Ajay conspires with some of the cast members. They catch hold of Sanam Kumar and throw him in the pool.

A short while later, Sanam staggers out in front of us, dripping colored water on the dance floor. Complaining bitterly, his voice cracks with despair, saying he has no other clothes to wear. For a moment it looks as if Sanam is seriously upset, until someone shouts, "He's only acting!" and hands him a drink.

In the party scenes during the film, everyone had beer or whiskey glasses in their hands but nobody was allowed to drink. Now the alcohol flows freely, even if tomorrow's call sheet lists 7:00 AM as the time for setup. It will take more than one shower to rinse the color out of the actors' hair and the unit is probably going to suffer a collective hangover. At this moment, however, none of that matters. Most of the shooting is completed and the tragedy of *Omkara* is about to come to a depressing end. But right now it's Holi. As a full moon comes up over the Panchgani plateau, and Billo's *beedi* song is played for the tenth time, we seem to be celebrating the film itself, in all its festive colors.

Omkara's gang dancing in celebration.

THE TRADE

KENNEDY BRIDGE, in central Mumbai, is little more than a flyover across railway tracks, about as characterless and utilitarian a memorial as one can find to America's former president. The offices of PLA Entertainment lie just where the bridge descends into Nana Chowk, an ulcer of traffic in the bowels of the city. An elevator takes you above the clamor of the street to a quiet, air-conditioned suite decorated with posters and stills from *Chupke Se* (Quietly), released a couple years ago.

Jayshree Makhija owns and runs the family company, started by her brother Gul Anand. Her elder daughter, Shona Urvashi, wrote and directed *Chupke Se.* Younger daughter, Masumi Makhija, starred in the film, which also featured Shona's husband, Raman Lamba—one of Mumbai's top models. *Chupke Se* is a lively, entertaining film that offers a satirical perspective on modeling and glamour. Being industry insiders, the family knows and recognizes the faults and foibles of the world they live in. Jayshree now spends most of her time in Pune.

"I have to escape the city," she says. "It gets too much for me."

PLA Entertainment is primarily a distributor and one of the rooms in the office is stacked with metal film canisters. Today

Jayshree has come to the office to sign checks and from time to time our conversation is discreetly interrupted by PLA's manager placing sheaves of paper in front of her.

"Look at this," says Jayshree, handing me an oversize glossy brochure announcing a film. "This is what they spend money on. It's incredible. Most of this goes in the wastebasket."

The brochure has a female actor swooning on the cover. On the other side an actor slurps maraschino cherries off a woman's back, as if she were a human sundae.

"These are sent out to all the distributors to try and attract interest and funding. In many cases, all they've shot is a single reel at the *mahurat.* There's no certainty that these films will ever get made."

Jayshree shuffles through the magazines on her desk and brings out copies of *Complete Cinema,* a trade journal.

"Here you can check and see exactly how much they've actually shot of the film."

Complete Cinema is the opposite of the glossy brochures. Printed on cheap newsprint, it is full of charts and statistics about the progress and earnings of films. There is a list of productions, with specific numbers as to how much is completed. There are also charts showing which films are in postproduction and where they are being dubbed and mixed. Another list titled "Censor News" provides weekly information on the ratings of films. For example: "Hollywood Bollywood International's *Garam Garam* has been issued CC.C. No. CIL/3/33/2005 (A) Mumbai. Dated 31/3/2005 Length 3884.64 meters in 12 reels." It makes sense that a film with a title that means "Hot Hot" should get an A (adult) rating. The final print has been measured down to the last centimeter so the producers can't sneak in another illicit frame.

The most important part of the trade journal is the revenue reports. This is where all the hype and brochures are set aside and the film is gauged purely on box-office take. The listing is done regionally, beginning with the Mumbai circuit and spreading out across western U.P. In the town of Ghaziabad, a film titled *Lucky: No Time for Love* "opened at all multiplexes with good response," while in Bilaspur in the C.P. circuit a film called *Sexy Khiladi* (Sexy Player) "ran for four days" only. Charts called "Transactions of the Week" give a summary of which distributors have taken which films. The movie reviews in *Complete Cinema* are aimed at the bottom line. *Lucky: No Time for Love,* which stars Salman Khan, is described as follows:

> Production values are of very high order. Technically good effort. Script is weak at times. Dialogues are good, musically though songs look forced at times, they are melodious . . . Background score is top class. Cinematography is very good. Action is breathtaking. Choreography is imaginative. Performancewise Salman Khan shines. He carries the film on his shoulders. Without him the film would have been a total nonshow. Debutant Sneha Ullal looks cute and does her job well . . . Directorially, Radhika Rao and Vinay Sapru show spark at places. They have potential to do well with better scripts.

Another film is described as "woefully lacks the required treatment. It gives an impression that the film was directed by a group of immature minds."

THE SALT OF LOVE

SHOOTING WAS supposed to be finished by the first week of April but there has been a delay of more than a month. At the end of March, Saif took a break from *Omkara* and traveled to Australia, where he performed in a Bollywood stage show, part of the closing ceremonies for the Commonwealth Games. On his way home, he stopped in Malaysia to shoot an ad film. While he was there, he suffered an appendicitis attack and was rushed to a hospital. The *Times of India* and other papers reported that he was recovering safely after an emergency operation. However, the final week of the *Omkara* schedule had to be postponed. Of the scenes that remain to be shot, the most important is a dance sequence in which Bipasha performs at a police station. At the end of the song, Omkara, Langda, and Kesu burst in and kill Kichlu, the only surviving member of Surinder Captaan's gang. Fortunately, not all of the stars are needed for the shoot, though it still requires adjusting dates and commitments.

"I was actually relieved to take a break," Vishal admits. "We had been shooting continuously and when Saif got sick, I was ready to stop."

During the interruption, marketing and postproduction have

gone forward, so that when the final days of shooting begin, the movie is already ahead of itself. Meghna Manchanda has now moved from her temporary editing studio in a hotel room at Panchgani to Vishal's studio in Mumbai. Most of the first cut is done, though the remaining scenes will need to be integrated into the film.

The title is still up for debate. Vishal is holding out for *Omkara,* while Kumarji and the distributors prefer *Issak* or *O Saathi Re,* arguing that these are more romantic titles. To break the deadlock and help market the film, a contest has been organized. Through Web site voting and mobile phone SMS responses, fans are invited to choose between the three titles. The contest winner will attend the film's music release in June. The Web site displays three mock-ups of posters, one for each title.

"We should have a decision by next week," Vishal tells me. "But seventy percent of the vote has gone to *Omkara.* Even Kumarji now says he likes the title."

The big news is the *Omkara* cast is going to Cannes on May 17, which is one of the reasons the title needs to be resolved. Kumarji and his family, as well as Vishal and Rekha, will accompany the stars to the south of France. Though the film is still months away from release, a ten-minute showreel has been prepared for Cannes. More than participating in the film festival, it's a matter of making their presence felt and gaining advance publicity.

After Cannes, Vishal travels to London for the final mixing of the songs. Rather than doing it in his own studio in Mumbai, he's chosen to work with Steve Fitzmaurice, a sound stylist who mixes the music of bands like U2 and Depeche Mode. Asked if Fitzmaurice has done any Hindi film music before, Vishal shakes his head.

"We're trying something new," he says, "It should be interesting."

Vishal still needs to compose the background score for the film and at least two months of postproduction work remains.

The final cut must be ready by June 5, so the film can be sent for DI processing. K. J. Singh will take the location recordings done by Subhash Sahu, polishing and refining these into a final mix. Though *Omkara* has been shot in synch-sound, which means dubbing will be minimal, there is still an enormous amount of work to be done, matching visual images with audio tracks.

In many ways, the final week of shooting is a reunion for the unit. During the break, Tassaduq went back to Los Angeles. He has returned for only a couple of weeks and leaves again for the United States immediately after the shooting is over. Ajit's leg is now out of its cast and he no longer needs to walk with a cane. Abhishek and he have had to handle the logistics of finding new locations and revising the schedule. As always, the stars' dates pose a challenge, with Ajay commuting between Bangkok, Mumbai, and London. Viveik has shoots in Muscat and New Zealand. Saif is off in Europe. Bipasha must squeeze in her dance number between other commitments. Some of the unit have taken a holiday or are already starting on other projects.

Originally, the final song and dance were scheduled to be filmed in Wai, but the Cypra set has already been dismantled. There's a wistful look in people's eyes when they talk about the village being destroyed. Omkara's *haveli* is gone, the props removed and the plaster walls torn down, lumber and other materials reclaimed by construction contractors. Samir Chanda's installation art is preserved only on celluloid and digital imagery. Cypra is a place that no longer exists except within the fiction of the film.

A new set has been built inside an old mansion in Khandavilli, one of the northernmost suburbs of Mumbai. The building has been used in numerous films but the art crew have disguised an inner courtyard as a police station, with appropriate signage and official-looking façades, including a bulletin board where photographs of wanted criminals are on display. One of the mug shots is of Abhishek, whose only crime may be abetting a satire of the U.P. police. By setting the dance sequence in a police station, Vishal underscores the corrupt, dissolute arm of the law. A painted banner announces celebrations in honor of a police officer's promotion. Billo Chamanbahar and her orchestra have been hired to perform for the cops, all of whom are drinking and carousing. This satire doesn't necessarily stretch the limits of credibility.

"There's an expression in the film industry: 'Take a liberty,'" explains Shyamali Dey, one of the director's assistants. "It's an old joke," Shyamali continues. "If a director shoots a scene that's completely inconsistent, we say, 'Not only has he taken a Liberty, but also Eros and Metro!'" (Liberty is a famous Mumbai cinema, as are Eros and Metro.)

In this case, the setting and choreography of the *namak* song add an element of parody and comic relief to a film that is often brutally realistic. For the picturization, Vishal has chosen another choreographer, Bhushan Lakhandri, who worked with him on *Maqbool* and *The Blue Umbrella.*

"He's less hard-core than Ganesh Acharya. More traditional, classical," Vishal explains. "But it's still a *dhamaka* dance." A performance with a bang.

On the first day of the final shoot, a delicate problem arises. Bipasha's blouse is cut so low it shows far more cleavage than Vishal had anticipated.

"Much too revealing," he says, "actually embarrassing . . . and it didn't fit her character. Half a day has been wasted repairing the blouse."

Bipasha's costume contrasts with the colorful outfit she wore in the *beedi* song. Mostly black, accented with sequins and embroidery, her pleated skirt helps show off the silver girdle that she wears—the gift from Omi to Dolly that Langda has given to

Kesu, who unknowingly bestows it on Billo. This is the evidence of Dolly's infidelity that drives Omi into a fatal rage of jealousy.

Before the gangsters arrive, however, Billo entertains the police with a dance number that swings between classical Kathak and cabaret. Bhushanji blocks out each move with his assistant, a dancer named Sharmila, who performs the steps and gestures. Unlike Bipasha, Sharmila wears no costume or makeup but everyone in the unit is transfixed by her poise and grace. Sharmila and Bipasha repeat the steps together, a subtle shadowing that Bhushanji refines—suggesting a tilt of the head or a flutter of the hands. Once Bipasha is comfortable with the choreography, Sharmila moves aside and background action is added. To create a haze of cigarette smoke, incense is lit and blown onto the set through the fans. Planted within the police force are ten members of Bhushanji's dance troupe, disguised in khaki uniforms. While Billo sways her hips, they leer and try to grope her—a slapstick routine of seduction and desire. Even with her "repaired" blouse, Bipasha sets the police station ablaze. She literally knocks one constable off his feet, then steals an inspector's hat and pistol, lip-synching to the lyrics.

Once again, Gulzar's words tease us with innuendoes of passion. The salt of love—"*namak isk ka.*" Most of the song is about taste, the burning *chaunk* of spices relieved only by the sweetness of honey, the irresistible itch of salt on the tip of your tongue.

Rekha is the playback singer for this song and she joins Vishal on the set to watch the dance. As her voice flows out of the speakers, she gently taps her fingers on the arm of a chair, while Bipasha's lips move to the words.

"It's strange to hear myself," Rekha says. "Of course, I wouldn't dance like this but it's interesting to see how she emotes to the music." Though the song is seductive, Rekha's voice conveys more romance, more "*shringar,*" as she defines it.

"You could say the music is a combination of *thumri* [light classical] and *mujra,* which is basically meant to entertain. This song lies somewhere in between," Rekha explains. "It's very different from the *beedi* song, which was livelier, less romantic."

While the music is playing, several unit members compliment Rekha, telling her the *namak* song is their favorite number in the film.

"It's very encouraging," she says, with shy pleasure. "When I recorded this song in the studio, we only had a percussion track over which I sang. Afterward, it has been replaced with the complete orchestration."

Rekha's voice, embellished by guitar, keyboard, and drums, accompanies the dancer—a layered synthesis of song, movement, and story. While Rekha does not appear in the film, some of the musicians who accompany her are cast as members of Billo's orchestra. In one of the cutaway shots, a male vocalist sings a phrase. Though a professional musician, he is not an actor. As Bhushanji directs him, there is a stiffness to his manner when he lip-synchs his own words. After several unsuccessful takes, Bhushanji stops and suggests a rehearsal, while quietly signaling to run the camera. In rehearsal the singer is more relaxed and gives a successful shot, filmed unaware.

Though Bhushanji exhorts the dancers with commands of "More mood! Full mood!" he brings a more restrained style to his choreography. He doesn't start and stop the action with a wolf whistle. Between takes, he often sits in a circle with his troupe and discusses the dance steps. Whenever someone's performance pleases him—whether it's Bipasha or a minor, background dancer—he calls out, "All clap!" then leads the unit in applause.

The song takes three days to film and ends with the shootout between Omkara's gang and Kichlu, who is in the audience. Escaping from the police station, Kichlu is pursued through a market nearby, where he is finally killed.

Though he knows his end is near, Pankaj Tripathi seems happily resigned to his fate. A theater actor, trained at Delhi's National School of Drama, Pankaj has had small roles in a couple of films. He shrugs as he tells me, "One can't make a living onstage."

Throughout the dance sequence, an army of carpenters and painters are preparing the market set in a narrow yard outside. Within forty-eight hours an arched gateway leads into a crowded bazaar full of butcher shops and vegetable vendors. Once again, Samir Chanda and his team have worked magic, filling a vacant space with an elaborate set. The entire area is enveloped in black plastic to create a night scene. Artists are busy weathering and aging the market. One man's job is simply to scratch old film posters that are glued to the walls, making them look authentically defaced.

The film set in Khandavilli has several restrictions. Shooting is not allowed beyond 10:00 PM because it's located in a residential area. The owners of the property have also imposed a rule that all food served on the set must be vegetarian. Nevertheless, nobody is complaining about the food. Three times a day, the crew lines up and heaps their plates.

"It's like the army, a film crew marches on its stomach," says Robin, who has dropped by to watch the shooting. "Food on the set always tastes best. There's a special masala to it you'll never find anywhere else." After finishing our meal in Vishal's makeup van, we eat *mishti dohi*—caramelized yogurt that Bipasha has brought as a treat. This is followed by ice cream and mangoes, which are just coming into season.

Nobody on a film set has ever gone hungry.

While the shooting proceeds, Vishal arranges for me to view the first cut of *Omkara.* His recording studio in Andheri has been transformed into an editing room. Where nine months ago we brainstormed during the monsoon, Meghna has set up her computer. Every frame that's been shot is saved on the hard drive. This makes the editing process much easier and the negatives will only be handled during DI processing. Essentially, Vishal and Meghna create an exact replica of the film on the computer. Only after being digitally processed is the final print produced. Unlike earlier systems, with cumbersome editing tables and spools of film that needed to be spliced, the latest technology is much more flexible and less complicated.

At the same time, however, cutting and pasting a film remains one of the most instinctual and creative aspects of filmmaking. It's a process of elimination, constantly trimming scenes until they fit and flow together in a pattern that matches the screenplay. The story, as it was conceived, adapted, written, narrated, and filmed, has been disassembled throughout the shooting. Now Vishal and Meghna have put it back together again, the final retelling of *Omkara,* before the film is released.

When I ask Vishal about the length he estimates, "It will be about two and a half hours. A little longer than I had hoped . . . My original target was two twenty. Ideally a film should be two ten or two fifteen."

As Meghna starts the computer, which is hooked up to a plasma-screen TV, she tells me, "Even though this is my first feature film, the editing is not so difficult because Vishal has a very clear visual sense of what he wants. I sit with the script in front of me and try to match the cuts. Usually, it's quite close to what Vishal pictured, though he has a very crisp sense of narrative. He recognizes a false cut immediately and will point it out."

Though Vishal has a definite vision of what he wants, he also invites suggestions. Over the past two days, Gulzar has been at the studio making his own cut of the film. Working with Meghna he has prepared a slightly different version of the story, his own retelling.

"It's interesting because it suggests some new routes to follow," says Vishal.

Instead of showing me the whole film, he has decided that I should see the first hour and only selections from the second half—those parts he feels are close to being the final cut. As always, we begin with Langda's voice-over and the opening scenes in which Rajju's marriage to Dolly is stopped. Though I have already watched most of this on video, during the shooting, the images are much more dramatic on a large-screen TV. Until now the story has been shown to me in fragments but here it comes together, organized in sequence. The lines Vishal wrote after meeting the gangster in Meerut jail have an added impact as Naseer delivers them with a malicious drawl. Scenes I haven't watched before surprise me, such as Bhaisaab having his head shaved while Dolly's father pleads his case.

Even those shots that I remember watching when they were filmed have a different feel, now that they are fitted together in the narrative, framed by what precedes and follows them. Tassaduq's cinematography is rich with color and action, catching the bruised features of a stunt double as he falls to one of Langda's bullets, or tracing the dull red stripes on the brick kiln's chimney. When the fight was being filmed, it seemed disjointed, but set to music it becomes a dance of destruction. At the end, after Surinder Captaan lies dead, blood flowing from his wounds, Omkara picks up a water vessel. He rinses his hands then pours the rest of the water over his face, as the sun goes down behind the mango trees.

All of the actors' faces now seem to belong to their characters—the glamour of stars giving way to the crude personalities of criminals. Only Kareena retains a filmi gloss, but as she rides a rickshaw through the streets of Lucknow there is no hint of celebrity. Ajay seems to have a harsher edge in this role than in other movies, though he breaks into a smile at the sight of Dolly. Saif is almost unrecognizable from the face that appears in TV advertisements, and even Viveik's features are roughened by the part he plays. These transformations lie in the language as much as the gestures of the actors. Konkona becomes a village housewife through her words and accent, rather than the cow dung she holds in her hands.

Even when the second half of the film is interrupted, as Meghna skips over scenes that haven't been fully edited, the tension and tragedy continues building. I know the end of this story too well—having read and reread Shakespeare's play and the script, having listened to Vishal's narrations, having witnessed the actors perform their scenes.

But this time the image that holds my attention is the silver belt that Omkara gives to Dolly, an ornament of desire, decorated with filigree and chains, a web of silver strands. In *Othello* this is the handkerchief of Egyptian cotton, an "antique token" tainted with the magic of a pharaoh's tomb. In *Omkara* the cummerbund is the family heirloom of a man whose lineage and caste have been questioned. The first time we see it, Dolly wears the cummerbund over a red petticoat, fastened low across her hips. Later, Indu takes the belt and holds it in front of her blue sari, admiring herself in the mirror. And now, even as I watch these scenes on the screen, the same cummerbund is draped around Billo's waist, glistening against the black fabric of her skirt as she whirls to the music of the *namak* song.

As we jump forward to the climax of the film, the cummerbund appears again. This time, Omkara discovers it in Kesu's room, the false proof of his bride's betrayal. The camera follows his hand as he picks it up, fingers clenched in anger around the tarnished silver chains. Overcome with jealousy, Omkara carries the ornament in his fist as he enters the room where Dolly lies asleep on her wedding bed . . .

This image freezes on the screen, as Meghna pauses. She apologizes for stopping but tells me that the last ten minutes of the film remain unedited. Though I desperately want to see the rest, I will have to wait until *Omkara* is released.

Billo performs the *namak* song in a police station.

CREDITS ROLL

SHEMAROO PRESENTS

BIG SCREEN ENTERTAINMENT'S

OMKARA

A **VISHAL BHARDWAJ** film

Based on William Shakespeare's

OTHELLO

Produced by

KUMAR MANGAT

Starring

AJAY DEVGAN as Omkara (Othello)

KAREENA KAPOOR as Dolly (Desdemona)

SAIF ALI KHAN as Langda (Iago)

VIVEIK OBEROI as Kesu (Cassio)

KONKONA SEN SHARMA as Indu (Emilia)

BIPASHA BASU as Billo (Bianca)

NASEERUDDIN SHAH as Bhaisaab (the Duke)

DEEPAK DOBRIYAL as Rajju (Roderigo)
SANAM KUMAR as Mental
AVTAR SAHANI as S.S.P. Babulal
MAANAV KAUSHIK as Surinder Captaan
PANKAJ TRIPATHI as Kichlu

Screenplay by
VISHAL BHARDWAJ, ROBIN BHATT, ABHISHEK CHAUBEY

Dialogues
VISHAL BHARDWAJ

Music
VISHAL BHARDWAJ

Lyrics
GULZAR

Directed by
VISHAL BHARDWAJ

Associate Director
ABHISHEK CHAUBEY

Director of Photography
TASSADUQ HUSSAIN

Sound Designer
K. J. SINGH

Location Sound
SUBHASH SAHU

Production Design
SAMIR CHANDA

Editor

MEGHNA MANCHANDA

Costume Designer

DOLLY AHLUWALIA

Dance Directors

GANESH ACHARYA

BHUSHAN LAKHANDRI

Makeup

VIKRAM GAIKWAD

First Assistant Director

AJIT AHUJA

Second Assistant Director

LARA BHALLA

Casting Director

HONEY TREHAN

Executive Producer

PUNAM SAWHNEY

HOUSE FULL

ON JULY 26, anniversary of the deluge of 2005, when Mumbai was hit by the worst monsoon storm in memory, I find myself flying back into the city for the premiere of *Omkara.* A month earlier, on June 27, a gala event to mark the release of the film's music CD had to be canceled because of a torrential downpour. But far more disturbing, fifteen days ago a series of bomb blasts were set off in the city's commuter trains, leaving more than two hundred dead and countless injured. For all its resilience, Mumbai feels besieged.

Though the music release was washed out, *Omkara*'s songs are now playing everywhere, on radio and television, as well as being downloaded as ringtones on mobile phones. Promos for the film appear every fifteen minutes on different TV channels, like Zee Muzic and Zoom, MTV and ETC. Starting near the flyovers just beyond the airport and extending to the southern tip of Nariman Point, billboards have been erected featuring the all-star cast. Ajay's grim features glower over the streets of Mumbai like a vindictive thundercloud. Saif's malicious scowl is as threatening as a bolt of crooked lightning. Kareena. Viveik. Konkona. Bipasha. Not a smile among them. *Omkara*'s posters and billboards seem to reflect the pervasive sense of tragedy looming over Mumbai.

As my taxi inches through traffic, I see the faces go by—Omi, Dolly, Langda, Kesu, Indu, Billo. The film has been imprinted on every available surface of the city—plastered onto mildewed walls, stuck to electric junction boxes, glued onto the flanks of buses, unfurled above the entrance of cinemas like Maratha Mandir—different versions of the poster but always those ominous faces.

The marketing of *Omkara* may not be as aggressive as for a film like *Krrish,* which blanketed the country with hype, but it is as persistent as the rain. The *beedi* song with Billo's seductive item number comes on the TV screen with relentless rhythms, as well as the theme song—*Dham Dham, Dharam Dhariya Rey!... Omkara! Hey Omkara!*

Vishal's phone is constantly busy but when I eventually get through to him, he invites me to a special screening of the film on July 27—the eve of its release. Instead of a flashy premiere in a downtown cinema or multiplex, *Omkara* will first be shown to an exclusive audience of industry insiders at Yash Raj Studios.

On the way, I pick up Robin Bhatt, who directs our driver through the back lanes of the city. Robin tells me that he learned all of the shortcuts in Mumbai when he got his first job, years ago, as a Vicks VapoRub salesman. Now he navigates through slums and alleys to a strip of studios in Lokhandwala. First we pass Mukta Arts, then the famous Balaji Studios, and finally come to the heavily guarded gates of Yash Raj Studios. On the way, Robin points out where his car was stranded a year ago and he had to wade through the rising floodwaters.

Yash Raj Studios is where M. F. Husain's mural on the history of Indian cinema now hangs. We are ushered upstairs to a crowded lobby, jostling with cast and crew. More than three months have passed since shooting ended but most of the assistant directors are here—Ajit, Lara, Honey, Debashree. Punam and K.J. are also in the crowd, as is Subhash. Tassaduq has flown in from California with his wife. Today there are no call sheets, no props or lighting, no walkie-talkies, sound booms, or microphones. Everyone looks relieved, relaxed, but also unsure of what to do with themselves now that the film is complete. Abhishek leans casually against the wall, joking and chatting.

When asked if he is happy with the film, he shrugs. "I've seen it so many times, I don't know what to think."

There seems to be the same feeling among the rest of the unit, who have lived within this film for the past nine months. "I can't be objective anymore," Debashree echoes.

Throughout the making of the film there was anxiety about the obscenities in the dialogue, words like *chootiya,* but the censors only objected to a single phrase, a crude reference to tearing a petticoat—which struck them as too demeaning for women. When Vishal suggested replacing it with "pant coat," the censors agreed.

"They were cool with it," says Abhishek, "because we were ready to accept an 'A' certificate." Many more cuts would have been demanded if they had wanted anything below an adult rating.

Nevertheless, anticipating problems, Vishal had already redubbed potentially offensive lines, particularly Saif's dialogue, replacing obscenities with innocuous expressions. This sanitized version will be used when the film is eventually shown on television for a general audience.

All of the debates about *Omkara*'s title have finally been resolved and Vishal has gotten his way. Until the last minute there were problems with the sound and over the past few days, he and K.J. have been working frantically to polish the final tracks. Spotting Vishal on the far side of the crowd, I go across to greet him.

"The bullet is out of the barrel now," he says with a philosophical smile. "There's nothing more to be done."

Kumarji passes us and when I ask how he's doing, he replies with an enthusiastic "First class! First class!"

Every few minutes the elevators open as someone else arrives—friends, media, filmmakers, stars. The screening was scheduled for 9:30 but it's already 10:00, still early for nightlife in Mumbai. Kareena has come with her mother and boyfriend, Shahid Kapoor. His family also arrives, including his father, Pankaj Kapoor, who played Abbaji, the gang lord in *Maqbool.* A few photographers wander about taking pictures but the event is organized to be low-key, discreet. None of the male stars attend. Ajay is off in Pune shooting another film. He has two releases this month—*Omkara* and a comedy called *Golmaal,* which has been running successfully for the past three weeks. Nobody seems to know where Saif might be, but Viveik has organized a separate screening for his family and friends at Fun Republic, another cinema nearby. Naseer is busy with the release of his own film, *Yun Hota To Kya Hota* (If This Happened, What Might Have Happened?), the first Hindi film to focus on 9/11. Konkona, who also has a lead role in that film, arrives unobtrusively, greeting the unit members with affection. Bipasha doesn't attend. She is busier than ever after the release of *Corporate,* for which she has received a lot of positive attention. Deepak Dobriyal, whose career is riding on *Omkara,* mingles in the crowd sporting a new bleached hairstyle. The person who is completely transformed, however, is Maanav Kaushik, who plays Surinder Captaan. Instead of the mud-stained dhoti and disheveled sweater, stubble beard and close-cropped scalp, he is dressed in jeans and a dark green shirt, looking more like an ad executive than a villain.

Maanav is seeing the film for the first time and speculates about the ending. "Supposedly, Vishal has done something that would have surprised even Shakespeare," he says.

At half past ten, the lights are dimmed and we enter the hall. The screening room has less than a hundred seats but there are many more people than that. Those who cannot find a place to sit make themselves comfortable in the aisles. Even Kareena gives up her seat for some of her guests and watches the film standing at the back.

Before the movie, we're shown a short, ten-minute public service announcement made by Ajay. It's an appeal for people to collect trash so it doesn't clog drains and lead to the monsoon flooding that claimed so many lives last year. Ajay also acts in the short along with a waiflike child actor with baleful eyes.

As soon as this ends, the screen is filled with the censor's certificate, issued to every film in India. Though the form is in English, the title is written by hand in Hindi. "A" for adult appears prominently in one corner, above the censor's seal and signature. Moments later, Saif's voice intones, "*Bewakoof aur chootiya mein dhaga bhar ka pharak hota haiga bhaiya . . .*" Looking into the camera, he seems to be speaking directly to the audience, abusing us for being either fools or fucking idiots.

Whatever thread of difference there might be is soon forgotten as the story begins to unravel. Omi has abducted Dolly on her wedding day, the love thief claiming his bride. From the first cut, which I saw in May, to the final print there are a number of significant changes. An opening sequence at Pinky's Beauty Parlor is gone. So is most of the footage filmed at Lucknow University and the scene between Bhaisaab and Auntyji. Dolly Ahluwalia's role has been completely erased. Each of these scenes involved days of filming but have been excised in the final editing, like lost memories. The action sequences and fight scene at the brick kiln have been shortened and other cuts are much tighter, quickening the pace but also leaving the viewer guessing at points. By removing sections, Vishal has heightened the suspense.

The most powerful moments are still there, when Omi pours water over his face after defeating Surinder Captaan; the crowning of Kesu as *bahubali,* when his forehead is smeared with vermilion and the crowds throw clouds of color; and Dolly's arrival at Omkara's village, when Indu takes a smudge of kohl from the corner of her eye and touches it to the bride's cheek, warding off evil glances.

At intermission, when the lights come on, smokers are the

first to leave, ducking out the doors. Others mill around the refreshment tables in the lobby. A few comments and congratulations are exchanged. Someone slaps Deepak encouragingly on the back, but having seen only half the film the response is subdued. No one wants to sound too enthusiastic just yet.

There is always a disorienting feeling when you step out of the picture hall into the real world and your eyes adjust to the fluorescent lights in the lobby. But the strangest part of this intermission are the familiar faces that appear. The youthful man in the baseball cap sitting near the drinks buffet is Aamir Khan, as big a star as you can find in Bollywood. A beautiful woman edges by and only a moment later, it dawns on me that this is Priyanka Chopra, who sizzled in *Aitraaz* and stars in *Krrish*. And there in the corner, an unlit cigarette pressed between his lips, is Shah Rukh Khan, hero of *DDLJ* and so many other big films. Karan Johar walks past. His film *Kabhi Alvida Naa Kehna* (Never Say Goodbye), already abbreviated to *KANK* and starring Shah Rukh Khan, opens in two weeks. Malaika Arora Khan, who performed the item number with Shah Rukh in *Kaal*, is dressed in shredded jeans. Her husband, Arbaaz Khan, attends as well, along with directors Farhan Akhtar, Mani Ratnam, and more than a dozen other Bollywood personalities who keep the gossip columns and society pages churning. For them, tonight is not an opportunity to be seen but a chance to watch. After the intermission, when the lights go down and the film begins again, they settle back into the anonymity of their seats.

For most of *Omkara*, the editing follows the screenplay closely. Because it was so tightly written, the script provides a firm scaffolding for the film. Some of the juxtapositions now make more sense on the screen, held together with music and song. For the final editing, Vishal, Abhishek, and Meghna had retreated to Aamby Valley—an exclusive resort near Pune—where they locked themselves away for a week and produced the final cut. Meghna has watched the film more often than anyone else.

"At least two hundred times," she says.

The speed at which this film was produced is astonishing, less than a year from conception to release. Yet the finished print is carefully crafted, no hints of cutting corners or missing links. In an industry that often takes two or three years to produce even a mediocre film, the pace that Vishal and his unit have set for themselves is record time for Bollywood.

In the second half, the earlier exuberance of the gangsters gives way to the inevitable weight of tragedy. Bipasha's second dance provides an interlude of comic romance, but Langda's bitterness taints the plot even as the wedding preparations are under way. A dead snake falls from the talons of a hawk and lands in a bowl of milk. Indore Singh, an opposing gangster, is killed on a train. As soon as Omi puts a bullet through his rival's brain, he turns on Langda, demanding the truth. Is Dolly having an affair with Kesu? Yes? No? These are violent men who will die a violent death but it is their human failings rather than the weapons they carry that determine their fate.

In Shakespeare, the tragedy is played out largely among the men and Desdemona seems almost absent in the scenes before her death. But as Vishal had told me earlier, Kareena was the actor who surprised him most. Bewilderment and pain show in Dolly's eyes, as she tries to comprehend why Omi has turned against her. Having sacrificed everything for him, she now faces the irrational force of his jealousy. The gradual changes in Dolly's expressions, from innocence and infatuation to confusion and anguish, are some of the most moving moments in the film.

Probably the greatest plot change from *Othello* to *Omkara* is Emilia's role. In the play, she curses her husband when she discovers what Iago has done, but Vishal takes her response a step further. Knowing that Langda has destroyed the lives of those she loves, Indu picks up a cleaver and kills him with a single stroke. Konkona's high-spirited village housewife is transformed into a vindictive goddess, a figure out of Hindu mythology rather than Elizabethan melodrama.

Wounded by Langda, Kesu staggers into Omkara's room to find the gang leader standing over Dolly's corpse. A pistol in one hand, Omi is confronted with the horror of his mistake. His monologue is short—a list of recent victims . . . Boom . . . Boom . . . Omkara turns the pistol on himself, fires, and falls to the floor. The swinging couch, on which Dolly lies, rocks back and forth like a fatal metronome.

When Ajay Devgan first heard the narration of this story, he told Vishal, "This is the kind of movie in which the last ten minutes I wouldn't want to watch." It is depressing. Four of the main characters are dead, and those who survive have nothing left to live for.

In an industry that banks on happy endings, where even the most tragic moments are often soaked in pathos and maudlin emotions, to make a film like *Omkara* involves a high level of risk. As the end credits spill down the screen and the house lights go up, there is complete silence. Later, in the lobby and out in the parking lot, there will be plenty of congratulations as the audience disperses—enthusiastic handshakes, embraces, the usual chatty praise one hears within the industry. But far more meaningful is that hollow silence, the stunned moment of catharsis in which the film ends and we touch ourselves to make sure we're still alive.

ENCORE!

"SAIF" BET

OMKARA RAISES THE BAR(D)

BEND IT LIKE BHARDWAJ

While copy editors at most of India's dailies worked overtime to try and think of clever headlines, virtually all of the reviewers come out in favor of *Omkara.* Nikhat Kazmi, writing in the *Times of India,* gives it a rating of four out of five stars and gushes:

> Vishal lives up to the Bard. For not only does he skillfully capture the netherworld of the human psyche—those ambiguous grey areas of conventional morality—which formed the playground for Shakespearean drama, he manages to lift the bar of Indian cinema with his unique adaptation. Here's a film that breaks the conventional mould of Bollywood into smithereens and does it with a panache that encompasses all departments of filmmaking . . . And yes, kudos to the Censor Board for dusting the cobwebs off its walls and coming of age. No blips, no cuts, just an 'A' certificate.
>
> Here's looking at you, Bollywood.

The *Mumbai Mirror*'s Mayank Shekhar also gives the film four stars and calls it "an immaculate achievement." Tushar Joshi of *Mid-Day* ups the ante with four and a half stars and concludes, "Mr. Bhardwaj, please take a bow. Not just for making a masterpiece but also for bringing Shakespeare into mainstream cinema with such eloquence."

Omkara opens on July 28 at more than forty cinemas in Mumbai and almost the same number in Delhi, as well as thousands of picture halls throughout the country, from Meerut to Mysore. At the same time, the film has a worldwide release in places like Dubai, Sydney, and Los Angeles. In London it is greeted with a full-page spread in *The Guardian.* British journalists seem flattered that Bollywood should resurrect the Bard. The crowds at theaters are enthusiastic. For an "A" rated picture, it pulls in large numbers, though family audiences are wary because of the strong language. While *Omkara* may not become a super hit, the film does well at urban and small-town cinemas across north India. Not bad at all, for a "round unvarnish'd tale."

Film has never been a static medium and Bollywood is constantly changing. *Omkara*'s success proves that Hindi cinema can break free of its own stereotypes, even as it exploits the ironies embedded in traditional clichés. Song and dance do mix with tragedy, while heroes may appear in different guises, and language need not always be polite. The production of this film combines the latest technology and professional rigor of modern moviemaking, together with the storytelling of the *Arabian Nights,* the drama of Shakespeare, and the exuberance of a Nautanki performance. It also meets the test of any art form by using familiar material to create something completely new.

Langda on the village set.

NOTES

6. *claimed by at least one journalist:* Janet Fine, *Hollywood Reporter* (January 1992), n.p.

11. *Like so much else in Bollywood:* Barbara Stoler Miller, *Phantasies of a Love Thief* (New York: Columbia University Press, 1970).

12. The intriguing expression "podoerotic" is used by Patricia Uberoi in "Dharma and Desire, Freedom and Destiny: Rescripting the Man-Woman Relationship in Hindi Cinema," cited in Woodman Taylor, "Penetrating Gazes: The Poetics of Sight and Visual Display in Popular Indian Cinema," in *Beyond Appearances?: Visual Practices and Ideologies in Modern India,* ed. Sumathi Ramaswamy (New Delhi: Sage, 2003), 310.

21. *Shakespeare himself adapted:* Introduction by Kenneth Muir, in William Shakespeare, *Othello* (Harmondsworth: Penguin, 1968), 7.

24. *According to biographer:* Dorothee Wenner, *Fearless Nadia* (New Delhi: Penguin, 2005), 2 and 98–99.

25. *the longest-running film in Indian cinema history:* Anupama Chopra, *Dilwale Dulhania le Jayenge: The Making of a Blockbuster* (New Delhi: Harper Collins, 2004), 9.

47. *October 22. While the team is in Mussoorie:* "Bollywood's Own Desdemona," the *Times of India,* October 22, 2005, 2.

61. *Storytelling has a long tradition:* Madhu Jain, *The Kapoors* (New Delhi: Viking, 2005), 100.

98. "*the Corleones of Bollywood*": Ibid., n.p.

168. *In an earlier interview he has said:* Javed Akhtar, *Talking Songs: Javed Akhtar in Conversation with Nasreen Munni Kabir and Sixty Selected Songs* (New Delhi: Oxford, 2005), 26.

169. "*Saagar Kinare*": Ibid., 105.

221. "*Hollywood Bollywood International's* Garam Garam . . .": *Complete Cinema* (April 9, 2005), 56.

222. *In the town of Ghaziabad . . .* : *Complete Cinema* (April 9, 2005), 72–74.

222. "*Production values are of very high order . . .*": *Complete Cinema* (April 9, 2005), 7–8.

INDEX

Note: *Italicized* page numbers indicate photographs.